SPIRITS & LIQUEURS
IN THE KITCHEN

SPIRITS & LIQUEURS
IN THE KITCHEN

A DEFINITIVE GUIDE TO ALCOHOL-BASED DRINKS AND HOW TO USE THEM WITH FOOD

STUART WALTON AND NORMA MILLER

LORENZ BOOKS

This edition is published by Lorenz Books, an imprint of Anness Publishing Ltd,
Hermes House, 88–89 Blackfriars Road, London SE1 8HA
tel. 020 7401 2077; fax 020 7633 9499
www.lorenzbooks.com; www.annesspublishing.com

If you like the images in this book and would like to investigate using them
for publishing, promotions or advertising, please visit our website
www.practicalpictures.com for more information.

UK agent: The Manning Partnership Ltd; tel. 01225 478444;
fax 01225 478440; sales@manning-partnership.co.uk
UK distributor: Grantham Book Services Ltd; tel. 01476 541080;
fax 01476 541061; orders@gbs.tbs-ltd.co.uk
North American agent/distributor: National Book Network;
tel. 301 459 3366; fax 301 429 5746; www.nbnbooks.com
Australian agent/distributor: Pan Macmillan Australia; tel. 1300 135 113;
fax 1300 135 103; customer.service@macmillan.com.au
New Zealand agent/distributor: David Bateman Ltd;
tel. (09) 415 7664; fax (09) 415 8892

Publisher: Joanna Lorenz
Senior Cookery Editor: Linda Fraser
Copy Editors: Jane Hughes and Jenni Fleetwood
Indexer: Hilary Bird
Designer: Sara Kidd
Photography: David Jordan and Janine Hosegood (cut-outs)
Food for Photography and Styling: Judy Williams
Illustrator: Madeleine David

ETHICAL TRADING POLICY
Because of our ongoing ecological investment programme, you, as our customer, can
have the pleasure and reassurance of knowing that a tree is being cultivated on your
behalf to naturally replace the materials used to make the book you are holding. For
further information about this scheme, go to www.annesspublishing.com/trees

A CIP catalogue record for this book is available from the British Library.

Previously published as *Spirits & Liqueurs Cookbook*

NOTES
Bracketed terms are intended for American readers.
For all recipes, quantities are given in both metric and imperial measures and, where appropriate, in standard cups and spoons.
Follow one set of measures, but not a mixture, because they are not interchangeable.
Standard spoon and cup measures are level. 1 tsp = 5ml, 1 tbsp = 15ml, 1 cup = 250ml/8fl oz.
Australian standard tablespoons are 20ml. Australian readers should use 3 tsp in place of 1 tbsp for measuring small quantities.
American pints are 16fl oz/2 cups. American readers should use 20fl oz/2.5 cups in place of 1 pint when measuring liquids.
Electric oven temperatures in this book are for conventional ovens. When using a fan oven, the temperature will
probably need to be reduced by about 10–20°C/20–40°F. Since ovens vary, you should check with your
manufacturer's instruction book for guidance.
Medium (US large) eggs are used unless otherwise stated.

Main front cover image shows Crêpes Suzette with Cointreau and Cognac - for recipe, see page 202

CONTENTS

INTRODUCTION

A T WHAT POINT IN HISTORY alcoholic drinks were first used in cooking, quite apart from fulfilling their time-honoured role as intoxicants, is a question that may never be answered. It seems a fair guess, however, to suggest that it was related to the discovery of fermentation.

The ancient Egyptians used fermented grains for making prototype forms of beer. These grains also enabled them to refine the techniques for producing raised breads. It was found that adding beer sediment – which was still full of live yeasts – was the quickest and easiest method of encouraging the start of fermentation in a new batch of dough. It was still going strong in the English Middle Ages when dough fermentation was initiated by the addition of froth from the head of the finished beer. Without being fanciful, it could plausibly be argued that this use of beer in bread-making represented the first appearance of alcohol in the culinary arts.

Wine, too, played its part in the foods of classical Greece and later Rome, not initially for adding flavour but for its acidity. The action of acids in softening the fibres of tough-textured meats led to the invention of marinating, which is still an indispensable procedure in kitchens the world over for tenderizing the meat of older animals. As well as making tough meat more supple, marinating would have removed excess salt from meats that had been encrusted with it, or soaked in brine, for preservation. Wine vinegar, its alcohol lost to acetic acid, may have been the first recourse, but wine itself appears in sauce recipes in the historically important late Roman cookery book of Apicius (3rd century AD). The wine itself was commonly infused with spices to mask the rank flavours of oxidation or acetification.

Today, adding wine to a sauce or using beer in casseroles are commonplaces of the domestic kitchen. The drinks featured in this book, however, spirits, liqueurs and fortified wines, are quite different types of drink. What they have in common is that they all depend to some degree on distillation. Even the fortified wines – sherry, port, Madeira and the others – are made stronger, and in some cases naturally sweeter, than ordinary table wine by the addition of a distillate.

Distillation (from the Latin *destillare*, to drip) is the extraction of higher alcohols from fermented drinks by using the action of heat to vapourize them. Compared to fermentation itself, distillation is a remarkably simple process, largely because it is much more readily subject to external control. Whereas freshly pressed grape juice needs the right ambient temperature to begin the process of turning into good wine, a spirit can be produced from wine simply by applying heat to it. Alcohol has a lower boiling point than water (about 78°C compared to 100°C), so it vapourizes into steam some time before the water content in the wine starts to boil. When the alcohol-laden steam hits a cool surface, it forms a dripping condensation, and reverts to a liquid of which the alcohol constitutes a much higher proportion than it did in the wine. Boil that liquid up again, and the same procedure will yield an even higher alcohol, and so on.

Much academic debate has been generated in the last 30 years or so as to when and where distillation was first discovered. The Greek philosopher Aristotle, who lived in the 4th century BC, writes of distillation as a way of purifying seawater to make it drinkable. He comments in passing that the same treatment can be given to wine, which is reduced thereby to a sort of "water". He

Right: Turning the drying germinated barley in the peat kiln at Glendronach Distillery near Huntly, Banffshire, Scotland.

Right: This burbling stream provides one of the essential ingredients for whisky distillation – clear spring water.

was tantalizingly close to the breakthrough, but the experiment did no more than prove for him that wine is just a form of modified water, and that a liquid can only derive flavour from whatever happens to be mixed with the water that forms its base.

The documented beginnings of systematic and scientifically founded distillation, at least in Europe, come from the celebrated medical school at Salerno around 1100 AD. Wine itself was held to have a range of medicinal properties (a view that has once again found favour in the 1990s), and the extraction of what was held to be the soul or spirit of the wine, through distillation, is what led to the naming of distillates as "spirits". Alcohol was believed to be the active ingredient in the healing powers of wine. Up to that time, the word "alcohol" was applied as a generic term to any product that had been arrived at by a process of vapourizing and condensation. Its origin from the Arabic word *al-kuhl* refers to the Arab practice of producing a black powder by condensing a vapour of the metal antimony. The powder was then used as eye makeup, which is why eyeliner is still occasionally known as kohl. It was not until the 16th century that "alcohol" was used specifically in reference to distilled spirits.

Not only medicine but the ancient practice of alchemy were involved in the European origins of distillation. Alchemy was a respected branch of the physical sciences, and was chiefly concerned with finding a means of transforming ordinary metals into gold. It was wholeheartedly believed that if such a process could be discovered, it might well be possible to apply it to the human body and extract the essential life force from its mortal shell, thus guaranteeing eternal youth. With the realization that alcohol could be repeatedly distilled to a greater and greater purity, it was thought that spirits

could be the Holy Grail.

Although it can't have taken long for the Salerno doctors to ascertain that whatever other remarkable properties distilled spirit had, the power to confer everlasting life wasn't one of them, the medical uses of spirits were to endure for hundreds of years. It was Arnaldo de Villanova, a Catalan physician of the 13th century, who first coined the Latin term *aqua vitae*, "water of life", for distilled spirits, indicating that they were still held to be associated with the promotion of vitality and health. (That term lives on in the Scandinavian aquavit, the French eau de vie and other spirituous names.)

Undoubtedly, the earliest distillates were of wine, since it had a more salubrious and exalted image than did beer, but grain distillation to produce the first whiskies and neutral spirits followed later in the Middle Ages.

Many of these prototypes contained herb and spice extracts, or were flavoured with fruit, in order to enhance the medicinal properties of the preparation. The additives also conveniently masked what must have been the fairly raw taste and off-putting aroma of the unadulterated liquor. Anybody who has smelt and tasted clear spirit dribbling off the still in a brandy distillery (or, for that matter, has had a brush with illicit Irish poteen or American moonshine) will know how far such untreated spirit is from the welcoming smoothness of five-star cognac or single malt Scotch. The infused distillates were the antecedents of many of the traditional aromatic liqueurs and flavoured vodkas of today.

That, for centuries, was the official account of the birth of distilled spirits. In 1961, however, an Indian food historian, O. Prakash, argued that there was evidence that distillation of rice and barley beer was practised in India around 800 BC. Others have argued that, if so, it probably arrived there from China even earlier. Thus, current theory cautiously credits the Chinese as the discoverers of the art.

It seems unusual that distilled alcohol was not remarked on or even apparently encountered by soldiers engaged in the European invasion of India, led by Alexander the Great in 327 BC. His campaign is reliably credited with having brought back rice itself to Europe, but any rice spirit appears to have been overlooked. Perhaps, if it was drunk at all by the invaders, it was in a diluted form, and was not therefore

Right: An original pot still has become a museum piece at the Jameson Heritage Centre, Midleton, County Cork.

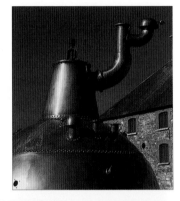

perceived to be any higher in alcohol than the grape wine with which they were familiar. Then again, it may just have been rejected as smelling or looking unclean. Whatever the explanation, if the Chinese or Indians did

Above: The final character, precise colour, and the richness and roundness of flavour of both cognac and whisky are derived from the final maturation period in wood.

Left: Copper pot stills – the original distillation vessel – are widely used in the Cognac region of France as well as by the whisky distillers of Scotland.

practise distillation as long ago as is claimed, the expertise they had stumbled on centuries before the Europeans remained specific to that part of the world.

The original and still widespread distillation vessel, used in the Cognac region of France, as well as by the whisky distillers of Scotland, is the pot still. It consists of the only three elements absolutely essential to the process: a pot in which the fermented product (malted grains, wine, cider, etc.) is heated; the alembic, or tube, through which the alcohol vapour driven off is sucked up; and the condenser where the steam is cooled and reliquified. To obtain a better quality product, spirits are generally distilled at least twice for greater refinement, so the still has to be started up again. Moreover, not all of the condensed vapour is suitable for use in fine liquor. The first and last of it to pass through (known as the "heads" and "tails") are generally discarded for the relatively high level of impurities they contain. The invention of the continuous still in the early 19th century, in which the process carries on to a second distillation uninterrupted, made spirit production more economical and easier to control. This is the method used in France's other classic brandy, armagnac, and it is now the preferred apparatus for most spirits production worldwide.

Probably the first spirit to be taken seriously as an object of connoisseurship, as distinct from being purely medicinal or just a method of using up surplus grape or grain production, was the brandy of the Cognac region of western France. It was noticed that the superior, mellower spirit produced by the light wines of Cognac responded particularly well to ageing in oak casks. The casks were traditionally fashioned out of wood from the Limousin forests of the region. Cask-aged spirits derive every bit of their final character, from the precise shade of tawny in the colour to their richness and roundness of flavour, from the maturation period they undergo in wood. They will not continue to develop

in the bottle. The complex classification system in operation today for cognac is based on the length of time the spirit has been aged. It is testimony to a reputation for painstaking quality that dates back to around the end of the 1600s.

Scottish and Irish whiskies rose to similar prominence soon after. Their differing production processes resulted in quite distinct regional styles, depending on the quantities of peat used in the kilns where the malted grain is dried, on the quality of the spring water used in the mash and, some have claimed, on the shape of the still.

Varieties of whisky are made across the world these days, from North America to Japan, but all attempts to replicate the precise taste of great Scotch – for all that the ingredients and procedures may be identical – have inexplicably foundered.

Where a distilled drink stops being a spirit and turns into a liqueur is something of an elusive question. The one constant is that, to be a liqueur, a drink should have some obvious aromatizing element (perhaps even a hundred or more in the case of certain celebrated products). This doesn't mean that all flavoured distillates are liqueurs –

flavoured vodkas are still vodka – but there are no neutral liqueurs. Some of these products have histories at least as venerable as those of cognac and Scotch. The most notable are those produced by the old French monastic orders. Bénédictine, the cognac-based, herb-scented potion that originated at the monastery in Fécamp, in Normandy, can convincingly lay claim to a lineage that rolls back to the beginning of the 16th century.

The first and greatest cocktail era, that arrived with the advent of the Jazz Age in the 1920s, rescued a lot of the traditional liqueurs from the niches of obscurity into which popular taste had relegated them. The Benedictine monks may have been a little shocked to hear that their revered creation was being mixed with English gin, American applejack, apricot brandy and maple syrup, shaken to within an inch of its life and then rechristened the Mule's Hind Leg, but at least it was drunk – as were the giggling flappers after knocking back three or four of them.

Gradually, spirits and liqueurs found their way into cookery too, either as enriching ingredients, such as the brandy

Above: The all-important water that flows through an old-fashioned water wheel at a traditional distillery in Northern Ireland.

used in coq au vin, or to boost flavouring, as with the fruit liqueurs used in ice creams and mousses. Certain dishes are constructed entirely around a particular drink: there would be no rum baba without rum, no zabaglione without Marsala.

In this book, we shall look first at the histories and compositions of all of the most important spirits, liqueurs and fortified wines, and then at ways in which they may be used classically and creatively in the kitchen. We hope that you will come to see these renowned products not just as drinks in themselves, but as indispensable elements of gastronomy too, so that you may need to clear a passage between the drinks cabinet and the kitchen cupboard. And, unlike other cookbooks that use alcohol in their recipes, this one allows you to learn something about the drinks you are using while the casserole is cooking, the mousse is setting or the sorbet is freezing.

May the spirits be with you.

SPIRITS

THE EARLIEST SPIRITS were almost certainly fairly straightforward, rough-and-ready distillations of ordinary wine. For centuries, a form of distillation had been practised using herbs and flowers infused in water, then cooked and condensed. The resulting essence was used medicinally, in cooking or just as a perfume. As we saw in the Introduction, the discovery in Europe of the art of distilling alcohol arose as a result of alchemical experiments designed to find the "elixir of life". The powerful brew that was arrived at by distilling was thought to contain the "soul" or "spirit" of the wine.

When it was realized that anything that had been fermented to produce alcohol could in turn be distilled into spirit, the process came to be applied to materials that were fermented *specifically* for distillation, rather than being consumable products in themselves. So, mashed malted grains were responsible, in regions that lacked the climate for wine-making, for the first drinks definable as whiskies.

As wine itself was held in high esteem, and was imported in great quantity by the cooler countries of northern Europe, such as England and Holland, the spirit produced from wine was the

first to receive true acclaim. Traders on ships putting in at La Rochelle and other ports in the Charente region of western France had no particular taste for the acidic, flavourless wines of the area, but the strong spirit the wines could be turned into was considered a lot better than other such distillates found elsewhere. Thus did cognac first come to prominence.

A memory of the alchemical quest to find the magic elixir was preserved in the Latin name first given to the product of distillation: *aqua vitae*, water of life. That phrase has remained inseparable from spirits terminology: the French call their spirit *eau-de-vie,* the Scandinavians *aquavit,* and the Celts *uisge beatha,* which was eventually corrupted by non-Gaelic speakers into whisky. In Russian, it became, more humbly, "little water" or vodka. The alternative medieval Latin name was *aqua ardens,* "burning water", for reasons that are not hard to fathom. The association with fieriness, both in the method used to extract the alcohol and in the sensation that drinking it produced, lived on in the naming of distilled wine *Gebranntwein* ("burnt

Above left: Scotland's smallest distillery in Pitlochry, Scotland was built in 1837.

Below left: Traditionally whisky was aged in used oak sherry casks.

Below: The dark berries of the juniper tree contribute the characteristic perfume of gin.

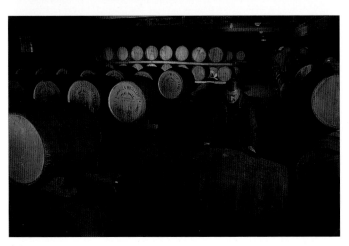

wine") in German, *brandewijn* in Dutch and eventually brandy in English.

Despite being highly prized, these early spirits would not have tasted particularly pleasant to us. They would only have been distilled once and would therefore have contained high concentrations of fusel oil, a group of compounds known in scientific parlance as the "higher alcohols", the "higher" referring to their greater acidity. It was only in 1800 that a physicist named Adam discovered the benefits of redistillation or rectification. This dispensed with a large proportion, though not all, of the raw-tasting higher alcohols and resulted in a purer spirit. It also stripped away a lot of the positive by-products of distillation that gave the drink its character, and so for a while the infusions of herbs, spices and fruit extracts that had originally been used to disguise the roughness of the

alcohol came back into favour in order to give it flavour.

Eventually, the correct balance was struck. The products that needed some distillation character – brandies and whiskies – retained it (undergoing a double distillation) and had it enhanced by ageing in wooden casks, while those that were intended to be as neutral as possible, such as vodka and gin, were subject to repeated redistillation. (In the case of gin and similar products, a neutral spirit base is created by prolonged rectification, so that the aromatic ingredients that are added can stand out the more boldly.) Most commercial spirits produced today have been thoroughly rectified, which is not necessarily a blessing: one thinks of the relentless blandness of some brands of white rum. The trend owes much to the fact that most of the white spirits are drunk with mixers these days.

Above: This modern distillery produces the neutral spirit base for both gin and vodka.

When tasting a fine spirit – aged cognac, single malt whisky, sour-mash bourbon or old demerara rum, for example – the procedure that is used for tasting wine clearly won't do. Try rolling a liquid with 40% alcohol around your mouth and you'll soon wish you hadn't. Some tasters judge them on the nose alone; others add a similar quantity of water, which many feel emphasizes their aromatic subtleties. I prefer to be brave and taste them undiluted. If you follow this route, the trick is to take in only a very little liquid, keep it at the front of the mouth just behind the lips by lowering the head after sipping, draw some air over it quickly and spit it out before it starts burning. The whole exercise is much brisker than tasting a mouthful of wine.

AQUAVIT *no recipe included*

AMONG THE VARIOUS spirits whose collective names are derived from the phrase "water of life", Scandinavian aquavit or akvavit has a particularly ancient history. It is known to have been distilled in northern Europe since medieval times, and its use as a drink – as distinct from its purely medical application – dates back at least to the 15th century.

Production of aquavit is very similar to that of flavoured vodkas. Its base is a neutral grain and/or potato spirit, which is rectified to a high degree of purity and then aromatized, usually with fragrant spices. The Scandinavian countries and Germany are the production centres of true aquavit. Its alternative name, schnapps, derives from an old Nordic verb *snappen*, meaning to snatch or seize. It denotes the way in which it is traditionally drunk, snatched down the throat in a single gulp.

HOW IT IS MADE

Potatoes are boiled in a contraption rather like a huge pressure-cooker, and the resulting starchy mass is then mixed with malted grains. After fermentation with yeasts, it is double-distilled to obtain a neutral spirit. Dilution reduces it to a drinkable strength, and contact with charcoal – as well as accepted flavouring elements – gives it its final character. Much commercial schnapps is sold at a reduced alcohol level and flavoured with various fruits.

AALBORG
A premium high-strength aquavit from Denmark

FLAVOURINGS
Aniseed
Fennel seeds
Dill
Cumin seeds
Caraway seeds
Bitter oranges

HOW TO SERVE
Aquavit should be served like good vodka – that is, ice-cold and neat from a receptacle no bigger than a shot-glass. The bottle should be kept in the freezer prior to serving. It makes a superb wintertime aperitif, especially for guests who have just come in from the cold.

MIXING
Try substituting aquavit for the vodka in an otherwise textbook Bloody Mary.

OTHER NAMES
Germany: Schnapps *Denmark*: schnaps
Sweden/Norway/Netherlands: snaps

TASTES GOOD WITH
Despite its cinematic association with reckless drinking sessions, aquavit has a genuine gastronomic history. It formed an integral part of the original Swedish *smörgåsbord*, which was a more modest feast than the lavish spreads of today. It consisted of just bread, fish (generally herring) and perhaps cheese, washed down with aquavit. The dry savouriness of the spirit complemented the appetizing role of the salty food. Divorced from its edible accompaniments, aquavit lives on today as an aperitif, knocked back in one and followed by a chaser of local beer.

BOMMERLUNDER
An acclaimed aquavit from Germany, which is immortalized in the popular drinking song Eisgekühlter Bommerlunder *(Ice Cold Bommerlunder)*

ARAK

ALTHOUGH THE DISCOVERY of distillation is still hotly disputed, it is just possible that some form of arak, or raki, was the very first spirit. There are claims that it was made in India around 800 BC, and certainly the production of a fiery, clear spirit on the sub-continent, and down in the South Pacific too, goes back many centuries.

Arak is not really one drink, but a generic name for a group of clear distillates, for which the base material and method of production vary according to the region of origin. In Java, Sumatra and Borneo, the fermented juice of sugar-cane provides the base, but there are also rice versions. The sap of palm trees, which ferments very readily in sultry temperatures, is popular as a source of arak in India.

The drink came to the Middle East and the Mediterranean with the

OTHER NAMES
Arrack, arraki, racki, raki, rakija

HOW TO SERVE
Arak or raki should be drunk in fairly abstemious measures, preferably with highly seasoned eastern Mediterranean meze (appetizers). Owing to its rough potency, it is safer to sip it than to down it in one.

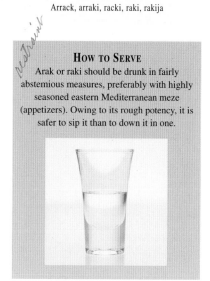

FLAVOURINGS
Figs, dates, grapes, raisins and plums

RAKI
Simple Turkish raki that has not been cask-aged

45 % VOL.

YENİ RAKI

HERGESTELLT AUS TRAUBEN UND ANIS

TÜRKISCHE SPEZIALITÄT
DESTILLIERT UND ABGEFÜLLT DURCH TEKEL
GENERALDIREKTION DER TABAK TABAKPRODUKTE
SALZ UND ALKOHOL BETRIEBE
ISTANBUL

0.7 L.

SPIRITUOSE - PRODUCE OF TURKEY

early Arab spice trade; its common name is derived from the Arabic word for juice or sap, *araq*. Other easily fermentable products such as dates and figs gradually infiltrated the making of arak, and are still used in parts of North Africa and the Middle East. Finally, grape wine came to play its part in the old wine-making cultures of Greece and Cyprus, including that made from raisins.

In the West today, arak is most commonly encountered in the form of raki, the aniseed-tinged spirit of Greece and Turkey. Some coloured raki is very fine, and is based on old cask-aged brandies, but most is a colourless and pretty raw-tasting spirit that can be anything up to 50% alcohol by volume (ABV). The Turks know it as Lion's Milk. Raki is made throughout the Balkan countries of southeast Europe, sometimes from figs or plums rather than grapes.

TASTES GOOD WITH
Around the Mediterranean region, raki is nearly always drunk as an aperitif, but if you are lucky enough to find a particularly mellow example, it may be better drunk at the latter end of the meal, after coffee.

MIXING
If drunk as an appetizer, the more basic grade of raki may well be taken with ice in Greece and Cyprus.

BITTERS

FLAVOURINGS

Numerous herbs and roots impart greater or lesser degrees of bitterness to all of these drinks.
Gentian is quite common. It is a flowering alpine plant, the root of which is rendered down to a bright yellow essence that has been used as a tonic and anti-fever remedy in folk medicine for centuries.
Quinine was the New World alternative to gentian. It is an extract of the bark of the cinchona tree, a native of South America.
Seville oranges The dried peel of this bitter variety is essential in Campari.

THE TERM "BITTERS" refers to any one of a number of spirits flavoured with bitter herbs or roots, which are generally held to have medicinal properties. They range from products such as Campari, which can be drunk in whole measures like any other spirit, to those that are so bitter that they are only added in drops to season another drink.

Bitterness is the last of the four main taste sensations (the others being sweetness, saltiness and sourness) that developing tastebuds learn to appreciate. A fondness for bitter flavours is often thought to be a sign of the palate having reached its true maturity.

The link between bitterness and health is evident in the fact that tonic water was originally conceived as an all-purpose pick-me-up containing the stimulant

quinine, rather than as a mixer for gin, although these days its flavour tends to be drowned with artificial sweetening. The other unquestionably effective medicinal role of bitters is as an aid to digestion.

The origins of bitters lie in the flavouring elements that were commonly added to the very earliest spirits. These elixirs were taken as restoratives and remedies for any number of conditions, ranging from poor digestion to painful joints. The apothecaries who concocted them drew on the collected wisdom of herbal medicine, and added extracts of bark, roots, fruit peels, herbs and spices to enhance the healing powers of the drink.

Bitters are made all over the world. Perhaps the most famous of all is Angostura. An infusion of gentian root with herbs on a strong rum base, Angostura was invented in the 19th century by a German medic who was personal doctor to the South American revolutionary hero Simón Bolívar. He named it after a town in Venezuela, although today it is made exclusively in Trinidad, albeit still by the company founded by its inventor. Angostura is one of the few such medicinal drinks that can lay claim to actually having been formulated by a doctor.

In Europe the two major centres of production

UNDERBERG
An intensely pungent digestive bitter from Germany

CAMPARI
Italy's most famous bitter aperitif also comes in a ready-mixed bottle with a crown cap

MIXING

Negroni: Thoroughly mix equal measures of gin, Campari and sweet red vermouth with ice in a tumbler and add a squirt of soda.
Americano: As for Negroni, but leave out the gin and add a few drops of Angostura.
Pink gin (below): Sprinkle about half-a-dozen drops of Angostura into a goblet-shaped glass, roll it around to coat the inner surfaces, then dash it out. Add ice-cold gin, which will then take on the faintest pink tint.

of bitters are Italy and France. Italy has Campari – a bright red aperitif of uncompromising bitterness, which is made in Milan – and also Fernet-Branca. Like Germany's Underberg, this is a ferociously dark, pungent bitters that is often recommended as a hangover cure. France's famous bitters include Amer Picon (which was invented as an anti-malarial remedy by an army officer serving in Algeria), Toni-Kola and Secrestat.

English fruit bitters, such as orange and peach, were widely used in the cocktail era of the 1920s. Hungary's runner is Unicum, which balances its bitterness with a slight sweetness, while the Latvians add their own treacle-dark dry tonic, Melnais Balzams (Black Balsam), to their coffee.

FERNET-BRANCA
The Italian bitter much prized as a hangover cure

UNICUM
A deeply coloured bitter speciality of Hungary

ANGOSTURA
The most widely used bitter in the cocktail repertoire

HOW TO SERVE
Campari is classically served with soda water and a twist of lemon peel, but don't drown it. Amer Picon may be served the same way, or perhaps as a bittering element with gin for those whose need to be picked up requires more than a straight dry Martini. Underberg and Fernet-Branca can be quaffed straight as stomach-settlers or just to aid digestion, while Angostura is essential in a pink gin – the drink of officers and gentlemen.

BRANDY

STRICTLY SPEAKING, the term brandy applies to any grape-based spirit distilled from wine. There are "brandies" made from other fruits – such as Normandy's calvados, made from apples – but we shall deal with these under their own headings. The English name is a corruption of the Dutch *brandewijn*, in turn derived from the German *Gebranntwein*, meaning burnt wine, which is an apt term for the product of distillation.

The most famous of all true brandies is cognac, named after a town in the Charente region of western France. It was to here that traders from northern Europe, particularly the Netherlands, came in the 17th century, putting in at the port of La Rochelle to take delivery of consignments of salt. They inevitably took some of the region's thin, acidic wine with them as well. Because of tax regulations, and to save space in the ships' holds – always a major consideration – the wines were boiled to reduce their volume by evaporation. On arrival at their destination, they would be reconstituted with water. However, it came to be noticed that the Charente wines positively benefited from the reduction process. It was but a short step from there to actual distillation.

HOW TO SERVE

The finest and oldest brandies should not be mixed. Younger products mix reasonably well with soda; the vogue for brandy-and-tonic being assiduously promoted in Cognac, of all places, is not one that finds favour with the author. In the Far East, brandy is mixed with plenty of iced water as a very long drink, and consumed with food.

MARTELL
The oldest house in Cognac is still a brand leader

HOW TO SERVE

Fine cognac should be drunk just as it comes, without mixers and certainly without ice. It is traditionally served in balloon glasses that allow room for swirling. Tradition is often an unreliable guide, and the aromas are much better appreciated in something resembling a large liqueur glass, which mutes the prickle of the spirit. The bouquet is also encouraged by a gentle warming of the glass in the hand (for which the balloon was indisputably better designed), but recourse to those lovely, old, silver brandy-warmers, which allowed you to barbecue the tilted glass over a little petrol flame, is not recommended.

Such was the fame and the premium paid for the distilled wines of the Charente that they came to have many imitators. None, however, could match the precise local conditions in which cognac is made. Its chalky soils, the maritime climate and the ageing in barrels fashioned from Limousin oak were the indispensable features that gave cognac the pre-eminent reputation that it enjoys to this day.

France's other brandy of note, armagnac, is made in the southwest of the country. Armagnac is based on a wider range of grape varieties and made using a slightly different method to cognac. Although not as widely known as cognac, it has its own special cachet in the spirits market and is preferred by many as the better digestif.

There are grape brandies produced all over Europe and the Americas, as we shall see in the succeeding pages. The best are generally made by the pot-still method of distillation. Some inferior spirit, artificially coloured and flavoured, used also to be known as brandy, but has been banned from using the term within the European Union following the introduction of a new law in 1989. *USA*

COGNAC

The Cognac region covers two *départements* on the western side of France near the Bay of Biscay: inland Charente, and Charente-Maritime on the coast. Cognac is a small town close to the border between the two. The vineyards are sub-divided into six growing areas, the most notable of which are Grande Champagne and Petite Champagne, just south of Cognac itself.

As we have seen, the fame of cognac had been well and truly established in the Dutch and British markets by the end of

HENNESSY X.O
Premium cognac in a decorative bottle designed in 1947

the 17th century. The industry's first great entrepreneur was Jean Martell, a Jersey-born opportunist who, in 1715, turned away from a life of crime (smuggling) in order to found the house that still bears his name. Cognac's other leading brands are Hennessy, Courvoisier and Rémy Martin. Smaller but no less distinguished companies include Hine and Otard.

The relative qualities of different cognacs depend almost entirely on the length of time they have been aged and the cognacs are classified accordingly. No brandy that has earned the right to the Cognac *appellation contrôlée* (AC) status may be blended from spirits that are less than two years old. At the bottom rung of the quality classification for the British and Irish markets is VS (historically known as three-star, and still designated by a row of three stars on the label). VS may contain brandies as young as three years old, but the basic products of most of the leading companies will contain some significantly older reserves.

The next stage up is VSOP, Very Special (or Superior) Old Pale, an old British term that arose in London in the 19th century to denote a particularly fine – but paradoxically light-coloured – batch of cognac. (Although cognac derives most of its colour from wood-ageing, caramel can also be added to influence the colour, provided it does not affect the taste. Any slight sweetness in the spirit derives from correction with sugar solution just before bottling.) VSOP is the five-star stuff because the youngest spirit it contains must have spent at least five years in wood.

Those blended from minimum six-year-old cognacs may be entitled XO, or given any one of a number of names the houses invent for themselves, such as Reserve, Extra, Cordon Bleu, Paradis or classically Napoléon – so named because the bottles supposedly contain brandies aged since the time of the *Empéreur*.

The prices that the oldest cognacs command are breathtaking, yet the enjoyment can never be proportionately greater than that to be had from good VSOP. In many cases, you may be paying for something that looks like a giant perfume

COURVOISIER
Along with Martell, this is one of the most widely drunk cognacs in the world.

REMY MARTIN
Remy's VSOP is a rich, fine, well-aged cognac.

bottle fashioned in cut crystal and presented in a silk-lined box. If you really want to try one of these luxury products, it makes sense to wait until your next trip through duty-free.

It is often thought that the optimum age for the best cognacs is about 40 years old, but it must always be borne in mind with any spirit that it can only age in cask. Once it is bottled, no further development takes place.

ARMAGNAC

Armagnac, which was thought of until about the middle of the 19th century merely as France's "other brandy", is made in the Pays de Gascogne in the far southwest of the country. There are three sub-regions – Bas-Armagnac, Ténarèze and Haut-Armagnac – of which the first is usually

considered the best. Despite its lesser renown, armagnac has a legitimate claim to be considered the more venerable product, distillation in the region having been reliably dated back to the 1400s. Its chief distinguishing characteristics compared to cognac are these: while cognac is made largely from the Ugni Blanc grape, armagnac's base wine is made from a blend of several varieties; a local black oak (as distinct from Limousin) is used for the maturation; and the continuous still (invented by Edouard Adam) is widely used to distil the spirit.

So inextricably bound up with armagnac production was Adam's patent still that, for a long period this century, it was the only authorized apparatus for producing armagnac. Continuous distillation yields a spirit rich in the aroma-containing impurities that give any brandy its character, which is why armagnac is noticeably more fragrant than cognac. Many tasters describe it as having a "biscuity" aroma, while others – by no means fancifully – detect a floral topnote like violets. The flavour tends to be drier because it isn't adjusted with sugar, and the absence of caramel as a colouring matter makes it generally paler than a cognac of the same age.

The labelling system is comparable to that of cognac. The exception is that the youngest armagnacs may be released in the British market after two years in cask rather than three. The designations VS, VSOP and XO are defined in exactly the same way. Vintage-dated armagnac – the unblended produce of a single year's harvest – has always been a peculiarity of the region (although vintage labelling has now been relegalized in Cognac). If the label on, say, a 1959 armagnac looks suspiciously new, remember that it is because it has probably only recently been bottled. The ageing can only take place in wood, not glass.

Part of the charm of the Armagnac region is that many of the producers are still rural artisans, rather than globally important companies catering to the luxury market, as in Cognac. Their brandies are often distilled in shared portable stills that are driven around the countryside at production time. As a result, prices for even the top armagnacs are considerably gentler.

NAMING

"Brandy" is just a generic term for any distilled grape spirit. They get very upset in Cognac and Armagnac these days, and perhaps understandably, if you refer to their products unceremoniously as brandy. It is happily used by quality producers in Spain, California and elsewhere. Note that none of these products contains any added flavouring element. If they do, they cease to be "brandy", at least in terms of the European Union definition of 1989.

ARMAGNAC
"Hors d'Age" on an armagnac label denotes very long cask-ageing

J.de Malliac
BAS ARMAGNAC
EXTRA
HORS D'AGE

PRODUCE OF FRANCE

OTHER EUROPEAN BRANDIES

Spain The most significant producer of grape brandy, in terms of both quantity and quality, outside France is Spain. The premium products are accorded the same attention to detail at every stage of their manufacture as the finest in Cognac and Armagnac and, as a result, are fully capable of withstanding comparison with their French counterparts.

Spanish brandy production is concentrated in the sherry region of Jerez, in the south of the country. Indeed, most of it is distilled by the sherry houses, such as Gonzalez Byass, Domecq and Osborne. The grapes from which the base wine is made generally come from La Mancha, the huge central plain that represents the grape basket of Spanish viticulture, but the wines are distilled and aged in sherry country. This entitles them to the designation of Brandy de Jerez – a dependable indicator of quality.

Maturation is by a process known as fractional blending, or the *solera* system, which is also used for the finest sherries. A *solera* consists of a stack of barrels piled up in rows. The new spirit enters the top row and, at intervals of several months, a quantity of it is drawn off and added to the next row down, where it displaces a similar quantity into the row below, and so on. The bottom row contains the oldest brandies which are drawn off in fractions for bottling. The brandy gains greater age characteristics by this process than it would if it were left to mature undisturbed in the same barrel, as in France, for a similar period.

Top brands include Lepanto, made by Gonzalez Byass, Sanchez Romate's Cardinal Mendoza and Osborne's Conde d'Osborne, which comes in an idiosyncratically shaped bottle designed by the mad genius of 20th-century Spanish art, Salvador Dali. The brand leader, though, is Fundador, a Domecq product, and one that deserves a much better reputation. In Catalonia, the pace-setting Torres winery makes its own exceptional brandy.

Germany The best German offering seen on export markets is Uralt, an aged product made by a distiller in the Rheingau called Asbach. It receives a maturation period of around 18 months. Like the country's less good sparkling wines, most German brandy is made from imported French or Italian base wine, and so it has no particular indigenous character.

Others Italy's brandies are fairly basic commercial spirits, most coming from the volume producer Stock. Portugal makes a handful of good brandies, but its industry is heavily geared to supplying grape spirit for the port shippers. In southeast Europe, Cyprus makes brandies of about the same level of sophistication as the fortified wines it once called "sherry", while Bulgaria still produces a decent aged brandy from base wine principally derived from the Ugni Blanc grape of Cognac.

LEPANTO
Spain's leading brandy, made by Gonzalez Byass of sherry fame

MIXING
Alexander: Shake equal measures of VSOP cognac, dark brown crème de cacao and thick cream with ice and strain into a cocktail glass. Sprinkle the surface with nutmeg or powdered chocolate for the most comforting cocktail in the repertoire.

B & B (Bénédictine and brandy): The traditional mix is half-and-half with good cognac, stirred not shaken, and not usually iced.

METAXA

Among the brandies produced on the mainland of Greece (and to some extent on the island of Samos), the abidingly popular Metaxa deserves a special mention. Despite the brouhaha with which it is treated in Greece itself, and a distinctly specious system of age-labelling, it is a fairly basic industrial product.

Greek brandy isn't ever going to fare well against aged cognac for the simple reason that the grape varieties that go into it are not generally of sufficiently high acidity to produce a suitable base wine. The mainstays are Savatiano (widely used in retsina) and the Muscat grape that produces the golden dessert wines of Samos and other islands, and the distillers are not above using base wines that contain some red grapes.

There are three grades of Metaxa, ascending in quality from three stars to

five and seven. The last is sometimes said to have been cask-aged for around half a century, a claim we can confidently take with a cask of salt. It is relatively pale in colour (which fact alone makes the age claim suspicious) and much sweeter on the palate than cognac, with a highly moreish toffee or caramel quality.

AMERICAN BRANDIES

USA Brandy has been made in the United States since the days of the pioneers, most of it in what is now the premier wine-growing state of California. At one time, brandy production was simply a convenient means of using up sub-standard grapes that were considered unfit for quality wine production, as it still is in many of Europe's viticultural regions. In the last 30 years or so, however, a turn towards producing finer aged spirits has been made, and a number of these American products are capable of giving some of the famous VSOP cognacs a run for their money.

Not all are made in the image of cognac; some are discernibly more orientated towards the Spanish style. The brandies are habitually matured in barrels of home-grown American oak,

MIXING
Never on Sunday
(from Michael Walker's *Cinzano Cocktail Book*): Stir a measure of Metaxa with half a measure of ouzo, a splash of lemon juice and a dash of Angostura over ice. Strain into a tall glass and top with equal quantities of champagne and ginger beer.

METAXA *Brandy*
The holiday maker's favourite

CARNEROS ALAMBIC
Brandy from the Napa Valley, California

MIXING

Brandy Blazer: Put two measures of cognac in a saucepan with one sugar cube and the thinly pared rind from half an orange and one lemon. Heat gently, then remove from the heat and light the surface of the liquid. The alcohol will burn with a low, blue flame for about one minute. Blow out the flame. Add half a measure of Kahlúa and strain into a heat-resistant liqueur glass. Decorate with a cocktail stick threaded with a twist of orange rind.

which gives a more pronounced aroma to the spirit, accentuated by the heavily charred inner surfaces of the barrels. These conditions result in brandies of great richness and complexity. Names to look out for include Germain-Robin and RMS (the latter brand owned by Cognac star Rémy Martin). Some of the top California wineries have also turned out some impressive efforts, while bulk producer Gallo in Modesto make a passable version intended for mixing.

Latin America There is a long tradition of drinking fiery spirits all over Central and South America, in which grape brandy plays its part – particularly in the areas where the early Spanish colonists first planted vines. Mexico is the most important producer. Its flagship is a big-selling global brand called Presidente, made in the light, simple style of a rough-and-ready Spanish brandy.

The peculiarly South American offering, however, is pisco. There is still much dispute over whether it originated in Peru or Chile, the two centres of production (with a modest

contribution from Bolivia). I shall forbear to come down on either side of the fence, except to point out that the Pisco valley and the seaport of the same name are in Peru, but the Chileans simply insist that that was one of the principal export destinations for their indigenous spirit, and the name just stuck.

Despite receiving some cask-ageing, pisco is always colourless because the barrels it matures in are so ancient that they have no colour left to give to the spirit. In Chile, the longer the maturation, the lower the dilution before bottling, so the finer grades (Gran Pisco is the best) are the strongest. Owing to widespread use of members of the Muscat grape family in the base wine, nearly all types and nationalities of pisco are marked by an unabashed fruitiness on the nose and palate.

The myth that pisco is a throat-searing firewater strictly for the peasants is probably based on the exposure of delicate European sensibilities to the lower grades. Top pisco has every right to be considered a world-class spirit.

PISCO brandy
A top-quality pisco from Peru

MIXING

Pisco Sour: Half-fill a small tumbler with smashed ice. Put in two measures of freshly squeezed lime juice and sweeten to taste with caster sugar. Stir well to dissolve the sugar. Add a measure of pisco, and give the drink a final stir.

CALVADOS

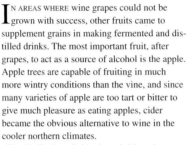

IN AREAS WHERE wine grapes could not be grown with success, other fruits came to supplement grains in making fermented and distilled drinks. The most important fruit, after grapes, to act as a source of alcohol is the apple. Apple trees are capable of fruiting in much more wintry conditions than the vine, and since many varieties of apple are too tart or bitter to give much pleasure as eating apples, cider became the obvious alternative to wine in the cooler northern climates.

The distillation of cider is probably quite as old as the practice of distilling wine for grape brandy. In its heartland – the Normandy region of northern France – the earliest reference to an apple distillate dates from 1553, but we have no means of knowing how long, prior to the mid-1500s, it had already been going on.

If the name of the Normans' apple brandy, *calvados*, sounds more Spanish than French, that is because it derives from a story that tells of a ship, the *San Salvador*, from the mighty Spanish armada, which was dashed to smithereens off

OTHER NAMES

USA: applejack
UK: apple brandy/cider brandy

the Norman coast. The *département* came to be known as Calvados, and its traditional spirit was named after it. There is no historical corroboration of the story, and no one in Normandy seemingly expects you to believe it.

Like cognac and armagnac, calvados received its *appellation contrôlée* status quite soon after the introduction of the AC system: 1942. At the heart of the region is one particularly fine area called the Pays d'Auge, prized for its soils and the lie of its land, which has its own designation. (The rest is straight appellation Calvados.) Both the pot-still double distillation and the continuous method are used, although the calvados of the Pays d'Auge area may only use the former.

There are hundreds of different varieties of cider apple, classified into four broad taste groups: sweet, bitter-sweet, bitter and acid. The bitter-sweet ones make up the lion's share of the blend in a typical calvados. After distillation, the spirit goes into variously sized barrels of French oak for maturation. Supposedly, the younger a calvados is, the more likely it is to smell and

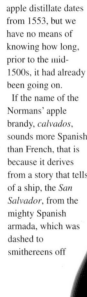

CALVADOS
The best calvados comes from the Pays d'Auge

APPLE BRANDY
A fine, powerful apple spirit from Somerset, England

MIXING

Depth Charge: Shake equal measures of calvados and cognac with half a measure of fresh lemon juice, a dash of grenadine and ice. Strain into a cocktail glass.

taste of apples; the older ones take on the vanilla and spice tones of the wood.

Age indications are not dissimilar to those of cognac and armagnac. Three-star (or three-apple) calvados spends a minimum of two years in cask, Vieux or Réserve three years, and Vieille Réserve or VSOP four years. Those aged for six or more years may be labelled Hors d'Age or Age Inconnu ("age unknown"!). If a calvados is labelled with a period of ageing, such as 8-year-old, then the age specified refers to the youngest spirit in it, not the average. Should you come across any of the small amount of vintage-dated calvados, note that the date refers to the year of distillation — the year *after* harvest.

In the United States, an apple spirit has been made ever since the first British settlers found that the apple trees they planted in New England proved hardier than grain crops. Applejack, as it is most commonly known, is made in much the same way as calvados, starting with good cider and distilling it twice in a pot still. The spirit is then aged in oak for anything up to about five years. The younger stuff is pretty abrasive, but on the eastern seaboard – as in Normandy – they like it that way. Laird's is one of the bigger-selling brands.

The alternative way of making applejack, now officially frowned on, was to freeze the cider. Water freezes before alcohol, so if the first slush to form was skimmed away, what was left would be virtually pure alcohol. (A derivative of this technique is used today in the making of both ice beers and ice ciders in order to strengthen them.)

Apple brandy, or cider brandy, is now being revived in the west of England. Somerset is, after all, considered by many to be capable of producing the world's best ciders. When properly aged, it can be quite impressive, although devotees of calvados are unlikely to be fooled by it in a blind tasting.

NOTE

HOW IT IS MADE

Apples are harvested from September through to December, depending on the variety. A precise blend of juices from the four types is fermented into cider at about 5–6% alcohol. This is subjected to a double distillation (or continuous distillation, except in the Pays d'Auge region of Calvados). The spirit is then aged in cask for anything up to 40 years, and bottled at 40–45% ABV.

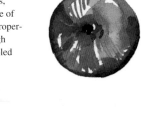

APPLEJACK
America's answer to calvados

HOW TO SERVE

In Normandy, there is a gastronomic tradition called the *trou normand* (literally "Norman hole"). A shot of neat calvados is drunk in place of a sorbet before the main course of a meal. The idea is that the spirit punches a hole through the food already consumed and allows you to go on eating in comfort.

EAU DE VIE

FLAVOURINGS
Numerous fruits, including strawberries, raspberries, pears, plums, bilberries, blackberries

HOW TO SERVE
Eaux de vie should be served extremely well chilled and neat. They blend well with neutral mixers like soda, but anything flavoured should be avoided because it will mask the attractiveness of the fruit aromas.

Eau de vie is the French phrase for the Latin *aqua vitae*, water of life. Strictly speaking, the term refers to all spirits distilled from fermented fruits, starting with wine-based cognac and armagnac. By the same token, calvados could therefore be considered an eau de vie of cider. Since the names of these individual spirits are legally protected by France's geographical *appellation contrôlée* regulations, they have come to be known by those names instead of being referred to as eaux de vie.

Spirits can be produced from many other fruits as well as grapes or apples, though, and these are

OTHER NAMES
The French also call colourless fruit brandies *alcools blancs*, or white spirits. Some of the fruit names in French are *framboise* (raspberry), *mûre* (blackberry), *prune* (plum), *poire* (pear), *fraise* (strawberry) and *myrtille* (bilberry)

much less precisely defined. The term eau de vie, therefore, tends now to be reserved for these other fruit brandies. Apart from their basic ingredients, the main attribute that distinguishes eaux de vie from cognac and armagnac is that they are colourless because they haven't been aged in wood like their more famous cousins. The theory is

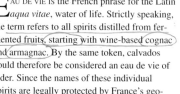

POIRE-WILLIAMS
Eau de vie flavoured with William pears

LA VIELLE PRUNE
Pascall makes this celebrated plum eau de vie

that they develop in glass, which rather flies in the face of what is scientifically known about spirits – namely, that development stops once they are in the bottle.

Of the variety of fruits used, the most often encountered – and those producing the most delicious eaux de vie – are the various soft summer berries. Alsace, a wine region of north-east France that has lurched from French to German domination and back again since the late 19th century, is a particularly rich source of these spirits. Some of them are made by winemakers, others by specialist distillers. What they have

in common is high alcohol (sometimes around 45% ABV), absence of colour and a clear, pure scent and flavour of their founding fruit. They are not sweetened, and should not be confused with the syrupy liqueurs of the same flavours, which tend to be coloured anyway.

Eau de vie of this kind is also made in Switzerland and Germany.

TASTES GOOD WITH

Served very cold in small measures, they can work well with certain desserts, particularly frangipane-based tarts topped with the same fruit as that used to make the eau de vie.

EAUX DE VIE
The firm of Bertrand makes a wide range of types, including mirabelle plum, fleur de bière (hop flower) and kirsch (cherry).

FRAMBOISE SAUVAGE
Eau de vie flavoured with wild raspberries

FRAISE
A popular eau de vie from strawberries

GIN

O F THE FIVE essential spirits (brandy, whisky, rum, vodka and gin), gin is the only one that really has a reputation to live down. Down the years it has been the calamitous curse of the urban poor, the Mother's Ruin by which young girls in trouble tried to inflict miscarriages upon themselves, the bathtub brew that rotted guts during American Prohibition, and the first resort of the miserable as the storm-clouds of depression gathered. It was all so different in the beginning.

Although the English often claim to be the true progenitors of gin (as well as, more convincingly, of port and champagne), its origins in fact go back to 16th-century Holland. Like many other distilled drinks, the first inspiration behind the creation of gin was medicinal. The blend of herbs and aromatics used in it was believed to guard against all the ills that flesh was heir to. Principal among the elements of these concoctions was juniper, the Dutch word

OTHER NAMES

Holland: genever *France*: genièvre (although almost everybody in France now calls it "gin")

for which – *genever* – is the linguistic root of the English word "gin".

The dark little berries of the juniper tree contribute to the characteristic strong perfume of gin. They are prized medicinally as a diuretic, to counteract water retention. Despite the predominance of juniper in the aroma and flavour of gin, however, it is not the only added ingredient. Precise recipes vary according to the individual distiller – each has their own secret formulae – but other common components include angelica, *parsley like* liquorice, orris root, dried citrus peel, and caraway and coriander seeds.

HOW TO SERVE
The age-old mixer for gin is of course Schweppes tonic, the production of which is almost exclusively sustained by gin-drinkers. A gin and tonic is usually offered as a long drink with a slice of lemon and plenty of ice, but equal measures is a more sensitive way of treating the gin. Gin rubs along with any old mixer, though: orange juice, bitter lemon, ginger beer, whatever. (It isn't very nice with cola perhaps, but then few things are.)

BOMBAY SAPPHIRE
More delicately aromatic gin than the commercial norm

GORDON'S
This is the brand leader among London gins

MIXING

The number of gin-based cocktails is legion, but here are a few of the more durable ones:

Gin Fizz: Shake a good measure of gin with a teaspoon of caster sugar and the juice of half a lemon. Pour into a tall glass and top with fresh soda water. (This is not noticeably different to a **Tom Collins**, except that the latter may have a little less soda added. Then again, leave out the soda altogether, stir it in a tumbler rather than shaking it and call it a **Gin Sour**.)

Gimlet (below): Stir equal measures of Plymouth gin and Rose's lime cordial in a tumbler with a couple of ice cubes.

reform of the excise system then produced an anomaly whereby beer was suddenly subjected to a much stricter levy than before, so that gin was actually cheaper. Not surprisingly, it became the staple drink of the poorest classes, who consumed it in much the same quantities as they had beer. The gin shops were born, and public drunkenness and alcohol-related illnesses soared.

For the great mass of the London poor, getting drunk was the only way of escaping grim reality. So began gin's long association with gloom and despond (which still persists today in the enduring myth that gin is more of a depressant than the other spirits). The purveyors of gin sold their wares in terms that no

BELGRAVIA
LONDON
DRY GIN
One of the
lesser-known
London
brands

MIXING

Gin Rickey: Half-fill a tall glass with ice. Add two measures of gin, the juice of half a lime or a quarter of a lemon and a generous dash of grenadine. Stir vigorously, then top with fresh soda.

White Lady: Shake a measure of gin with half a measure of Cointreau and half a measure of fresh lemon juice, with ice, and strain into a cocktail glass. (Some recipes also add a teaspoon of egg white. My bible, the *Savoy Cocktail Book*, clearly indicates the White Lady to be innocent of such a substance. It simply gives the drink a frothier texture, if that's what you like.)

It may well have been British soldiers returning home from the Thirty Years' War who first brought the taste for Dutch genever across the North Sea. Then again, it may simply have been travellers to the continent starting or ending their journeys in Amsterdam. However that may be, a form of gin was being distilled in London in the 17th century, using the basic beer ingredients – hops and barley – and the essential juniper berries.

The meteoric rise in gin's popularity in Britain had two main causes. Firstly, periodic hostilities with the French led to the application of punitive tariffs to their exports and, just as port came to be the wine of patriotic choice among the elite, so gin replaced cognac. To compound that,

FLAVOURINGS

Juniper berries
(essential)
Coriander seeds
Caraway seeds
Orris root
Dried orange and lemon
peel
Angelica
Liquorice, fennel or
anise
Almonds
Cardamom pods

advertiser today could get away with; the wording on one signboard famously ran: "*Drunk for a penny. Dead drunk for tuppence. Clean straw for nothing*". Such was the addiction of the masses to gin that it was actually made illegal other than in bulk by an Act of Parliament in 1736, but the law was hastily reversed six years later after it was predictably discovered that the contraband stuff that was now being drunk was considerably more toxic than the official spirit had been.

In 1750, the great social satirist William Hogarth produced his famous engraving *Gin Lane*. It depicted in minute detail the degradation and squalor that was being wrought by widespread consumption of gin. A century later, gin was still being blamed by critical commentators such as the author Charles Dickens as the corrosive solace of the destitute, although Dickens was more concerned to blame social inequity for the condition of the poor, rather than to see drink in itself as an evil. It was in this period, however, that the

great Temperance movements took root, and the poor were encouraged to fear drink as the devil's potion.

It was only in the late Victorian period that gin began to reassume a more dignified apparel. Because of its colourlessness and its absence of wood-derived richness, it was seen as a usefully ladylike alternative to Scotch whisky and cognac. The all-too-recent association with the sordid doings of the idle poor meant that some euphemism had to be found for it – a facility Victorian society was supremely practised in. For a while, it was improbably referred to as "white wine". Finally, the gin and tonic, the world's favourite aperitif, was born, and a new era in gin's fortunes was ushered in.

During the period of Prohibition in the United States (1919–33), gin became one of the more readily available sources of illicit hooch, largely because it was so

BEEFEATER
*One of the
most famous
London gins*

MIXING

Dry Martini: No cocktail recipe is more energetically argued over than the classic dry Martini. It is basically a generous measure of virtually neat stone-cold gin with a dash of dry white vermouth in it. But how much is a dash? Purists insist on no more than a single drop, or the residue left after briefly flushing the glass out with a splash of vermouth and then pouring it away. (They puzzlingly refer to such a Martini as "very dry", as if adding more vermouth would sweeten it. In fact, the terminology harks back to the original recipe, when the vermouth used was the sweet red variety.) Some go for as much as half a measure of vermouth, and I have at hand a book that suggests a two-to-one ratio of gin to vermouth – guaranteed to send the purist into paroxysms of horror. I have to admit I incline more to the purist philosophy, though: the vermouth should be added as if it were the last bottle in existence. The drink should properly be mixed gently in a separate jug, with ice, and then strained into the traditional cocktail glass (the real name of which is a martini glass). A twist of lemon peel should be squeezed delicately over the surface, so that the essential oil floats in globules on top of the drink, but *don't* put the lemon twist in the glass. And hold the olive. (Add a cocktail onion, however, and the drink becomes a **Gibson**.)

easy for amateur distillers to make. All that was needed was to add whatever flavourings you could lay your hands on to a basic grain spirit, and then bottle it as soon as you liked. It is sometimes said that a lot of the more outlandish cocktails of the Jazz Era owed their inspiration to the need to disguise the disgusting taste of home-made gin.

The reason that gin continues to provide the base for so many cocktails is that it is such a good mixer. Its lack of colour means that it doesn't turn an off-putting muddy hue when blended with fruit juices, as the brown spirits do, while its aromatic quality gives it something for the mixers to mingle with, as distinct from the absolute neutrality of vodka. Gin has inevitably lost a lot of ground to vodka in the more recent youth market, as its peculiar

PLYMOUTH GIN

The Blackfriar's Distillery in Plymouth is the only producer of this gin.

*TANQUERAY
A specialty gin,
produced since 1830,
is exported from the
UK to its major market
in the US*

perfume is something of an acquired taste to untutored palates. In the 1990s, however, it suddenly found itself gaining new cachet among certain American rap artists, becoming the preferred tipple enthusiastically celebrated in their lyrics as "juice and gin" (in other words gin and orange, known to the Scott Fitzgerald set in the 1920s as Orange Blossom).

TYPES OF GIN

English Gin There are two types. London dry gin is by far the more commonly known, although it doesn't necessarily have to be distilled in the capital. It is an intensely perfumed spirit, and varies greatly in quality between producers. Gordon's, Booth's and Beefeater are the most famous names, but some speciality products have established a conspicuous presence on the market in recent years, notably Bombay Sapphire in the pale blue, tinted bottle.

delicate

DUTCH GENEVER
The prototype for London Gin

The other type is Plymouth gin, of which there is only one distiller, Coates, at the Blackfriars distillery in the centre of the city, not far from the waterfront. Plymouth is a distinctly drier gin than the big London brands, its spirit is impressively rounded and the range of aromatics used in it somehow give it a subtler bouquet than most gin-drinkers may be used to. It makes an incomparable Pink Gin.

A very small amount of gin is cask-aged and referred to as golden gin after the colour it leaches out of the wood.

Dutch Genever This is quite a different drink to English gin, owing to the more pungently flavoured grain mash on which it is based. The mixture of barley, rye and corn is often quite heavily malted, giving the older spirits a lightly beery tinge in the colour. There are basically two grades, labelled either Oude (old) or Jonge (young), the latter looking more like the English article. They frequently come in an opaque "stone" bottle.

KIRSCH

(handwritten: Brandy eau de vie cherries)

KIRSCH IS THE ORIGINAL cherry spirit. It is a colourless pure distillate – a true brandy or eau de vie, in other words – made from cherries. It is included separately because it has traditionally been seen as a distinctive product from the other fruit brandies. A fair amount is made in the Alsace and Franche-Comté regions of eastern France, where they know a thing or two about such matters. It is also a particular speciality of the Schwarzwald, the Black Forest region of Bavaria in western Germany – hence its German name, which simply means "cherry". (Confusingly, Kirsch is not related to cherry brandy.)

When the cherry juice is pressed for the initial fermentation, the stones are ground up too and left to infuse in it. The stones impart a characteristic slightly bitter note to the spirit, and bequeath a minute and harmless amount of cyanide to it in the process. It is generally given a short period of ageing, but in large earthenware vats rather than barrels, so that it remains colourless. The true Kirsch cherry is the black Morello (the type that crops up in the Black Forest gâteau, Bavaria's gift to the world's

KIRSCH
A cherry eau de vie with an identity all of its own

OTHER NAMES
Germany: Kirschwasser, or Schwarzwalder

MIXING
Rose: Shake equal measures of Kirsch and dry vermouth with a dash of grenadine and plenty of ice. Strain into a cocktail glass.

dessert trolleys), but these days, red varieties are often used instead.

Kirsch is also made in Switzerland and Austria.

TASTES GOOD WITH
Use Kirsch to add a touch of alcoholic richness to desserts, whether for soaking the sponge base for a mousse, or moistening fresh fruit such as pineapple. Indeed, its flavour blends unexpectedly well with all sorts of fruits. Beware any bottle labelled "Kirsch de Cuisine". It is an inferior product, smelling more like candle-wax than cherries, whose roughness is supposedly disguised when used in cooking. And if you believe that…

HOW TO SERVE
Lightly chilled in small glasses, Kirsch makes a refreshing after-dinner tipple.

MARC

IN THE VINEYARDS of Europe, winemakers have long had to accustom themselves to the precarious existence that reliance on nature forces on them. A bumper harvest of ripe, healthy grapes means plenty of good wine and a healthy income. But what if frost decimates your crop in the spring and the sun doesn't shine when you most need it? In the lean years, you may well be grateful for a by-product you can fall back on to ease the financial squeeze.

For many thrifty wine producers, *marc* has traditionally been the answer. After the grape juice has been pressed for fermentation, a mass of smashed skins and pips, or pomace, is left, itself capable of fermentation. Marc is the distillate of this residue. In France, the most celebrated Marc is made in Burgundy and Champagne, frequently by producers enthusiastic enough to buy other growers' leftovers, but there is also some made in Alsace, Provence and the isolated eastern region of the Jura.

In Italy, Marc is known as grappa, and such is the connoisseurship surrounding it that varietal grappa, made from the skins of single grape varieties, has become

OTHER NAMES
Italy: grappa (also used in California)
Portugal: bagaceira
Spain: aguardiente (but that term may also
be applied to any fiery grape spirit,
including brandy)

something of a fad. An indication of its potential trendiness is that several producers in California (where the climate is sufficiently benign not to need such a stand-by) are making versions of grappa too. In all regions, the finer spirits may be treated to maturation in oak, resulting in a burnished golden colour, but most of it is clear.

TASTES GOOD WITH
I once ate a sorbet in Reims that had been made with Marc de Champagne, and anointed with yet more of it. It was acutely horrible, but in a somehow intriguing way. More beguiling is the use of Marc de Bourgogne for marinating the rind of the powerful local soft cheese of Chambertin.

HOW TO SERVE
Their strong tannins make marcs unsuitable for mixing. They are intended for drinking neat, though their pro-foundly earthy flavour may come as a shock to the uninitiated. On the calvados principle that a strong spirit aids digestion, the Burgundians in particular value them as after-dinner drinks.

MARC DE CHAMPAGNE
Made by the champagne giants Moët & Chandon

GRAPPA
A varietal grappa distilled in the Piedmont region of Italy

MESCAL

MESCAL, OR MEZCAL, is one of Mexico's indigenous drinks. It is a pale yellowish spirit made from the juice of a species of succulent called the agave. The pressed juice is fermented to make *pulque*, a kind of beer of around 5–6% alcohol, which is known to have been consumed in Aztec times. It is then distilled once by the continuous method to produce mescal. (A second distillation removes more of the off-putting impurities in the spirit and results in the more highly prized tequila.)

It would be fair to say that mescal doesn't have a particularly illustrious image. It is the rapacious firewater that contributes

to the downfall of the dissolute British Consul in Malcolm Lowry's celebrated novel of alcoholism, *Under the Volcano*. In the past, it was considered to be capable of inducing gruesome hallucinations, a feature Lowry's novel reports, but it is hard to account for this since the agave plant – or American aloe, as it is sometimes known – is not one of the hallucinogenic species.

Much mescal is often sold with a pickled white agave worm in the bottle. It is genuine, and is intended to be eaten as the last of the drink is poured out. Supposedly, ingestion of the worm encourages great heroism in those already brave enough to swallow it. Again, the myth persists that the worm, which feeds on the agave plant, contains hallucinogenic properties. If that is likely to be your only motivation for trying it, don't bother. (The psychedelic drug, mescaline, was derived from the peyote cactus, not the agave.)

HOW IT IS MADE

The unlovely agave plant has an enormous core, the shape of a pine-cone, which is surrounded by great, spiny fat leaves. This core, or heart, is hacked away and the expressed juice – which is milky-white and extremely bitter – is fermented into pulque. Mescal is the first rough distillation of the pulque. It may be given a short period of ageing in wood, but it is not intended to be a sophisticated product.

TASTES GOOD WITH

Agave worm.

MESCAL
A little white worm lurks at the bottom of every bottle

RUM

R UM IS PROBABLY the least understood of the
five main spirits, despite the fact that, in
its white version, it is one of the biggest-selling
of them all. Indeed, it is debatable whether
many of those knocking back Bacardi-and-
Cokes in bars around the world realize they are
drinking some form of rum at all. In the popular
mind, the drink is inextricably associated with a
rather antiquated pantomime idea of "Jolly Jack
Tars" and a life on the ocean wave.

There is some uncertainty over the origin of
the spirit's name, but the favourite theory is that
it is a shortening of a rather marvellous old
West Country English word "rumbullion", itself
of unknown origin, but generally denoting any
hard liquor.

The invention of rum probably dates from not
long after the foundation of the sugar planta-
tions in the West Indies, in the early 16th
century. Until the voyages of Christopher
Columbus, sugar was a luxury product, and
much sought after in southern Europe, having
originally been brought from India into Venice

OTHER NAMES
France: rhum
Spain: ron

by Persians and then by Arabs. When the
Spanish explorers landed in Hispaniola
(modern-day Haiti and the Dominican Republic) and the neighbouring Caribbean islands,
they saw in them promising
environments for cultivating
sugar cane and thereby
breaking the stranglehold
on the market that the
Arabs had.

If yeasts need sugar to
feed on in order to produce
alcohol, then the sugar
plant was always going to
be an obvious source for
some kind of distillate.

HOW TO SERVE
The best dark rums, and aged rums in
particular, should be served straight,
unchilled, as digestifs. They make stimulating
alternatives to malt whisky or cognac.
Premium white rums from the independent
producers are also best enjoyed neat, but they
should be served cold.

NOTABLE PRODUCERS
Appleton, Myers
(Jamaica);
CSR (St Kitts);
Green Island
(Mauritius);
Clément, Rhum St
James, La Mauny
(Martinique);
Havana Club (Cuba);
El Dorado (Guyana);
Cockspur, Mount Gay
(Barbados);
Barbancourt (Haiti);
Pusser's (British Virgin
Islands)

CAPTAIN
MORGAN
The leading
brand dark rum

MIXING

Rum is the base for many of the more way-out cocktail concoctions on offer today, its heady richness contributing to the explosive power required. Here are two classics:

Bacardi Cocktail: The original cocktail, named after the famous brand. Shake a double measure of Bacardi with the juice of half a lime, a teaspoon of grenadine, and ice. Strain it into a cocktail glass.

Cuba Libre (below): Mix a generous measure of light or golden rum with a tablespoon or so of freshly squeezed lime juice, pour over ice, and top up with cola.

When first pressed, cane juice is a murky, greenish colour and full of impurities. Boiled down, it eventually crystallizes into sucrose and a sticky, brown by-product, molasses, that would readily have fermented in the tropical conditions. Rum is the spirit derived from distilling the fermented molasses.

Sugar soon became a widespread everyday product in Europe. The astronomical demand for it was serviced by one of the most notorious manifestations of European colonial history – the slave trade – and rum played a crucial part in the circular trade that came to be established. Settlers in New England financed their trips to West Africa by selling rum. A consignment of African slaves would be delivered to the West

Indies and sold for molasses, which would then be shipped back to New England to be turned into more rum.

The association of rum with the British Navy in particular derives from the fact that rum was provided to the ratings as a standard daily ration in the 18th century. The tradition continued throughout the most glorious period of Britain's maritime history, basically because rum could withstand hot weather more sturdily than beer could. The initial allowance was a fairly rollicking half-pint a day, which eventually was watered down into the despised "grog"

WOOD'S 100
A particularly rich naval-strength dark rum

MIXING

Petite Fleur: (from Michael Walker's *Cinzano Cocktail Book*): Shake equal measures of white rum, Cointreau and freshly squeezed grapefruit juice with ice and strain into a cocktail glass.

Mai Tai (below): Blend a measure each of dark rum and light rum with half-measures of tequila, Cointreau and apricot brandy, a measure of freshly squeezed orange juice, a splash of grenadine and a few drops of Angostura and ice cubes in a liquidizer. Decant into a very large wine glass. Approach with trepidation.

growing sugar cane specifically for distillation.

Some rum is made from the pressed cane juice itself, but most is made from the fermented molasses. In the former French colonies in particular, there is a distinguished tradition of *rhum agricole*, speciality products made on small sugar farms, in which rums are produced with different strains of yeast. They are individually appreciated in the same way that a wine drinker appreciates wines made from single grape varieties.

Both methods of distillation are practised for rum

and then mixed with lemon juice as an antiscorbutic (but it was still not much less than a third of a pint of spirit). It was only as recently as 1970 that it was decided that perhaps encouraging the lads to drink around eight measures of spirit every day might not be the best guarantee of military efficiency.

Rum is today produced all over the West Indies and eastern South America, to a lesser extent in the Indian Ocean area – the Philippines and Mauritius – and in smaller quantities still in the United States and even in Australia. A lot of it is inevitably a by-product of the sugar-refining industry, but the best grades are made by smaller, independent companies

BACARDI
The world's
favourite white
spirit brand

MIXING

Hot Buttered Rum: In a tall glass, mix a teaspoon of demerara sugar in a good double measure of strong black rum. Add half a teaspoon of ground cinnamon and a knob of unsalted butter and fill with hot water. (Remember to stand a spoon in the glass to conduct the heat if the water has just boiled.) Stir well to dissolve the butter and sugar.

Pina Colada (below): Whizz up two measures each of white rum and pineapple juice, with a couple of teaspoons of shredded fresh coconut and ice, in a liquidizer. (For that tropical touch, the drink should ideally be poured into a pineapple shell with a good lining of fruit left in it and drunk through straws.)

important category commercially, and it is certainly where the superior products are found. Leading brands are Captain Morgan and Lamb's, but there are many others. Some of them are bottled at the original naval strength of more than 50% ABV (Wood's Navy Rum, for example, is 57%), the traditional name for which was "overproof". The everyday dark rums are a more standard 40%, while Bacardi is adjusted down to 37.5% to put it on a level with the other commercial white spirits.

In between the two styles is the increasingly

MOUNT GAY BARBADOS
A major Caribbean brand of golden rum

MIXING

Daiquiri: Shake a double measure of white rum with the juice of half a lime or a quarter of a lemon, a teaspoon of caster sugar and ice. Strain into a cocktail glass. (Adding half a measure of some fruit liqueur, together with 50g/2oz of the equivalent fresh fruit, puréed, is a popular spin on the original Daiquiri. A strawberry version made with fraise liqueur is especially enticing.)

and, as with other spirits, the premium versions are double-distilled in a copper pot still. Continuous distillation and thorough rectification are used mainly by the bulk producers, particularly for the relatively neutral-tasting white rums that lead the market. Freshly distilled spirit from the pot still method is very high in impurities and must be allowed to mellow through a period of cask-ageing, which in turn gives colour to the darker rums. Some companies adjust the final colour with caramel, but not to a degree that would affect the flavour.

After white rums, dark rum is the next most

FLAVOURINGS

A small amount of rum is aromatized with mixed spices and fruits such as raisins and plums. Some of Guyana's Demerara rums are flavoured in this way

MIXING

Zombie: Blend a measure each of dark rum, light rum and apricot brandy with half-measures of pineapple juice and freshly squeezed lemon and orange juices in a liquidizer, with ice, and pour into a large goblet.

of the residue of the first distillation – known as dunder – may be added to the molasses during fermentation. Commercial white rums are rectified and bottled immediately. Coloured rums are cask-aged, sometimes for decades, before they are bottled.

TASTES GOOD WITH

More than any other basic spirit, rum makes an excellent accompaniment to fruits of all kinds. A "salad" of orange segments in golden rum was already a traditional dish in the 18th century. Rum can be added to the syrup for all fruit salads, though, and works particularly well with pineapple and banana. It is excellent for adding an enriching note to sponge-based desserts such as charlottes. Rum baba – the soft sponge filled with raisins and soaked in light rum – would, of course, be nothing without it.

popular golden or light rum, which is a particular speciality of Cuba and Puerto Rico aged for less time in barrel. The darkest and heaviest rums, some not far from the colour of thick black treacle, traditionally come from Jamaica. Good white rum, such as the white Rhum St James from Martinique, is full of burnt-sugar richness, a world away from the blandness of commercial white. Some exporters make a virtue of selling rums with 30 or 40 years of cask age, and there is even a tiny production of vintage-dated rum for the true connoisseur.

HOW IT IS MADE

Juice from the sugar cane is pressed and either fermented straight, or else boiled down to extract the molasses, which itself forms the basis of the ferment. It is either continuously distilled or, for speciality products, double-distilled in a pot still. For a headier product, some

LAMB'S
One of the
leading brands
of dark rum

SLIVOVITZ

TRUE SLIVOVITZ IS, or was, the local fruit brandy, or eau de vie, of Serbia and Bosnia-Herzegovina. I say "was" because the ravages of the war in the early 1990s in the former Yugoslavia, of which those countries were once part, put paid to a lot of the production capacity of the distilleries. Indeed it put paid to whole distilleries in some cases. A little did continue to be made, however (its rarity value leading one London retailer at the time to triple the price of its remaining stocks), and with peace production has risen once more.

At its best, slivovitz is one of the most distinguished and delicious eaux de vie made anywhere in Europe. The base fruit is a particular variety of black plum called Madjarka, which imparts a richly heady scent to the spirit. For the best grades, the spirit is cask-aged, and steeped in yet more whole fresh fruit during maturation to emphasize the flavour. It comes in a variety of weirdly shaped bottles, some tall and thin, some round and flask-shaped, still others of faceted glass.

Slivovitz has always been made and drunk elsewhere in eastern and central Europe, notably Bulgaria, Hungary, Germany, Austria and Italy. In the Balkans, it may also go by its other name of *rakija*. This

name denotes its origin as one of the European fruit versions of the arak that came from the Far East.

HOW IT IS MADE

Black plums are crushed along with their stones and fermented very slowly over a period of around three months. A double distillation is carried out, and then the new spirit is aged in great casks of Slovenian oak. Sometimes, whole plums are thrown in to macerate in the spirit while it ages. It is generally bottled at about five years old and at 35–40% ABV.

TASTES GOOD WITH

A little slivovitz added to stewed plums, or even to a traditional Christmas pudding, will enrich the dish no end.

SLIVOVITZ
is heady with the
scent of ripe black
plums

OTHER NAMES

Bosnia, Croatia,
Serbia: sljivovica. Also
rakija/prakija/slivovka

SLJIVOVICA
A Croatian
slivovitz in a
flask-shaped
bottle

HOW TO SERVE
As with all such spirits, slivovitz is most commonly drunk unchilled, as a digestif.

TEQUILA

TEQUILA IS THE NATIONAL spirit of Mexico. It is one stage further down the road to refinement than its fellow succulent-based spirit, mescal, but several leagues ahead in terms of drinking pleasure. It starts life as *pulque*, the fermented beer-like juice of the agave plant, and is distilled twice before being aged in cask. It comes in two versions, clear like vodka, and golden (or Oro), which spends a longer period in contact with the barrels. Virtually unknown in Europe until comparatively recently, it made its first inroads into the world's drinks cabinet by travelling north-wards to the USA, and it is now something of a cult drink in the youth market.

The name, tequila, is echoed in the full botanical name of the

HOW TO SERVE

The correct way of drinking tequila: your drink is served to you cold and straight in a small shot-glass. You then season your tongue with citrus and salt, by first squeezing a wedge of lime (lemon for the wimps) and then pouring salt on to the back of the hand and licking at each in turn. To be anatomically precise, the hand should be held at a 45° angle away from the body, with the thumb extended downwards, and the juice and salt deposited along the groove between the bases of the thumb and forefinger. (Some make things easier by just sucking on the piece of lime.) The tequila is then thrown back in one gulp like schnapps, carrying the seasonings with it. The process is repeated ad infinitum.

Believe it or not, this really is how tequila is widely drunk on its native territory. If it sounds like a fiddly and indescribably messy procedure, the answer is that it is, but long practice induces a sort of head-tossing, devil-may-care sanguinity in experienced users.

MIXING
Tequila and Orange: Have done with the fuss, and drink it on the rocks with fresh orange juice. It makes an enlivening change for those grown weary of vodka-and-orange.

CUERVO TEQUILA
The white version of Mexico's national spirit

MIXING

Margarita: Shake equal measures of tequila
and Cointreau with the juice of half a lime
and plenty of ice. Dip a finger in and run it
around the rim of a cocktail glass. Up-end
the glass briefly in a saucerful of coarse-
ground salt, then strain the drink into it. (This
is the classic tequila cocktail, but it is just a
customized way of getting round the traditional salt-licking routine – with a slug of
Cointreau for sweetly counteracting the salt.
Some recipes add egg white too. No
accounting for taste.)

HOW IT IS MADE

Like mescal, tequila is distilled from the
chopped, pressed and fermented hearts of
agave plants. The juice is quite high in acidity,
which lends even the refined spirit a certain
piquancy. It is distilled a second time in a pot
still, and then matured in wooden casks, briefly
for the white version, and up to five years for
the Oro.

*GOLDEN
MONTEZUMA
Gold tequila has
aged in cask for
longer than white*

MIXING
Tequila Sunrise: Half-
fill a tall glass with
crushed ice. Put in a
goodly measure of
tequila and top up with
fresh orange juice.
Quickly dollop a tea-
spoon of grenadine into
the centre of the drink.
(The bright red grena-
dine sinks to the
bottom and then blends
upwards into the
orange in a very
becoming way, hence
the drink's name.)

plant from which it is sourced: *Agave tequilana*.
Perhaps what put everybody else off trying it for
so long was the thought of a spirit made from
succulents, and indeed even the finest grades
don't actually smell particularly inviting. It has
a sweaty, slightly muggy quality that must have
come as something of a jolt at first to tastebuds
honed on squeaky-clean vodka.

In recognition of its cultural importance, the
production of tequila has been strictly delimited
within Mexico. It may be distilled in only a
handful of towns, including Tequila itself, and
in the area immediately surrounding Guadala-
jara. Two of the brands most commonly
encountered on the export markets are Cuervo
and Montezuma, the latter depicting an Aztec
shield on the label.

VODKA

IN ONE SENSE, vodka is the closest thing to perfection ever conceived in the long history of spirits. Had it been invented in the 1990s, in the era of alco-pops and ice beers, it would be hailed as a supremely adept piece of marketing wizardry. Nobody, other than a confirmed teetotaller, could possibly dislike it, for the simple reason that it tastes of nothing whatsoever. It is pure, unadulterated, uncomplicated alcohol. At least, most of it is.

The word "vodka" is a Russian endearment meaning "little water", from their word for water, *voda*. It doesn't denote the flavourlessness of the spirit, however, but derives from the widespread linguistic practice in Europe of referring to all distillates originally as a form of water (as in the Latin *aqua vitae* and French *eau de vie*).

Precisely because it is such a simple drink, it is almost impossible to pinpoint the origins of vodka historically. A potent spirit distilled from various grains, and

OTHER NAMES
Poland: wodka

indeed potatoes – still wrongly believed in the popular imagination to be its main ingredient – has been made in Poland, Russia and the Baltic states of Latvia, Lithuania and Estonia since the very early days of distillation in Europe.

But as to where a drink specifically recognizable as vodka first arose is a matter for the Poles and the Russians to sort out between themselves. (Most outsiders, it should be said, tend to come down on the Polish side of the fence these days.) What is certain is that, by the time home distillation had become a favoured way of passing the long, grim northern winters in Poland, peasant families were producing their own vodkas on an extensive scale.

The discovery of rectification

SMIRNOFF
The basic red label brand is the market leader

ABSOLUT
Blue label Absolut is the unflavoured version

techniques did not take place until the beginning of the 19th century, and so these early distillates would have tasted pretty unclean, to say the least. Any herbs, seeds or berries that were to hand would be steeped in the spirit to mask its rankness. So the first vodkas were not the anonymous products preferred today, but the true ancestors of the flavoured vodkas that are sometimes greeted as nothing more than novelty items by modern drinkers.

Nonetheless, it was the neutral, ultra-purified grain vodka – made from wheat or rye – that came to commercial prominence in the West. So prevalent is it now, particularly among younger drinkers who have yet to discover and appreciate the taste of unrectified, cask-matured spirits such as good whisky and cognac, that it is hard to believe that hardly anyone in western Europe or America had heard of it until the late 1940s.

BLACK LABEL SMIRNOFF
A softer, mellower product

BLUE LABEL SMIRNOFF
The strongest at 45%

MIXING

Basic vodka has no scent or flavour, meaning it is not the most inspiring ingredient in the cocktail repertoire. All it can really do is confer an extra slug of alcohol for those hell-bent on the short-cut to oblivion. As a result, the sky's the limit.
Black Russian: The true Black Russian is simply equal measures of vodka and Tia Maria, or Kahlúa, mixed with ice cubes in a tumbler. However, the fashion in recent years has been to serve it as a long drink in a big glass, topped up with cola. Alternatively, leave out the cola, add a measure of single cream, shake it up and it becomes a
White Russian: Then again, substitute dark brown crème de cacao for the Tia Maria and create a **Piranha**.
Black Cossack (below): Add a good slug of vodka to a half-pint of Guinness.

It all changed with the first stirrings of interest in California during the period of the Beat Generation.

Not only did vodka possess the aforementioned neutrality that made it such an obvious beginner's spirit, but it was also seen as a provocatively dissident thing to drink in the era of the onset of the Cold War. Vodka was the favoured "hooch" of the Soviet bloc, and in the witch-hunting atmosphere of 50s America, nothing was more guaranteed to inflame bourbon-drinking patriots than to see young folks imbibing the spirit of Communism with such evident glee. The late Alexis Lichine,

FLAVOURINGS

Vodka will happily take up whatever flavouring a producer decides to give it, including:
Lemon peel
Bison grass
Red chilli peppers
Cherries
Rowanberries
Blackcurrants
Apples
Sloes
Saffron
Tarragon
Walnuts
Honey
Liquorice
Rose petals

LIMONNAYA
A leading lemon-
flavoured vodka

MIXING
Screwdriver: That
nightclub favourite,
vodka and orange. The
name, according to one
theory, originated
among workers on
American oil-rigs who
– finding themselves
short of swizzle-sticks
– resourcefully used
their screwdrivers to
stir the drink. In the
Baltic states, the
freshly squeezed
orange juice is served
to you in a separate
little jug and you mix
to taste. Even here the
cocktail name is in use,
although, as I discov-
ered in Riga, to make
yourself perfectly
clear, you must ask the
barman for a "skrew".
When first marketed
on the west coast of the
USA, it was suggested
that it be drunk with
ginger beer. Thus did
the first **Moscow Mule**
come to light.

drink historian, attributes the start of vodka's
meteoric rise in the West to the purchase of a
recipe for rectified vodka from a Russian
refugee called Smirnoff by an American
company, on the eve of the Second World War.
The rest is history.

Vodka is still very much the drink of gastronomic choice in its native lands, drunk as
aperitif, digestif and even as an accompaniment
to food. It is nearly always taken icy-cold,
preceded in Polish homes by the ritual wishing
of good health – *na zdrowie* – to one's family
and friends. The quantities consumed may raise
eyebrows in our Western unit-counting culture,
but a vodka hangover is very rare, owing to the
relentless clean-up job the drink is given during
distillation. This removes nearly all of its con-
geners, the substances that impart character to
the dark spirits.

Fruit flavourings are very common, and make
a drier, more bracing alternative to the equivalent liqueurs. Perhaps
the most celebrated
flavoured product is
Zubrowka, bison-
grass vodka, which is
generally sold with a

*ABSOLUT
Kurant is
solidly fruity
and flavoured
with black-
currants*

MIXING
Bloody Mary: Everyone has his or her own
proprietary recipe for the next best hangover
cure after aspirin. Some strange people even
put tomato ketchup into it. Others round out the
alcohol with a splash of dry sherry. Here is
my own formula.
Put a slice of lemon and two or three ice-cubes
in a tall glass, add a teaspoon of Lea &
Perrin's Worcestershire sauce, a teaspoon of
freshly squeezed lemon juice, a pinch of
celery salt, a generous dash of Tabasco and
about half-a-dozen twists of the black pepper
mill, and stir to coat the ice. Fill the glass to
about an inch-and-a-half from the top with
tomato juice and pour on a generous measure
of vodka. Stir well to combine
the alcohol.

blade of grass in the bottle. Bison grass is the
gourmet preference of the wild bison that roam
the forests of eastern Poland, and the beast is
usually depicted on the label.

Wisniowka (cherries), Limonnaya (lemon)
and the Swedish Absolut company's Kurant
(blackcurrant) are all appetizing drinks.
Pieprzowka, which is infused with chilli
peppers, is a variety for real aficionados: the
spirit is emphasized by the hot spice burn of its
flavouring component. Russia's Okhotnichya –
"Hunter's Vodka" – is impregnated with orange
peel, ginger root, coffee beans, juniper berries
and even a drop of white port.

Neutral vodkas are produced all over the

world now, although most grades are only intended to be served in mixed drinks. Russian Stolichnaya, particularly the Cristall bottling, is an honourable, silky-smooth exception. Smirnoff makes a wide range, with red, blue and black labels denoting varying strengths, and there are brands with such names as Black Death and Jazz Jamboree. Scandinavian vodkas such as Finlandia and Absolut have their deserved followings, while most British vodka tends to be little more than patent alcohol. At one time, vodka production had even travelled south from Russia into Iran, but the coming of Islamic rule brought that to a halt.

Also seen on the export markets is Polish Pure Spirit, bottled at around 70% ABV, and much beloved by reckless students as a dare.

HOW IT IS MADE

Although potatoes and other vegetables, and even molasses, have been used to make vodka at various times in its history, commercial vodka is nowadays virtually exclusively made from grains, the principal one of which is rye. A basic mash is made in the usual way by malting the grains and encouraging them to ferment with cultured yeasts. The resulting brew is then continuously

PIEPRZOWKA
This vodka has been coloured and flavoured with chillies

distilled in a column still apparatus to higher and higher degrees of alcoholic strength, thus driving off nearly all of the higher alcohols or fusel oil. As a final insurance policy against flavour, the finished spirit is then filtered through a layer of charcoal, which strips it of any remaining character. It is then bottled at around 37.5% for commercial strength and released without further ado.

In the case of flavoured vodkas, the aromatizing elements are added to the new spirit after rectification, and left to infuse in it over long periods – sometimes three years or more. Occasionally, a speciality vodka will be aged in cask and take on a tinge of colour; others derive their exotic hues from the addition of spices, flowers or nuts.

TASTES GOOD WITH

Ice-cold vodka is the classic accompaniment to finest Russian caviare, itself served on heaps of ice. In the Scandinavian countries, it is also drunk, like aquavit, with marinated and smoked fish such as herring, mackerel and even salmon. Superchef Martin Blunos who is based in England's West Country has created a sumptuously theatrical dish of scrambled duck egg served in the shell amid a slick of flaming Latvian vodka, topped with sevruga caviare and with blinis and a shot of freezing vodka on the side.

STOLICHNAYA
This smooth vodka should be sipped appreciatively

MIXING

Balalaika: Shake a measure each of vodka and Cointreau with half a measure of lemon juice and plenty of ice, and strain into a cocktail glass.

Barbara: Shake a measure of vodka with half-measures of crème de cacao and single cream, with ice, and strain into a cocktail glass. (This is essentially a vodka-based **Alexander**.)

Katinka (from Michael Walker's *Cinzano Cocktail Book*): Shake a measure-and-a-half of vodka with a measure of apricot brandy and half a measure of fresh lime juice with ice, and pour over a heap of slivered ice in a cocktail glass.

Vodkatini: Basically a classic Martini, but with vodka replacing the gin.

Czarina: Stir a measure of vodka with half-measures of apricot brandy and dry vermouth and a dash of Angostura with ice in a mixing jug. Strain into a cocktail glass.

WHISKY

WHISKY (OR WHISKEY, depending on where it hails from) is one of the world's leading spirits. Its history is every bit as distinguished as that of cognac and, like the classic brandies of France, its spread around the world from its first home – the Scottish Highlands, in whisky's case – has been a true testament to the genius of its conception. Tennessee sour mash may bear about as much relation in taste to single malt Scotch as Spanish brandy does to cognac, but the fact that they are all great products demonstrates the versatility of each basic formula.

Whiskies are produced all over the world now. As the name is not a geographically specific one, they may all legitimately call themselves whisk(e)y. In Australia and India, the Czech Republic and Germany, they make grain spirits from barley or rye that proudly bear the name. The five major whisky-producing countries are Scotland, the United States, Ireland, Canada and Japan, which are covered in this chapter.

The name "whisky" itself is yet another variant on the phrase "water of life" that we have become familiar with in the world of spirits. In translation, the Latin *aqua vitae* became *uisge beatha* in the Scots branch of Gaelic and *usque-baugh* in the Irish; it eventually was mangled into the half-Anglicized "whisky"

and was in official use by the mid-18th century.

In countries that lacked the warm climate for producing fermented drinks from grapes, beer was always the staple brew and, just as brandy was the obvious first distillate in southern Europe, so malted grains provided the starting-point for domestic production further north. Unlike brandy, however, which starts life as wine, whisky doesn't have to be made from something that would be recognizable as beer. The grains are malted by allowing them to germinate in water and then lightly cooking them to encourage the formation of sugars. It is these sugars on which the yeasts then feed to produce the first ferment. A double distillation by the pot still method results in a congener-rich

LAPHROAIG
One of the richest of the peaty styles of Scotch produced in Islay

MACALLAN
This 18-year-old whisky is one of the best-loved Highland malts

spirit that can then be matured – often for decades for the finer whiskies – in oak barrels.

Just as with other spirits that haven't had the life rectified out of them, whisky is nearly always truly expressive of its regional origins and the raw materials that went into it. For that reason, a passionate connoisseurship of this spirit has arisen over the generations, similar to that which surrounds wine. Even more than brandy, whisky handsomely rewards those who set out with a conscientious approach to the tasting and appreciation of the spirit.

SCOTLAND

Home distillation in Scotland can be traced back to the 15th century, when the practice of distilling surplus grain to make a potent drink for clan chieftains was established. Initially, the drink was – like all spirits – primarily valued

for its medicinal powers, and early examples were no doubt infusions of herbs and berries rather than the pure grain product we know today. Although other cereals would at first have been used, the pre-eminence of malted barley was acknowledged relatively early on in the development of Scotch.

Before the Act of Union that brought England and Scotland together politically in 1707, Scotch was hardly known in England. Gin was the national drink south of the border. Once the English laid their administrative hands on Scotland, they did their level best to bring whisky distillation under statutory control, but with only very partial success. Those whisky-makers within striking distance of the border fled northwards with their stills into the Highlands, and the production of Scotch continued unabated as an almost wholly illicit activity.

Eventually, by a combination of threats and bribes, the authorities managed to place the whole enterprise under licence so that, by the 1870s, there

GLENLIVET
A 10-year-old Spey-
side malt from the
Scottish Highlands

TASTES GOOD WITH
Scotch is naturally the only accompaniment to the ceremonial haggis on Burns Night (January 25). Whether it is a precise gastronomic match may be open to question, but to order a bottle of Rioja would be missing the point somewhat. Uniced Scotch is also great with hearty soups: thick, barley-based Scotch broth or cock-a-leekie should ideally have a fair amount of whisky in them anyway.

TALISKER
Talisker whisky is the only malt whisky produced on the island of Skye.

AUCHENTOSHAN
A Lowland malt distilled not far from Glasgow.

MIXING
Rusty Nail: Equal measures of Scotch and Drambuie mixed with ice and strained into a small glass, or poured over crushed ice.
Whisky Mac (below): The classic cold remedy is half and half good Scotch and green ginger wine (preferably Crabbie's) with no ice.

were just half-a-dozen arraignments in Scotland for illegal distilling (as against nearly 700 only 40 years earlier).

The advent of continuous distillation came to Scotland courtesy of Robert Stein, who invented a rudimentary version of the column still in 1826. Although Scotch had traditionally been characterized by the richness and depth of flavour that marks all pot-still products, the development of the new method allowed a lighter spirit of more obvious commercial appeal to be produced. By the late 19th century, the habit of blending true malt whisky with straight grain spirit made by continuous distillation from unmalted barley (and maize, or corn) was widespread. These were the types of Scotch that were introduced to cautious English palates.

In the early years of this century, a Royal Commission was set up to determine the parameters for Scotch whisky production, i.e. the methods of distillation, rules on blending, minimum maturation times and, of course, the salient geographical point – that Scotch could only be distilled and aged in Scotland. The Commission reported in 1909, its conclusions were refined slightly in 1915, and it remains in force today as the legal textbook for an industry of worldwide importance that is also a central support of the Scottish economy.

THE FAMOUS GROUSE
One of the leading brands of blended Scotch

TYPES OF SCOTCH
The most highly prized of Scotch whiskies are the single malts. These are whiskies that are produced entirely from malted barley, double-distilled, and made exclusively at a single one (hence the terminology) of Scotland's 100 or so working distilleries. Some of these products are aged for many years. Twenty-five-year-old Scotch will be shot through with all sorts of profoundly complex flavours and perfumes picked up from the wood in which it has matured and perhaps, according to some, from the sea air that wafts around the coastal distilleries. Remember that – as with other spirits – aged malt can't continue to develop once bottled.

Some malts are the blended produce of several single malts, in which case they are known as vatted malts. They are often assembled from several distilleries within a particular region in order to illustrate the local style comparable to specific regional subdivisions in a *vin de pays* wine area.

Whiskies made from corn or unmalted barley are known as grain whiskies and are always

WHYTE & MACKAY
This whisky is re-blended for a second period of maturation

considerably lighter in style than the malts. They could be described as beginner's Scotch since they have far fewer of the aromatic components that account for the pedigree of great malt, but they should by no means be seen as worthless imitations. They have their role to play.

The greater part of that role is in the production of blended Scotch, whisky made from a mixture of malt and grain spirits. This is the market-leading category, occupied by virtually all of the big brand names, such as Bell's, J&B, Johnnie Walker, Ballantine's, Whyte & Mackay, The Famous Grouse, White Horse and Teacher's. Most of these have fairly low concentrations of malt in the blend, although Teacher's and Johnnie Walker's Black Label

J&B
This blended whisky
is popular in the
American market;
J&B stands for
Justerini &
Brooks

bottling are notable exceptions.

Scotch whisky is mostly retailed at the standard dark spirit strength of 40% ABV, or perhaps slightly above (avoid any that are below). A small proportion of the best grades are bottled from the barrel undiluted. These are known as "cask-strength" whiskies. You are not intended to drink them as they come, but the distiller is inviting you to dilute them with water yourself and find the precise level of potency that suits you.

AREAS OF PRODUCTION
For the purposes of whisky production, Scotland is divided up into four broad regions: the Lowlands, south of Stirling; the tiny Campbeltown, on a narrow peninsula west of Ayr; Islay and the Western

GLENMORANGIE
One of the most
celebrated Northern
Highland malts.

TEACHERS
One of the maltier blended whiskies.

GIFT WRAPPING
Malt whiskies are often sold in elegant presentation cartons.

Isles, comprising Jura, Mull and Skye; and the Highlands. The Highlands can be further subdivided into the Midlands, the Western, Northern and Eastern Highlands and Speyside.

As a (very) rough guide to the regional styles, Lowland whiskies are the gentlest and sweetest styles of Scotch, while Campbeltown's are fresh and ozoney. Islay produces an instantly recognizable pungent spirit, full of seaweed aromas, and particularly marked by the influence of the peat that fires the drying kilns for the grain, while many Highland malts have a soft smokiness to them. There are numerous distilleries, though, and each has evolved its own style.

How It is Made

In the case of the malts, the grains of barley are soaked in water to encourage them to germinate. Soon after they have begun sprouting, the process is arrested by heating them in a kiln, in which variable quantities of peat will be added to the fuel, depending on

the intended final flavour of the whisky. After kilning, the grain is mashed and drained and then poured into large tanks to begin fermentation, either with natural or cultured yeasts. (Yeast strains have a pronounced effect on the flavour, too.) The resulting brew is then double-distilled in the traditional copper pot still.

The other factor of huge significance in determining the character of a whisky is the type of maturation vessel. Scotch was traditionally aged in casks that had previously been used for shipping sherry, and some still is, but used bourbon casks from Kentucky are now quite common. In both cases, the wood is American oak, capable of imparting great richness to a whisky. (There is at least one product on the market that has been aged in old port casks.) Whiskies aged for long periods will derive a certain character from the action of oxygen seeping through the pores of the wood.

WHITE HORSE
A pronounced peatiness marks the flavour of this blended whisky

JOHNNIE WALKER
Red Label is the biggest selling whisky of all.

JOHNNIE WALKER
The Black Label has a higher malt content than the red

UNITED STATES

In North America, where whiskey is mostly spelled with an "e" as it is in Ireland, production of the drink goes back only as far as the 18th century. Its roots are embedded in the era leading up to Independence. Before that, the staple spirit in America was dark rum, made from molasses transported from the West Indies by the slave ships. It was British and Irish settlers, bringing their own whisky with them from the old countries, who provided the impetus for the development of what is today America's national spirit.

The first American whiskies were made with malted barley and rye, in vague imitation of the European archetypes. Soon, however, a group of distillers in Bourbon County, Kentucky, began producing pure corn whiskey. By happy chance, their little communities were descended upon from 1794 onwards by droves of tax refugees who were fleeing from revenue officers in Pennsylvania, after staging an armed uprising against the new State excises on liquor. Suddenly, the Kentuckians had a ready-made new market for their own product and, before

too long, Kentucky bourbon was well on its way to assuming a place in the ranks of the world's fine spirits.

Rye whiskey is still made in the eastern states of Pennsylvania, Maryland and Virginia, but seemingly in ever-decreasing quantities. It is the whiskeys of Kentucky and Tennessee that represent the cognac and armagnac, if you will, of American spirit production.

BOURBON

Nowadays, most bourbon distilleries are concentrated not in Bourbon County, but around the towns of Louisville, Bardstown and Frankfort. Nonetheless, only whiskeys from the state of Kentucky are entitled to be called bourbons. Bourbon is not a straight corn whiskey, but one made from a mixture of not less than 51% corn with malted barley, like a blended Scotch. Some may contain a little rye. The chief distinguishing taste characteristic of bourbon, however, derives from the barrels in which it matures. They are made of American oak, as one would expect; unlike the barrels used for Scotch, however, they are always brand new. Furthermore, they are heavily charred, or toasted, on the insides to a depth of about 5mm/¼

WILD TURKEY BOURBON comes from Lawrenceburg, Kentucky

FLAVOURINGS

Discounting the whisky-based liqueurs, the only case of a straight whisky being flavoured is that of certain Canadian products that have minute amounts of other drinks added to them: grape wine, wines from other fruits (prunes are a favourite), unfermented fruit juices, even sherry

MIXING

Old-Fashioned: Grind up a sugar lump with a good shake from the Angostura bottle in the squat tumbler that is named after this drink. Add plenty of ice and a cheering quantity of Canadian or straight rye whisky. Throw in a twist of lemon peel, a slice of orange and a cocktail cherry, and serve with a stirring implement in it.

in, which allows the spirit freer access to the vanillin and tannins in the wood. Nobody quite knows where the charring tradition came from, but it seems quite likely that it was the result of a happy accident.

There are two distinct styles of bourbon, sweet mash and sour mash, the differences arising at the fermentation stage of the grains. For sweet mash, the yeasts are allowed to perform their work quite quickly over a couple of days, while for sour mash, some yeast from the preceding batch augments the brew. This doubles the length of the fermentation and ensures that more of the sugars in the grain are consumed.

Most bourbon is labelled "Kentucky Straight Bourbon", which means it is made from at least 51% corn, is aged for a minimum of two years in charred new barrels and has been made and matured within the prescribed areas. It is the equivalent category to single malt Scotch. Some, sold as "Blended Straight", is made from more than one lot of straight bourbon, and corresponds to vatted malt. Most bourbon is bottled at a slightly higher strength than standard Scotch – about 43–45% ABV.

The leading brand by a long chalk is Jim Beam, made at Bardstown and virtually synonymous with

bourbon on the export markets. Other brands include Wild Turkey, Evan Williams, Early Times, Old Grand-Dad and the pace-setting Maker's Mark (the one with the top dipped in red sealing-wax).

TENNESSEE

South of the bourbon state of Kentucky, in neighbouring Tennessee, an entirely different but equally distinctive style of whiskey is made. Tennessee sour mash is represented by just two distilleries – Jack Daniel's in Lynchburg, and George Dickel in Tullahoma. Their various bottlings represent some of the richest and smoothest whiskeys made.

Whereas bourbon is matured in charred barrels, Tennessee takes the principle a stage further by actually filtering the newly made spirit through a mass of charcoal. In the yards behind the distilleries, they burn great stacks of sugar maple down to ash and then grind it all into a rough black powder. This is

JACK DANIEL'S
By far the bigger
brand of the two
Tennessee whiskeys

MAKER'S MARK
Small-volume
production allied
to top quality

piled to a depth of around 3 metres/10 feet into so-called mellowing vats, all sitting on a fleecy woollen blanket. The whiskey drips at a painfully slow rate from holes in a gridwork of copper pipes above the vats, and filters gradually through the charcoal bed, before being cask-matured in the usual way.

Jack Daniel's is one of the world's best-loved whiskey brands. Its market-leading Old No. 7, in the famous square bottle, first established the kudos of JD by winning a Gold Medal at the 1904 World's Fair in St Louis. Its great rival, Dickel (which spells its product "whisky" in the Scottish way), matures its No. 12 brand for several years longer, and the results are evident in a more discreet and mellower nose and deeper colour. It is bottled at 45% ABV.

One of the great ironies of Tennessee whiskey is that both producers have their distilleries in "dry" counties where it is forbidden to sell alcohol, which means that they may not avail themselves of

JIM BEAM
A particularly popular bourbon

the doorstep custom they could enjoy from public visits. A glass of soul-saving spring water is offered instead.

IRELAND

The origins of distillation in the Emerald Isle are lost in swathes of Irish mist, but are certainly of great antiquity, at least as old as those of Scotch. There are those who have claimed that it was Irish missionaries who first brought the knowledge of distilling to France, and thus made brandy possible. Whether that is true or not, Irish whiskey once enjoyed an unrivalled reputation as a more approachable style of spirit than Scotch malt. It was only when blended Scotch began to be made on any significant scale towards the end of the 19th century that Irish whiskey was nudged out of the frame.

The reasons for the greater accessibility of Irish whiskey lie in its production process. No peat is used in the kilns, so that there is none of the smoky pungency that is present in some degree in most Scotch. Secondly, punitive taxes on malted barley in the mid-19th century meant that the Irish distillers began to use a mixture of malted and unmalted grain in their mash, making it traditionally a blended product long before the recipes for today's

PADDY
This whiskey is distilled at Midleton, just outside the city of Cork

JAMESON
The brand leader on the export market

MIXING

Whisky Sour: Mix the juice of half a lemon with a level teaspoon of icing sugar in a tumbler with two or three cubes of ice. When the sugar is dissolved, add a generous measure of whisky and stir again – American whiskeys are best for this preparation. (Some add a brief squirt of soda. If you find this formula a little *too* sour, add a little more sugar, but this is the way I like it.)

CANADIAN CLUB
The leading brand of Canadian whisky.

standard Scotch brands had even been dreamed about.

Most famously of all, Irish whiskey is subjected to a triple distillation by the copper pot still method. The third passage of the spirit through the stills results in a product with a softer, ultra-refined palate profile while still retaining all of its complexity. By law, the whiskey must then be cask-aged for a minimum of three years, although in practice most are aged for two to three times that period. It is usually bottled at 40% ABV.

The brand leader on the export markets is Jameson's. Other notable names include Bushmills, John Power, Murphy's, Paddy, Dunphy's and Tullamore Dew. All but one are made in the Republic, mostly in the environs of Dublin or Cork. The exception is Bushmills, which is located in County Antrim in Northern Ireland.

(There is another Irish "whiskey" of course, made on illegal travelling stills that the authorities have always found notoriously difficult to track down. Perhaps they have more constructive things to do. For all its reputation as toxic brain-scrambler, poteen – pronounced "*pocheen*" – is an unassailable part of Ireland's folk history, and will continue to be so for as long as taxation rates on the official stuff are as rapacious as they are.)

CANADA

Canada's whiskies are made from blends of different grains, the greater proportion of each brand based on an original mash that combines rye, corn and malted barley. They nearly always contain some spirit, however, that is produced entirely from the heavier-tasting rye, but it usually accounts for less than a tenth of the final blend. As a result, they have the reputation of being among the lightest classic whiskies of all, even more so than the triple-distilled Irish.

The whisky industry in Canada dates back only to the last century, when it arose as an offshoot of the agricultural production of grain. It was quite common at one time to pay the millers in kind with some of the grain, and distillation has long been a traditional way of using up surpluses the world over. The earliest

producers – and, despite the country's size, there are still only a handful – were Hiram Walker, Seagram's and Corby's, all in the province of Ontario.

Distillation is by the continuous process, in gigantic column stills. Different spirits produced from different mashes, or fermented from different yeast strains, are painstakingly blended by the distiller – before the maturation in some cases, afterwards in others. All whiskies must spend at least three years in the barrels, which are of new wood, but there is a noble tradition of aged products in Canada for whiskies that are 10, 12, even 18 years old on release. As elsewhere, the standard blends are sold at 40% ABV, but speciality aged bottlings may be somewhat stronger.

A curiosity of Canadian whisky is that the regulations permit the addition of a tiny quantity of other drink products, such as sherry or wine made from grapes or other fruits. While this may account for no more than a hundredth part of the finished product, it makes its presence felt in the fleeting suggestion of fruitiness in the flavours of some whiskies.

CROWN ROYAL
A Canadian brand owned by Seagram's

Most of the distilleries are situated in the eastern provinces of Ontario and Quebec. The leading label is Hiram Walker's Canadian Club, first blended in the 1880s, and is supported by the Burke's and Wiser's ranges from Corby's, McGuinness's Silk Tassel, Alberta Springs and Seagram's Crown Royal.

JAPAN

Of the countries under consideration here, Japan has by far the youngest whisky industry – of even more recent provenance than its efforts at wine making. The first distillery was established only in 1923, and it is only in the last 30 years or so that its products have come to the attention of whisky-drinkers other than the Japanese themselves.

The model for Japan's whiskies is single malt Scotch, but there are equally successful spirits made in the idiom of blended Scotch. The base is a mash of malted barley, dried in kilns fired with a little peat (though considerably less than is the case in Scotland, and so yielding a less aromatically defined product). Distillation is by the pot still method. Some of the brands are aged in used sherry or bourbon casks, as for Scotch, others in heavily charred new American oak barrels, as for bourbon itself. Some distilleries buy in a proportion of unused Scottish spirit for blending in with the home-grown whisky. The premium brands

SUNTORY
The 12-year-old
Yamazaki is a
kind of Japanese
single malt

are generally bottled at around 43% ABV.

The giant drinks company Suntory, which has a finger in all sorts of pies from classed-growth Bordeaux to the green melon liqueur Midori, is also the biggest producer of Japanese whisky, accounting for virtually three-quarters of the industry's annual output. Behind Suntory comes the Nikka company, and then the smaller producers Sanraku Ocean and Seagram's, which is anything but small everywhere else.

In Japan, whisky is nearly always taken heavily watered. Whereas in Scotland, the mix is usually half-and-half, the Japanese prefer to take it as a long pale-yellowish drink in tall glasses filled to the top with spring water and with plenty of ice – about the most denatured form in which fine whisky is commonly drunk anywhere in the world. It is drunk both as an aperitif and as an accompaniment to food.

Among the more illustrious products are Suntory's 12-year-old Pure Malt from its Yamazaki distillery on Honshu, the principal island; Nikka Memorial 50, Sanraku Ocean's single malt Karuizawa (also from Honshu); and Seagram's top labels Crescent and Emblem.

LIQUEURS

Since we are clearly distinguishing between spirits and liqueurs, it would be useful to arrive at a working definition of what constitutes a liqueur. Why is Kirsch a spirit, for example, but cherry brandy a liqueur?

The distinction lies in the way that the various flavours of these drinks are obtained. Essentially, a liqueur is any spirit-based drink to which flavouring elements have been added, usually by infusion, and – in the vast majority of cases – enhanced by sweetening. Sometimes the flavourings are themselves subjected to distillation; sometimes they are merely soaked or macerated in an alcohol base. Although there are flavoured spirits, such as lemon vodka (or, for that matter, gin) there are no unflavoured liqueurs. To answer the question in the first paragraph, Kirsch is a spirit because it is a straight, unsweetened distillate of cherries, whereas cherry brandy is a neutral spirit from other sources to which cherry flavour is added by infusion of the fruit.

Liqueurs have their origins in the practice of adding aromatic ingredients – herbs, fruit extracts, seeds, spices, nuts, roots, flowers, and so forth – in order both to mask the unappealing flavour of the impurities that had not been rectified out of them, and to endow the resulting potions with medicinal value. Given a source of basic spirit, they could and often would be concocted in domestic kitchens for use in cooking as well as for drinking – a tradition carried on in this book. As various proprietary liqueurs came on to the market during the course of the 19th century, so home liqueur-making declined.

When the science of distillation was still in its infancy in Europe, the Catalan physician Arnaldo de Vilanova advanced the theory that steeping them in alcohol extracted the beneficial qualities of certain medicinal herbs. This was a logical progression of the non-alcoholic distilling of essential oils that had been practised in ancient Egypt and classical Greece. As an offshoot of the alchemical arts, distilling was intimately bound up with the doomed enterprise of attempting to turn base metals to gold, and so gold itself came to play a part in the formulation of alcohol-based remedies. (Arnaldo was saved from the Inquisition, it is said, because he had cured the Pope of life-threatening illness by means of a tonic containing flakes of

Left: Le Palais de Bénédictine. Until recently Bénédictine was still made by the monastic order. Chartreuse is one of the few liqueurs still produced in the traditional way in the distillery (below) at Voiron, near Grenoble.

Above: Even today, small producers, such as this French artisan distiller, produce a wonderful variety of flavoured liqueurs.

gold.) The tradition lives on today in the form of a drink called Goldwasser.

It was in the religious orders that many of the traditional liqueurs were first formulated, since the medicinal ingredients used were often grown in the monastery gardens. By the late Middle Ages, the Italians had become the most celebrated practitioners of the art of liqueur-making. The marriage of Catherine de Medici to the future French king Henri II in 1533, brought a wave of Italians into France, bringing their expertise with them. Some of the more notable products, such as Bénédictine, were made by French monastic orders until relatively recently. (Chartreuse still is.)

In the last century, liqueurs had an aura of being soothingly palatable after-dinner digestifs for those – women essentially – who were not fond of the stronger alternatives such as cognac.

Indeed, they were seen as more ladylike drinks altogether, an image enhanced by the introduction of the tiny glasses that are still depressingly enough seen as the appropriate receptacles. By now, they had shed most of their health-giving claims and become honest-to-goodness drinks, although it was still popularly believed by imbibers that they had pro-phylactic properties.

The cocktail era of the 1920s and 30s that had doggedly to contend with uni-versal prohibition in the USA, but suffered no such constraints in London, Paris, Berlin and Venice, freed liqueurs from the straitjacket of cultured polite-ness in which the Victorian period had imprisoned them. At a stroke, they trans-formed the old slings and fizzes, fixes, sours, punches, cups and smashes into drinks that were worthy of their names. A mixture of gin with lemon juice, sugar

Above: The museum of La Grande Chartreuse Monastery, Isère, France.

and soda may have been a pleasant way of taking gin, but add a slug of cherry brandy to it and it became an altogether more exciting and hazardous proposi-tion. That sense of playing with fire is inscribed in the names of the great cock-tail recipes of the 1920s, in their evocations of gambling (Casino), sex (Maiden's Blush), spiritual danger (Hell, Little Devil) and even First World War munitions (Whizzbang, Depth Bomb, Artillery).

No drinking culture was ever happier or more heedless than that of the origi-nal and greatest cocktail era, and it couldn't have happened without the liqueurs. The following pages are a taster's tour of the famous and the not so famous.

ADVOCAAT

ADVOCAAT IS A Dutch speciality. It is essentially a customized version of the humble egg nog, without the milk: a mixture of simple grape brandy with egg yolks and sugar, as thick and as yellow as tinned custard. Most of it is sold in this natural form, although it is possible in the Netherlands to buy vanilla- and fruit-flavoured versions. As a result of its velvety texture and bland wholesomeness, advocaat is often thought of as a drink for the elderly, and is commonly added to mugs of hot chocolate or strong coffee.

There are a few widely available brands of advocaat on the market: the red-labelled Warninks is probably the most familiar, but Fockinks, and the liqueur specialists, Bols and De Kuypers, also make it. The standard bottled strength is quite low for a liqueur – around 17% ABV, which is about the same strength as the average fortified wine.

WARNINKS
Probably the
most famous
advocaat brand

ADVOCAAT ORIGINAL WARNINKS PRODUCE OF HOLLAND

17.2% vol. 70cle

MIXING
Snowball: Put a generous measure (a couple of fluid ounces) of advocaat in a tall glass and top up with ice-cold sparkling lemonade. If you require a bit more of a kick, add a dessertspoon of sweet brown sherry to it as well. (This is the kind of "cocktail" generally considered safe to give to minors, since it resembles nothing so much as a particularly rich milkshake.)

HOW IT IS MADE
Commercial grape spirit is bought in and sweetened with sugar syrup. Only the yolks of the eggs are added, along with an emulsifying agent to prevent the mixture from separating.

TASTES GOOD WITH
As the ready-made basis of an egg nog, it can be made into a long drink by topping it up with whole milk and a sprinkling of nutmeg.

ADVOCAAT
This is the only manufactured drink in this book to contain egg yolk.

BOLS ADVOCAAT PRODUCE OF HOLLAND

AMARETTO

O F ALL THE LIQUEURS that rely on almonds for their principal flavouring, amaretto is the most famous. It has become widely associated in people's minds with one particular Italian brand, Disaronno Amaretto, made by a company called Illva, although there are other liqueurs that may properly be called amarettos. The famous amaretto comes in a rectangular bottle, with a label in the form of an old scroll and a disproportionately large, square screwtop. The flavour is not entirely derived from almonds but from the stones of apricots too. Resembling a kind of liquid marzipan, the taste is strong and sweet and is quite assertive even when mixed in a cocktail.

Legend has it that the recipe was given to an Italian painter, Bernardino Luini, in the 16th century by an innkeeper who was the model for the Virgin Mary in his wall-painting of the Nativity at Saronno. Whether or not there is much truth in the tale, the original domestic concoction was probably grape brandy in which apricot kernels – with their strongly almondy flavour – had been steeped.

HOW IT IS MADE

Almond extracts, along with apricot kernels and seeds, are steeped in brandy, and the resulting drink is sweetened with sugar syrup and coloured to a deep brown.

MIXING

Godmother: Mix Disaronno Amaretto with an equal measure of vodka in a tumbler full of ice. **Godfather** (below): As above, but substitute Scotch for the vodka.

TASTES GOOD WITH

Just as a frangipane mixture, full of ground almonds, makes a good base for almost any fruit tart, so amaretto works well in the syrup for a fruit salad, or added to whipped cream or ice cream for most fruit-based desserts. It also marries deliciously with chocolate in super-rich *pot au chocolat*, and is excellent in a liqueur coffee, and perhaps with cognac too.

CASONI AMARETTO Amaretto's flavour is like marzipan in a bottle

OTHER NAMES
France: crème d'amandes

FLAVOURINGS
Almonds
Apricots

DISARONNO AMARETTO The most famous brand of Italian amaretto

HOW TO SERVE
Although sweet, the flavour of Disaronno Amaretto is quite complex enough for it to be enjoyable on its own, but it works better chilled. Serving it *frappé* (poured over crushed ice) is highly refreshing.

ANIS

CONFUSION REIGNS as to the precise differ-ences between anis and pastis, and indeed whether there are any meaningful differences at all. They are both flavoured with the berries of the aniseed plant, originally native to North Africa, and are popular all around the Mediter-ranean. They both turn cloudy when watered, and are both claimed as the respectable successor to the once outlawed absinthe.

One august authority claims that pastis should be flavoured with liquorice rather than aniseed, although the two are very close in taste. Another claims that anis is simply one of the types of pastis. Still another claims that, whereas anis is a product of the maceration of aniseed or liquorice in spirit, pastis should properly be seen as a distillation from either of the two ingredients themselves.

They can't all be right of course, but for what it's worth, I incline to accept the last definition. For one thing, anis tends to be lower in alcohol than pastis – liqueur strength rather than spirit strength. The one thing we can be sure of

FLAVOURINGS

Anise berries (aniseed). Sometimes the seeds of star anise – an oriental shrub that bears a fruit in the shape of an eight-pointed star – may be used. The flavour is fairly similar, though by no means identical

HOW TO SERVE

The only true way to serve anis is to take it ice-cold in a little thick-bottomed tumbler. The addition of a small amount of water – usually about as much again – turns it milky but with a faint green-ish tinge. It is considered a great appetite-whetter.

p 9l

is that pastis is always French (the word is old southern French dialect), whereas anis – particularly with that spelling – can also be Spanish. In Spain, there are sweet and dry varieties, whereas French anise tends mainly to be dry.

Ever since the days of the medical school of Salerno, and probably earlier, extract of anise has been seen as a valuable weapon in the apothecary's armoury. It is thought to be especially good for ailments of the stomach.

ANISETTE

Anisette is quite defi-nitely a liqueur. It is French, sweetened, and usually some-what stronger than anis. The most famous brand is Marie Brizard, from the firm named after the Bordelaise who, in the mid-18th century, was given the recipe by a West Indian acquaintance.

ANIS
This liqueur is made in Spain as well as France

ANISETTE
The sweet liqueur form of anis, typified by this Marie Brizard anisette

AURUM

Orange
very special
see 67 & 73
Brandy taste

IF THE NAME of Argentarium evokes silver, that of Aurum hints at gold. One glance at its colour will explain why. Made in the Abruzzi mountains, on the Adriatic coast of Italy, Aurum is a brandy-based proprietary liqueur in which a mixture of orange peel and whole oranges is infused, and the lustrous golden intensity of its appearance enhanced by saffron. It is claimed that the basic formula is of great antiquity. Aurum was given its Latin name by the celebrated Italian writer Gabriele d'Annunzio. The name hints that it may at one time have contained particles of genuine gold, harking back to the alchemical origins of distillation, and it has logically been argued that Aurum was the true forerunner of Goldwasser. *p 78*

HOW IT IS MADE

No mere industrial spirit is used in Aurum. The brandy in it is distilled by the makers from vintage Italian wines, and the distillate is cask-aged for around four years to take up wood colour. The oranges (and other citrus fruits) are infused separately in more brandy, and then the infusion is triple-distilled. This, and the first brandy, are then blended and allowed another period of oak maturation.

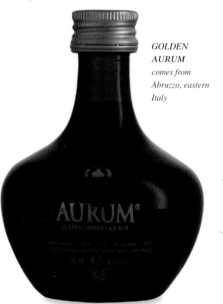

GOLDEN
AURUM
comes from
Abruzzo, eastern
Italy

ARGENTARIUM

One of a handful of liqueurs that are still produced by religious orders, Argentarium is made in a monastery in the Lazio region of Italy, north of Rome. It is based on grape brandy, flavoured with a collection of herbs that grow wild on the surrounding hillsides, some of which are gathered by the monks themselves. Most of it is consumed locally.

BENEDICTINE

"DEO OPTIMO MAXIMO" (Praise be to God, most good, most great), exclaimed the Benedictine monk, who formulated the liqueur that now bears his order's name, on first tasting the results. Or so the story goes. It was reputedly in 1510, so it isn't easy to verify. What is certain is that his monastery at Fécamp, in the Normandy region of northern France, produced this cognac-based herbal liqueur until the time of the French Revolution in 1789, when the monasteries were forcibly closed and production banned.

Bénédictine was officially extinct until the 1860s, when it was revived by a descendent of the monastery's lawyers, Alexandre Le Grand. On finding the secret recipe among a bundle of yellowing papers, he was inspired to build an extraordinary new distillery in the high Gothic style at Fécamp, and the now secularized liqueur – first christened Bénédictine by Le Grand – lived to fight another day.

Bénédictine is a bright golden potion of honeyed sweetness, containing a herbalist's pantheon of medicinal plants and spices. The exact formula is known only to three people at any given time, but it is thought to contain as many as 75 aromatizing ingredients.

BENEDICTINE
One of the old
monastic liqueurs

HOW TO SERVE

It is imperative to serve a speciality product such as **Aurum** (below) by itself as a digestif. It should not be chilled but rather warmed in the hand like fine cognac, and served in the same sort of glass to appreciate its aromas.

Bénédictine should ideally be served straight in a large liqueur glass at the end of a meal, but its makers clearly have no qualms about its use as a mixing ingredient by those who find the sweetness of classic liqueurs too much to take *au naturel*.

CHARTREUSE

UNLIKE BENEDICTINE, CHARTREUSE really is still made by monks – of the Carthusian order – at Voiron, near Grenoble, not far from the site of their monastery, La Grande Chartreuse. Expelled from France at the time of the French Revolution, the order was allowed back into the mother country after the defeat of Napoleon, only to be kicked out again in 1903. It was then that a second branch of the operation was founded at Tarragona, in eastern Spain, and it continued as Chartreuse's second address until 1991, long after the production was finally re-established in France in 1932.

The Carthusians are a silent order, which has no doubt helped to keep the recipe a secret; like its Norman counterpart, it is known only to a lucky trio. Proceeds from the worldwide sales of Chartreuse are ploughed back into the order's funds, from where it goes to pay for all kinds of charitable works.

There is a premium version of Chartreuse (the original recipe is said to date from 1605) called Elixir, which is sold in miniature bottles at a fearsome 71% ABV, but it is principally sold in two incarnations today, green (55%) and yellow (40%). The latter is a deep greenish-yellow hue, sweet, honeyed and slightly minty in flavour; while the green Chartreuse is a pale, leafy colour, has a less pungent herbal scent and is distinctly less viscous. *resistance to flow*

Additionally, the order produces a rare higher grade of each colour, labelled VEP, for *vieillissement exceptionnellement prolongé* (exceptionally long ageing).

GREEN CHARTREUSE
Intensely powerful and aromatic.

YELLOW CHARTREUSE
Sweeter than green Chartreuse and of normal spirit strength.

MIXING
Alaska: Shake three-quarters gin to one-quarter yellow Chartreuse with ice and strain into a cocktail glass.

Bijou: Stir equal measures of Plymouth gin, green Chartreuse and sweet red vermouth with ice and a dash of orange bitters in a mixing jug. Strain into a cocktail glass. Add a cherry and a twist of lemon.

HOW IT IS MADE
By varying processes of distillation, infusion and maceration, over 130 herbs and plants are used to flavour a base of grape brandy. They were all once gathered from the mountains surrounding the monastery, but some are now imported from Italy and Switzerland. It is aged in casks for up to five years, except for the VEP, which receives twice that long.

TASTES GOOD WITH
The French sometimes fortify their hot chocolate with a reviving splash of the green Chartreuse. The yellow is thought more suitable for coffee.

HOW TO SERVE
If you find Chartreuse overwhelming on its own, do as the French do and serve it mixed as a long drink with tonic or soda and plenty of ice.

ELIXIR VEGETAL
This is the original Carthusian elixir, bottled at very high strength

COINTREAU *Orange*

O NE OF THE MOST POPULAR branded liqueurs
of all, Cointreau is, properly speaking, a
variety of Curaçao. This means it is a brandy-
based spirit that has been flavoured with the
peel of bitter oranges. When it was launched in
1849 by the Cointreau brothers, Edouard and
Adolphe, it was sold under the brand name
Triple Sec White Curaçao, but so many other
proprietary Curaçaos began to be sold as Triple
Sec that the family decided to give it their own
name instead.

The centre of operations, as well as a distillery,
are located in Angers, in the Loire valley, but it
is also made in the Americas. A variety of different bottlings is made at different strengths,
including a cream version, but the best-loved
Cointreau is the one that comes in a square
dark-brown bottle
at 40% ABV.

COINTREAU
One of the
best-loved
liqueurs of
them all

MIXING
Cointreau is so versatile in cocktails that a
list of recipes could easily fill a whole book.
Suffice to say it can successfully be mixed in
equal quantities with virtually any spirit
(except perhaps whisky) and the juice of half
a lemon and shaken with ice. Start with gin
and you have a **White Lady** (below), brandy
for a **Sidecar**, vodka for a **Balalaika** and
even tequila for a lemon (as opposed to lime)
Margarita.

Brandy base

Despite its spirit strength, Cointreau tastes
deliciously innocuous. It is sugar-sweet and
colourless, but has a powerful fume of fresh
oranges, with an underlying vaguely herbal note
too. The oranges used in it are a clever blend of
bitter green Seville-style varieties from the
Caribbean (the island of Curaçao itself is close
to Venezuela) and sweeter types from the south
of France.

HOW IT IS MADE
Cointreau is a double distillation of grape
brandy, infused with orange peel, sweetened
and further aromatized with other secret plant
ingredients.

TASTES GOOD WITH
If the balance of other seasonings is right, it
works admirably in the orange sauce classically
served with duck. It is excellent in a range of
desserts, particularly so in rich chocolate mousse.

HOW TO SERVE
Absolutely everybody's
favourite way of
serving Cointreau is
either on the rocks or
frappé, depending on
whether you like your
ice in chunks or
crystals. The cold then
mitigates some of the
sweetness of the
liqueur, while the pure
citrus flavour is exquis-
itely refreshing.

CREAM LIQUEURS

These LIQUEURS ARE an ever-expanding category in the contemporary market. Whether the makers acknowledge it or not, cream liqueurs all owe something of their inspiration and appeal to the archetypal brand, Bailey's Irish Cream. The manufacturers tend to push them particularly at Christmas, where they occupy a niche as the soft option for those who feel they need a spoonful of sugar and a dollop of cream to help the alcohol go down.

Bailey's itself is a blend of Irish whiskey and cream with a slight coffee flavour. It became instantly chic when created in the 1970s, but was quickly saddled with the image of the kind of soft, svelte drink that unscrupulous boys plied unsuspecting girls with in nightclubs. Since then, cream liqueurs have gone on multiplying.

Coffee and chocolate flavourings are particularly common, and indeed some cream liqueurs are made by confectionery companies, such as Cadbury's and Terry's. Then again, some of the more reputable liqueur-makers have produced cream versions of their own top products (for example, Crème de Grand Marnier) in order to grab a share of this evidently lucrative market.

I have to say I decline to take these products seriously. At best, they are substitutes for real cream cocktails, but they are always sweeter and less powerful than the genuine home-made article, and many of them contain an artificial stabilizer to stop the cream from separating. In any case, why rely on somebody else's formula when you can follow your own specifications? Once you have made your own brandy Alexanders, you won't want chocolate cream liqueur.

The extreme was reached when another Irish drinks company of some repute launched a product called Sheridan's in the early 1990s. It came in a bifurcated bottle with two tops, one half filled with a black liquid that was coffee-flavoured Irish whiskey, the other with white vanilla liqueur. The idea was that you poured first from one side of the bottle and then from the other – remembering to close the top on the first half – in order to simulate the appearance of a liqueur coffee. (Little matter that Irish coffee is supposed to be served hot.) I am told the product has not so far proved conspicuously successful, perhaps because it involves such a fandango when it comes to serving it in bars.

FLAVOURINGS
Coffee
Chocolate

HOW TO SERVE
Both the sweetness and the texture of these products need the mitigating influence of ice to make them attractive.
A brandy glass is the best receptacle.

*MOZART
BLACK
An intense blend
of dark chocolate
and bourbon
vanilla*

*BAILEY'S
The daddy
of all cream
liqueurs*

CREME LIQUEURS

No cream inside

A WHOLE RANGE OF liqueurs that use the prefix "*crème de*" may be bracketed together here. They are nothing at all to do with cream liqueurs, despite the terminology. They nearly always consist of one dominant flavour indicated in the name, often but not always a fruit, and are usually appropriately coloured. In the main, they are bottled at 25–30% ABV, and may be considered among the more useful building-blocks of the cocktail-mixer's repertoire.

Originally, the term "crème" was used to indicate that these were sweetened liqueurs, as distinct from dry spirits such as cognac or calvados. They were mainly French in origin – the Marie Brizard

FRAISE DES BOIS
This version of crème de fraise uses wild strawberries

MIXING

The use of these liqueurs in cocktail-making is as limitless as the flavours themselves. Sometimes they work well with each other (try brown cacao and fraise, or banane and noyau, for example) but they will need a very dry base to counteract the cumulative impact of the sweetness. They all work well in cream cocktails, but one flavour is usually quite sufficient. Let your imagination off the leash.

Fruit Daiquiri: The original Daiquiri recipe of white rum shaken with the juice of half a lemon and a pinch of sugar can be adapted by adding a measure of any of the fruit liqueurs to it (and perhaps some puréed fruit as well), but you may then want to leave out the sugar.

Stinger: The adaptable Stinger is simply a half-and-half mixture of any spirit with white crème de menthe, shaken with ice and served over smashed ice in a cocktail glass. The prototype version is probably with cognac.

Alexander: The recipe for this given in the brandy chapter can be adapted with other spirits too – gin is particularly successful – but it is always the brown crème de cacao that must be used.

FLAVOURINGS

The flavours of such liqueurs are numerous, and the following list does not pretend to be exhaustive. The French names are given first, since that is how they are labelled. Most commonly seen are: crème de banane (banana), cacao (cocoa or chocolate – comes in dark brown and white versions), cassis (blackcurrant), fraise (strawberry), framboise (raspberry) and menthe (mint – comes in bright green and white versions).

---

company founded in the mid-18th century in Bordeaux is still important in this field – but production soon spread to other specialist liqueur manufacturers such as Bols and De Kuypers of Holland.

Before the widespread availability of such products, the sweetening element in a cocktail used to be sugar, pure and simple, or perhaps a sugar syrup. The crème liqueurs had the advantage of not only providing that sweetness, but also of introducing another flavour into the drinks they were added to. They have since become indispensable in extending the horizons of both the professional and amateur bartender, and are usually a recommended purchase in any guide giving advice on starting your own cocktail bar at home.

Most of these products will be based on a neutral-tasting, un-aged grape brandy, with the various flavouring ingredients either infused or

CREME DE FRAISE

A basic strawberry liqueur from Marie Brizard of Bordeaux.

HOW TO SERVE

If these drinks are to be taken as befitted their original purpose, as pleasant aids to digestion at the end of a grand dinner, they are best served *frappé* – i.e. poured over shaved ice – rather than neat. In that way, some of their sugary sweetness is mitigated.

MIXING

Oracabessa: Shake a measure of dark rum with a measure of crème de banane and the juice of half a lemon with ice and strain into a tall glass. Float some thin slices of banana on the surface of the drink and top it up with sparkling lemonade. Garnish lavishly with fruits.

Silver Jubilee: Shake equal measures of gin, crème de banane and cream with ice and strain into a cocktail glass.

Blackout (from Lucius Beebe's *Stork Club Bar Book*): Shake a measure and three-quarters of gin and three-quarters of a measure of crème de mûre with the juice of half a lime and plenty of ice and strain into a cocktail glass.

Stratosphere: A few dashes of crème de violette are added to a glass of champagne until a mauve colour is obtained. The scentedness is then enhanced by adding a whole clove to the glass. (An American violet liqueur, Crème Yvette, was at one time the only correct product to use in this very ladylike aperitif.)

English Rose: Shake a measure and a half of London gin with three-quarters of a measure of crème de roses, the juice of half a lemon, half a teaspoon of caster sugar and half an egg-white, with ice, and strain into a wine glass. (Alternatively, you can make this in an electric blender for that extra frothiness.)

CREME DE CACAO

Cacao – cocoa or chocolate – is available in two versions, dark and white, to please the chocoholics.

NOT LIKE KIRSCH

macerated in the spirit rather than being subject to distillation themselves. The difference, essentially, between infusion and maceration is that the former involves some gentle heating action, while the latter is just a cold soaking of the flavouring element in the spirit until it has been broken down and has imparted its aromatic compounds. Maceration is obviously a considerably slower process than infusion. In both cases, the ingredient has to be rendered water-soluble, in the case of maceration particularly so.

Since these are intended to be rich but simple products, with one overriding flavour, the crème liqueurs are not generally treated to ageing in wood.

CREME DE BANANE

Banana is one of the more versatile flavours

Oak maturation would interfere anyway with the often bold primary colours of the drinks, as well as obscuring the tastes.

They are more often than not sold in 50cl bottles. You will find as you use them that a certain amount of powdery sugar deposit builds up underneath the screw tops; simply give them a good wipe down every now and then.

HOW THEY ARE MADE

After the infusion or maceration, during which take-up of flavour is obtained, the aromatized spirit may then have to be strained to remove any solid particles caused by making the flavouring agent water-soluble. It

CREME DE CASSIS
Cassis is also a speciality of Burgundy

MIXING
Kir: The world-famous aperitif created in Burgundy, and originally named after a mayor of Dijon, consists of a glass of light, dry, acidic white wine with a teaspoon or two (depending on taste) of crème de cassis. The classic wine to use is a Bourgogne Aligoté of the most recent vintage, but any fairly neutral-tasting but *sharp* white wine will do. Add the cassis to a glass of non-vintage Brut champagne and the drink becomes a **Kir Royale** (below).

CREME DE FRAMBOISE
Red fruit liqueurs, such as framboise, are very good if added by the teaspoon to a glass of basic champagne or sparkling wine.

FLAVOURINGS
More obscure flavours include: crème d'ananas (pineapple), café (coffee), mandarine (tangerine), mûre (blackberry), myrtille (bilberry), noyau (almond), roses (rose-petal), thé (tea), vanille (vanilla), violette (violet)

is then sweetened, usually by means of the addition of sugar solution, or sometimes with a sugar and glucose mix. Unless it is possible to achieve a striking colour naturally (which is in fact quite rare), the colour is then created by the addition of vegetable-based colouring matter such as carotene or beetroot. Red colourings are often created by adding cochineal. These colourings do not affect the flavour. The liqueur is then subjected to a heavy filtration to ensure a bright, crystal-clear product. It is transferred into neutral, stainless steel tanks to await bottling.

CREME DE MENTHE
The white version of the mint liqueur is similar in taste to the green variety.

CREME DE MENTHE

Green crème de menthe is sweet and spearminty

TASTES GOOD WITH
The most obvious way to use these liqueurs is as boosting ingredients in desserts that are themselves flavoured with the same principal ingredient, especially in the case of the fruit ones. Enliven your strawberry mousse with crème de fraise, your blackberry cheesecake with crème de mûre, and so forth. (On the other hand, a richly gooey *pot au chocolat* can get along quite well without crème de cacao if you have used top-quality chocolate.) The flowery crème liqueurs make exotic additions to the syrup for a simple fruit salad.

CREME DE PECHE
Peach is an unusual flavour to find in a crème liqueur.

BRAMBLE
Fruit liqueurs are also made in the UK.

CURACAO

Orange bitters [handwritten]

FIRST INVENTED BY THE DUTCH, Curaçao was a white rum-based liqueur flavoured with the peel of bitter green oranges found by the settlers on the Caribbean island of the same name, not far off the coast of Venezuela. Desipte its geographically specific name, the liqueur has never been subject to anything like appellation regulations. It is made by many different companies in a number of countries, where brandy is used as the starter spirit.

A variant name in common use

ORANGE CURACAO
All Curaçao is flavoured with bitter oranges

MIXING

Olympic: Shake equal measures of cognac, orange Curaçao and freshly squeezed orange juice with ice and strain into a cocktail glass. Decorate with a twist of orange peel.
Oasis: Pour a double measure of gin over ice-cubes in a tall glass. Add half a measure of blue Curaçao. Top up with tonic water and stir well. Garnish with a slice of lemon and sprig of mint.

was Triple Sec, the most famous example being Cointreau, although confusingly Curaçao is not at all *sec* but always sweet. The bitterness of the oranges – which are green simply because they are not quite ripe, not because they are some notably exotic variety – balances the sweetness, however, to the extent that drinkers may have been prepared to consider it dry.

Curaçao comes in a range of colours in addition to the clear version. The orange Curaçao, especially from companies like Bols, is often particularly bitter, its colour a deep, burnished tawny orange. Curaçao also comes in bright blue, dark green, red and yellow versions for novelty value, but the flavour is always of orange. The strength is generally somewhere between 25–30% ABV.

The name of the island is not, of course, Dutch but Portuguese, after the original discoverers. More perplexity is occasioned over the correct way to pronounce "Curaçao" than over the name of any other liqueur. It should properly be "curashow" (to rhyme with "miaow"), but it is corrupted by English speakers into something like "cura-say-oh".

FLAVOURING
Bitter oranges *white rum* [handwritten]

HOW TO SERVE
The bitterness of the fruit mixes well with other bitter flavours, so orange Curaçao and tonic makes a particularly appetizing long drink. Alternatively, use a not-too-sweet sparkling lemonade, if you can find one. It also goes well in equal measures with either dry or sweet vermouth. Curaçao is not especially pleasant taken neat.

OTHER NAMES

Triple Sec (only for the colourless version, strictly speaking)

HOW IT IS MADE

The blossom and dried peel of wild oranges are steeped in grape brandy or even neutral spirit; the resulting infusion is then sweetened, clarified and coloured according to style.

CURAÇAO

Blue Curaçao enjoyed something of a vogue in the cocktail renaissance of the early 1980s, though its colour makes it hard to mix with.

TRIPLE SEC
The term tends to be used for the colourless Curaçao

MIXING

Whip: Shake equal measures of cognac, dry vermouth and white Curaçao with a dash of pastis (e.g. Pernod) and plenty of ice and strain into a cocktail glass. (It should be noted that this lethal cocktail contains no non-alcoholic ingredient. Caution is advised.)
Rite of Spring (below): Mix a double measure of vodka and a measure of green Curaçao with ice in a mixing-jug. Decant into a tall glass and top up with clear lemonade. Dangle a long twist of lemon peel in the drink.

TASTES GOOD WITH

Indispensable in the classic crêpe Suzette. In the recipe given by the great French chef Auguste Escoffier, the pancake batter is flavoured with tangerine juice and Curaçao and the cooked crêpe sauced with butter, sugar and tangerine zests. These days, it is generally Cointreau that is used in this ever-popular dessert.

CUARENTA Y TRES

Cuarenta is a sweet liqueur made in the Cartagena region of eastern Spain, based on a recipe that supposedly dates from classical times when the Phoenicians founded Carthage, in North Africa, and introduced viticulture. It is concocted from a brandy base with infusions of herbs, but has a noticeably predominant flavour of vanilla, which rather torpedoes the Carthaginian theory since vanilla was only discovered in the 16th century by Spanish explorers in Mexico. Not much seen outside its region of production, it is nonetheless held in high regard locally.

DRAMBUIE

Drambuie is Scotland's (and, for that matter, Britain's) pre-eminent contribution to the world's classic liqueurs. Hugely popular in the United States, it is a unique and inimitable concoction of Scotch whisky, heather honey and herbs. The story goes that the recipe was given as a reward to one Captain Mackinnon in 1745, after the defeat at Culloden by Charles Edward Stuart – or Bonnie Prince Charlie, as the pretender to the English throne has ever since been better known. The lad that was born to be king was of course ferried to Skye, and from thence to France, away from the clutches of the nefarious English. Captain Mackinnon was his protector.

That story has inevitably since been debunked by meticulous historians. The truth is almost certainly the other way round. It was the Mackinnons who revived the spirits of the fugitive Prince with their own Scotch-based home concoction, which was very much a typical blend of the period, an unrefined spirit disguised with sweet and herbal additives.

Today, the spirit is anything but unrefined, being a mixture of fine malt and straight grain whiskies, to which the flavourings are added. The Mackinnon family still makes it, though near Edinburgh now rather than on Skye. They registered its name (from the Gaelic *an dram buidheach*, "the drink that satisfies") in 1892. It has been in private production since the time of the Bonnie Prince, but was only launched commercially in 1906 – with spectacular success.

Scotch
heather honey
herbs

TASTES GOOD WITH
A hunk of rich Dundee cake doused in Drambuie is a sumptuous cold-weather treat.

DRAMBUIE
Perhaps
Britain's
greatest
contribution
to the liqueur
world

CYNAR
Cynar is a liqueur for the very brave. It is a soupy, dark-brown potion made in Italy, flavoured with artichoke hearts (its name derives from the Latin for artichoke, *cynarum*). All of the savoury bitterness of the globe artichoke, boldly illustrated on its label, is in it, and if that sounds like fun, go ahead and try it. I once swallowed a modest measure of it in a little backstreet bar in Venice, and of all my shimmering memories of the watery city, Cynar is not, I have to say, the loveliest.

HOW TO SERVE
Serve Drambuie as it comes, over ice, or with an equal measure of Scotch as a **Rusty Nail**.

GALLIANO

ANOTHER OF ITALY'S liqueur specialities, golden-yellow Galliano is chiefly known on the international cocktail scene for its matchless role of livening up a vodka-and-orange in the Harvey Wallbanger cocktail, and for its tall conical bottle. It was invented by one Arturo Vaccari, a Tuscan distiller who named his new creation in honour of an Italian soldier, Major Giuseppe Galliano. In 1895 Galliano held out under siege at Enda Jesus in Ethiopia for 44 days against the vastly superior Abyssinian forces under the command of Haile Selassie's nephew.

The formula, as we are accustomed to hear in the world of liqueurs, is a jealously guarded secret, but it is said to be based on up to 80 herbs,

MIXING
Harvey Wallbanger:
Pour a generous measure of vodka over ice in a highball glass, top up with fresh orange juice and float a measure of Galliano on top.

GALLIANO
This Italian classic comes in a distinctive conical bottle

MIXING
Milano: Shake equal measures of gin and Galliano with the juice of half a lemon and ice, and strain into a cocktail glass.

roots, berries and flowers from the alpine slopes to the north of Italy. Among its flavours is a strong presence of anise or liquorice, and there is a pronounced scent of vanilla. It is also naturally very sweet. Despite the complexity of its tastes, it is a valuable addition to the bartender's battery.

HOW IT IS MADE
The various flavouring ingredients are steeped in a mixture of neutral spirit and water and then distilled; the resulting potion is then blended with refined spirits. It is bottled at 35% ABV.

FIOR D'ALPI
No liqueur makes more of a show of itself than Fior d'Alpi. Made in northern Italy, its name means "Alpine flowers", and those – along with a fistful of wild herbs – are its principal flavourings. It is a delicate primrose hue and comes in a tall narrow bottle. What catches the eye in the shop window, though, is the gnarled little tree that sits inside every bottle. If you leave the bottle undisturbed for a while, the sugar in the drink will form a crystallized frosting on the twigs that can look touchingly Christmassy. That, coupled with the agreeable sweetness of the liqueur itself, is what keeps it popular – at least in Italy. Similar products are sold as Millefiori and – what else? – Edelweiss.

GLAYVA *Orange*

LIKE DRAMBUIE, Glayva is a Scotch whisky-based liqueur made near Edinburgh, but it is of much more recent provenance. The drink was first formulated just after the Second World War. Its aromatizers are quite similar to those of Drambuie, although its flavour is intriguingly different. Heather honey and various herbs are used, and so is a quantity of orange peel, resulting in a noticeably fruitier attack on the palate.

The noble Scot commemorated in the case of Glayva is one Master Borthwick, the phlegmatic 16-year-old credited with carrying Robert the Bruce's heart back to Scotland after the King's defeat at the hands of the Saracens. Not content

MIXING

Saracen: Shake a measure of Scotch whisky, half a measure each of Glayva and dry sherry and a dash of orange bitters with ice. Pour into a tumbler and add a splash of soda. Decorate with a piece of orange rind.

FLAVOURINGS *Scotch*
Heather honey
Orange peel
Various herbs

with rescuing the regal heart, the indomitable lad cut off the head of a Saracen chieftain he had killed, impaled it on a spear, and brought that back too just to keep his spirits up. All of those pubs named the Saracen's Head recall the event, as did the Moorish head once depicted on the Glayva label.

TASTES GOOD WITH

Like the other Scotch-based liqueurs, Glayva is particularly good added to an ice cream, perhaps one flavoured with honey and/or orange, like the drink itself.

HOW TO SERVE
Glayva should be served just as it is, in a standard whisky tumbler. Its fruitiness makes it slightly better for chilling than Drambuie, but don't overdo it.

GLAYVA
The original formula for Glayva is much older than the product itself

GOLDWASSER

FLAVOURINGS
Aniseed
Caraway seeds
Citrus fruits

Goldwasser, or Danziger Goldwasser to give it its archetypal name, recalls the great Catalan physician Arnaldo de Vilanova who, in the 13th century, is reputed to have cured the Pope of a dangerous illness by giving him a herbal elixir containing specks of gold. In so doing, he also saved his own skin from the Inquisition. Since the search for the elixir of life was intimately bound up with alchemy's project of turning base metals into gold, it was only natural that gold itself should be seen as being beneficial to health.

OTHER NAMES
France: Liqueur d'Or or eau d'or

MIXING
Generally, there is no point in mixing Goldwasser because you then bury the gold flakes. However, I am indebted to Lucius Beebe's 1946 *Stork Club Bar Book* for the following recipe for a layered cocktail (to be used only if you are sure your eggs are free of salmonella):
Golden Slipper: A measure of yellow Chartreuse is poured into a *copita* or sherry glass. A separated egg yolk is then dropped whole on to the surface of it, and a measure of Goldwasser carefully poured on top of that. (I haven't tried this. I suspect it may look rather prettier than it tastes.)

GOLDWASSER
All Goldwasser came originally from Gdansk, like this one

The commercial prototype of the drink was first made in the Baltic port city of Danzig (now Gdansk in Poland). Based on the drink kümmel, it is flavoured with both aniseed and caraway seeds and is colourless, less sweet than many liqueurs, and it really does have a shower of real golden particles added to it, in memory of Arnaldo. When the bottle was poured, the gold specks flurried up to general approbation like the flakes in a snowstorm toy. (There was also for a time a silver version, Silberwasser.) Liqueur d'Or was a now-extinct French version of the same thing. Some brands also had a citric fruit flavour – sometimes lemon, sometimes orange.

HOW TO SERVE
The prettiness can be enhanced by serving Goldwasser in a little cut-crystal liqueur glass.

TASTES GOOD WITH
Soufflé Rothschild is a very classical, hot dessert soufflé made from crème patissière and crystallized fruits that have been macerated in Danziger Goldwasser. It is served in individual soufflé dishes surrounded by strawberries.

GRAND MARNIER *Orange*

GRAND MARNIER IS ONE of the best-loved of all the world's orange-flavoured liqueurs. The original product is a little younger than Cointreau, its big French rival, but the style is quite different. In the sense that the oranges used in it are bitter varieties from the Caribbean, it may be classed as another type of Curaçao, but it is a distinctly finer product than most ordinary Curaçao.

The house that owns it was founded in 1827 by a family called Lapostolle. Louis-Alexandre Marnier later married into the family business and it was he who, in 1880, first conceived the liqueur that bears his name. Encountering the bitter oranges of Haiti on a grand tour, he hit upon the idea of blending their flavour with that of finest cognac, and then giving it a period of barrel-ageing that basic Curaçao never receives.

Today, the production of the liqueur is split between two centres, one at Château de

GRAND MARNIER
Fully the equal of the higher grades of cognac

MIXING

Gloom Chaser: Shake equal measures of Grand Marnier, orange Curaçao, freshly squeezed lemon juice and a dash of grenadine with ice and strain into a cocktail glass. Decorate with a twist of orange.

Bourg in the Cognac region, the other at Neauphle-le-Château, near Paris. The initial blending is carried out at the former site, the ageing at the latter. What results is a highly refined, mellow full-strength spirit that has a warm amber colour and an intense, festive scent of ripe oranges. It is sweet, but the distinction of the Fine Champagne cognac on which it is based prevents it from being in any way cloying when served straight.

The Marnier-Lapostolle company also decided to try cashing in on the mania for cream liqueurs that has arisen in the last 20 years or so by launching a Crème de Grand Marnier at much lower strength, which I can't find it in my heart to recommend.

HOW IT IS MADE

The juice of Caribbean oranges is blended with top-quality cognac. After full amalgamation of the flavours, it is then re-distilled, sweetened and given a period of cask-ageing.

TASTES GOOD WITH

It is the classic ingredient in duck à l'orange, and may also be used in a whole range of desserts, particularly flamed crêpes and anything made with strong chocolate.

FLAVOURING
Oranges *Cognac*

HOW TO SERVE
As reverently as best cognac.

KAHLUA

K AHLÚA IS THE only liqueur of any note to
have been conceived in Mexico. It is a
dark brown coffee-flavoured essence packaged
in a round-shouldered, opaque bottle with
a colourful label. There are two versions, one
bottled at 20%ABV and a more concentrated
Especial at the original 26.5%. It is inevitably
often compared to the other, more famous
coffee liqueur, Tia Maria, but it is slightly
thicker in texture and somewhat less sweet than
its Jamaican counterpart.

p104

KAHLUA
A liqueur with the
stimulant properties
of strong coffee

HOW TO SERVE
Kahlúa makes a very good chilled alternative
to a liqueur coffee. Pour the Kahlúa over
crushed ice in a tall glass and float some
thick cream on top. Alternatively, add it to
hot black coffee, top it with cream and a
dusting of ground cinnamon. Some think it
mixes well with either Coca-Cola or
milk as a long drink.

TASTES GOOD WITH
To enhance the flavour of a coffee dessert such
as a soufflé or ice cream, Kahlúa somehow
gives a smoother result than the more
commonly used Tia Maria.

MIXING
Black Russian: Certain
aficionados insist on
Kahlúa rather than Tia
Maria with the vodka.
Either way, it is as well
not to adulterate the
drink with cola.
Alexander the Great:
Shake a measure-and-a-
half of vodka with half
a measure each of
Kahlúa, crème de cacao
and thick cream and
plenty of ice. Strain into
a cocktail glass. (This
drink is reputed to have
been invented by the
great Nelson Eddy.)

IZARRA
Izarra is a sort of Basque version of
Chartreuse, made in Bayonne in southwest
France. It is flatteringly imitative to the
extent that it comes in two colours – yellow
and green – both full of aromatic herbs gathered wild in the Pyrenees. Green Izarra is
higher in alcoholic strength. (It is in fact, at
55%, exactly the same strength as green
Chartreuse, but doesn't really have the same
complexity of flavour.) The name means
"star" in the local dialect. Izarra is based on
armagnac, which is given a redistillation
with the aromatizing ingredients, followed
by a period of cask-ageing. Not surprisingly,
it is not much seen outside its native region.

KUMMEL

KUMMEL IS ONE of the more ancient liqueurs. All we know is that it originated somewhere in northern Europe, although we do not know exactly where. The best guess is Holland, but the Germans have a respectable enough claim on the patent as well (its name is, of course, German). Certainly, it was being made in Holland in the 1500s, and it very much fits the image of such drinks of the time, in that it would have been an unrefined grain spirit masked by an aromatic ingredient.

The ingredient in this case is caraway seeds. A certain amount of needless confusion is created by the fact that the name looks as though it has something to do with the more pungent cumin. This is only because, in certain European languages, caraway is often referred to as a sort of cumin. They have nothing to do with each other, the misleading nomenclature only arising because the seeds are supposed to look vaguely similar.

KUMMEL
Wolfschmidt
is the leading
brand of
kümmel

FLAVOURING
Caraway seeds

A key episode in kümmel's history occurred at the end of the 17th century, during Peter the Great's sojourn in Holland. He took the formula for the drink, to which he had grown rather partial, back to Russia with him, and kümmel came to be thought of as a Russian product, or at least as a Baltic one. The Baltic port of Riga, now capital of Latvia, was its chief centre of production throughout the 19th century, and some was also made in Danzig (now Gdansk), where they eventually came to add flecks of gold to it and call it Goldwasser.

Versions of kümmel are today made not just in Latvia but also in Poland, Germany, Holland, Denmark and even the United States. Not the least valued property of caraway, valued since Egyptian times, is its ability to counteract flatulence, which is why it was one of the traditional ingredients of gripe water for babies.

HOW IT IS MADE
The base is a pure grain distillate, effectively a type of vodka, in which the seeds are infused. Most brands are fairly heavily sweetened but they are always left colourless.

TASTES GOOD WITH
Try adding it to the mixture for old English seed cake, which is made with caraway seeds.

HOW TO SERVE
Kümmel is nearly always served on the rocks in its countries of origin.

LIQUEUR BRANDIES

SOME FRUIT LIQUEURS have traditionally been referred to as "brandies", even though they are properly nothing of the sort in the sense that we now understand that term. There are essentially three fruit brandies – cherry, apricot and peach – and, although they are occasionally known by other names, it is as cherry brandy, etc. that drinkers know them best.

Strictly speaking, these products belong to the same large category as those liqueurs prefixed with the phrase "crème de", in that they are sweetened, coloured drinks, based on simple grape brandy that has been flavoured with the relevant fruits, as opposed to being

FLAVOURINGS
Apricots
Cherries
Peaches

CHERRY BRANDY
Indispensable in the making of a Singapore Sling

HOW TO SERVE
The best of these liqueur brandies make wonderful digestifs served in small quantities, provided they are not the very sweetest styles.

OTHER NAMES
France: Apricot brandy is sometimes known as Apry or Abricotine.
Liqueur brandies may eventually come to be known as apricot liqueur, etc. if the term "brandy" is enforced for grape distillates only. (The alternatives could well be crème d'abricot, de cerise and de pêche.)

MIXING
Paradise: Shake a measure of gin with half a measure each of apricot brandy and fresh orange juice and ice, and strain into a flared wine glass.

primary distillates of those fruits themselves. The maceration of the fruit usually includes the stones or pips as well, for the bitter flavour they impart and – in the case of apricot kernels especially – the distinctive flavour of almond.

Of the three, the apricot variant has probably travelled the furthest. There are true apricot distillates made in eastern Europe, of which the Hungarian Barak Pálinka is the most renowned, but they are dry like the fruit brandies of France. Good examples of sweet apricot liqueurs are Bols Apricot Brandy, Cusenier and Apry made by the Marie Brizard company.

Cherry brandy is one of the few liqueurs that may just have been invented by the English, the role of creator being claimed by one Thomas Grant of Kent. The original version was made with black morellos, although other cherry varieties may be used in modern products, depending on what is locally available. English

MIXING

Angel Face: Shake equal measures of gin, apricot brandy and calvados with ice and strain into a cocktail glass.

Singapore Sling: Shake a measure of gin, a measure of cherry brandy and the juice of half a lemon with ice and a pinch of caster sugar. Strain into a tall glass and top with soda. (Some like to put in a splash of Cointreau too, but that may be over-egging the pudding.)

Pick-Me-Up: Mix a measure each of dry French vermouth and cherry brandy with a couple of dashes of gin and a shovelful of ice in a tumbler and knock back. (This is but one of the many recipes for pick-me-ups. As with all of them, it is intended to be drunk PDQ or, as Harry Craddock – Cocktail King of the Savoy Hotel in the 1920s – used to put it, "while it's laughing at you".)

Wally (from the *Stork Club Bar Book*): Shake equal measures of calvados (or apple-jack), peach brandy and fresh lime juice with ice, and strain into a cocktail glass.

cherry brandy contributed to the downfall of the dissolute King George IV, who consumed it in ruinous quantities, perhaps to get over the memory of his doomed affair with Mrs Fitzherbert in Brighton.

Among the more famous cherry liqueur brands are Cherry Heering, now properly known as Peter Heering Cherry Liqueur, which was first formulated in the mid-19th century by a Danish distiller of that name. The Heering company grows its own cherries to make this product, which is cask-aged. Others include Cherry Rocher, de Kuyper, Garnier, and Bols, and there are brands produced in Germany and Switzerland.

Peach brandy is the one least frequently seen, its most famous manifestation probably being the one marketed by Bols.

HOW THEY ARE MADE

The pressed juice and stones of the respective fruits are generally mixed with a neutral grape spirit (more rarely a grain spirit), sweetened with sugar syrup and macerated until take-up of

flavour is complete. If the fruit juice itself has fairly high natural sweetness, correspondingly less syrup will be added. In some cases, the liqueurs may be treated to a period of cask-ageing, followed by adjustment of the colour with vegetable dyes.

TASTES GOOD WITH

They all work well in fruit-based desserts that use the same fruits, for example hot soufflés, tarts and charlottes.

APRICOT BRANDY
Cusenier's liqueurs all come in these distinctive bottles

HEERING
Named after a Danish distiller in the last century.

grows own cherries

MALIBU

FLAVOURING
Coconut

W**ITH THE GROWTH** of tourism in the Caribbean islands, it was only a matter of time before liqueurs flavoured with coconut began to make their presence felt on the international market. Of these, the most famous is Malibu. Presented in an opaque white bottle, with a depiction of a tropical sunset on the front, it is a relatively low-strength blend of rectified Caribbean white rum with coconut extracts. The flavour is pleasingly not too sweet. Malibu was a better product than most of the range of liqueur concoctions with totally tropical names that bombarded the market during the cocktail renaissance of the early 1980s.

Another reasonably good product was Batida de Coco, a coconut-flavoured neutral spirit made in Brazil that was also exported in quantity to the holiday islands of the Caribbean. Cocoribe was similar.

They are all colourless products, with an alcohol level slightly higher than that of fortified wine. Since the success of these proprietary products, some of the famous Dutch and French liqueur manufacturers have got in on the act and also marketed variants of crème de coco.

MIXING

Pina Colada: A sort of cheat's version can be made using Malibu instead of real coconut milk. Mix in equal measures with white rum and plenty of ice. Top up with pineapple juice.
Batida Banana: Mix equal measures of Batida de Coco with crème de banane and several ice-cubes in a tall glass. Top up with whole milk. (This is a dangerously moreish drink, effectively little more than a grown-up milkshake.)

HOW THEY ARE MADE

Most of the coconut liqueurs are based on ultra-refined white rum, although one or two are made with a neutral grain alcohol. The dried pulp and milk of the coconut are used to flavour the spirit, which is then sweetened and filtered.

TASTES GOOD WITH

A splash of coconut liqueur may productively be added to the sauces in Cajun or Far Eastern dishes, particularly those of Thai or Indonesian cuisine where coconut itself figures strongly. Otherwise, it is splendid as a flavouring in a richly creamy ice cream.

HOW TO SERVE

These drinks are not great on their own, but make excellent mixes with ice and fruit juices, which is how they were intended to be served in the first place.

MALIBU
Perhaps the best of the coconut liqueurs

BATIDA DE COCO

Brazil's contribution to the coconut collection.

MANDARINE NAPOLEON

MANDARINE IS ANOTHER TYPE of Curaçao, 73 this time made with the skins of tangerines as opposed to bitter Caribbean oranges. By far the most famous brand is Mandarine Napoléon, the origins of which really do derive from the drinking preferences of the Emperor Napoleon I. The key figure in its history is a French chemist, one Antoine-François de Fourcroy, who rose to prominence in France as a key figure in public administration after the Revolution.

Following the demise of the Jacobin regime, de Fourcroy found favour with Napoleon Bonaparte to the extent that he was made a member of his Imperial State Council. When the tangerine first arrived in Europe from China (hence its synonym, mandarine) at the end of the 18th century, there was something of a craze for it. The fashion was to steep the peel in cognac after eating the fruit, and Antoine-François records in his diary that many was the night he was called on to share in the Emperor's indulgence.

Mandarine Napoléon was launched in 1892 by a Belgian distiller, Louis Schmidt, who stumbled on the recipe in de Fourcroy's correspondence while pursuing

MANDARINE NAPOLEON

A French invention now made in Belgium

OTHER NAMES

France: Mandarine *Italy*: Mandarinetto

HOW TO SERVE

Despite its sweetness, it does work well as an after-dinner drink taken straight or *frappé* in a traditional brandy balloon.

some chemical researches. It was only after the Second World War, when the distillery was relocated from Belgium to France, that the Fourcroy family once again became involved, eventually taking on the worldwide distribution of Schmidt's liqueur. As it became ever more successful, they moved the production back to Brussels, where it remains.

The tangerines used in Mandarine come exclusively from Sicily. Other companies make versions of tangerine liqueurs – the Italians themselves of course make one from their Sicilian crop – but Mandarine Napoléon remains justifiably the pre-eminent example, a thoroughly individual product that has deservedly won international awards.

HOW IT IS MADE

For Mandarine Napoléon, tangerine skins are steeped in cognac and other French brandies. The spirit is then re-distilled, sweetened, coloured with carotene to a vivid yellowy-orange and matured for several months. It is bottled at 38% ABV.

TASTES GOOD WITH

Add it to tangerine-flavoured mousses or use it as the fuel to flame sweet pancakes.

FLAVOURING Brandy in cognac
Tangerines

p204 Poached Mandarines

MIXING

Titanic: Mix equal measures of vodka and Mandarine Napoléon over ice in a tumbler, and top up with soda water.

incomparable!

use instead
of our Kirsch?

MARASCHINO

THE ORIGINAL MARASCHINO (which should be pronounced with a "sk" sound in the middle, not "sh") was a distilled liquor of some antiquity made from a sour red cherry variety. The Italian name for the cherry was Marasca, which grew only on the Dalmatian coast. When the Italian-speaking enclave of Dalmatia was incorporated into the then Yugoslavia, Italian production of maraschino was continued in the Veneto, where plantings of the Marasca cherry were established from cuttings.

Maraschino is a clear liquer derived from an infusion of pressed cherry skins in a cherry-stone distil-

FLAVOURING
Marasca cherries

MIXING
Tropical Cocktail: Shake equal measures of dry French vermouth, maraschino and white crème de cacao with a dash each of Angostura and orange bitters and plenty of ice. Strain into a wine glass.

late. (This secondary infusion is why maraschino should technically be considered a liqueur rather than a spirit, as distinct from Kirsch.) After further distillation to obtain a pure, clear spirit, it is aged, ideally for several years. It always remains colourless, and should have a pronounced bitter cherry aroma, backed up by the nuttiness of the cherry stones.

A number of Italian firms are especially associated with the production of maraschino, notably Luxardo (which sells its product in straw-covered bottles in two strengths, 30% ABV and a more knee-trembling 50%), the venerable Drioli company and Stock.

HOW IT IS MADE
The pomace of pressed cherries is infused over gentle heat in a cherry distillate for several months. It is then rectified and transferred to neutral maturation vessels, made either from a light wood such as ash or from glass. It is sweetened with sugar syrup and left to age for several years.

spirit

liquor

TASTES GOOD WITH
It is incomparable for soaking the sponge in a layered cake, or poured over fresh cherries and many other fruits, such as peaches or apricots.

HOW TO SERVE
The best grades of maraschino should be smooth enough to drink on their own, but the sweeter it is, the more recourse to the ice-bucket you may feel is necessary.

MARASCHINO
The traditional straw-covered bottle of Luxardo

MIDORI

AN INSTANT HIT when it was launched in the early 1980s, Midori was another stroke of marketing genius from the giant Japanese drinks group, Suntory. Not content with its range of fine Scotch-style whiskies and classed-growth Bordeaux property, Château Lagrange, Suntory aimed for a slice of the cocktail action with this bright green liqueur in an idiosyncratic little bottle of textured glass.

The flavouring agent is melons,

MIDORI
Cornering the
market in melon
liqueurs

FLAVOURING
Melon *banana*

not a particularly common one in the liqueur world, but its vivid green colour is achieved by means of a dye. Indeed, its greenness is its principal sales pitch, since *midori* is the Japanese word for green. The colour is perhaps intended to evoke the skins of certain melon varieties, as opposed to the flesh that is actually used to flavour it. Having said that, Midori doesn't especially recall any melon variety; it is actually much closer to banana, in both aroma and taste. It is sweet and syrupy, and at the lower end of standard alcoholic strength for liqueurs.

TASTES GOOD WITH
It was seized on by chefs in some of the more adventurous restaurants for use in desserts that involve tropical fruit. Salads of mango, pineapple, melon, passion-fruit and so forth are perfect choices, although again, there is that unapologetic colour to contend with.

MERSIN *Orange*
Mersin is a Turkish version of Curaçao, a colourless liqueur based on grape spirit and flavoured with oranges and herbs. It is commonly taken with a chaser of the fierce black coffee of Turkey.

HOW TO SERVE
Midori is much better mixed than served straight, when its flavour quickly cloys. It blends beautifully with iced fruit juices, notably orange, except that the resulting colour is horribly lurid. Lemonade may make a more visually appealing marriage, but a sweet mixer with a sweet liqueur is never a brilliant idea.

NUT LIQUEURS

T HE NUT-FLAVOURED liqueurs deserve to be considered separately since they form quite a large sub-group. Drinks relying on coconut for their principal taste are dealt with elsewhere (see Malibu); the flavourings here are those of hazelnut, walnut and almond.

In their French manifestations, the first two of those are straightforward enough. They are named noisette and crème de noix, after the French words for hazelnut and walnut respectively. In the case of almonds, it all becomes a little more complicated, basically because certain fruit stones, such as those of apricots and cherries, have an almond-like taste. A liqueur that

contains almonds themselves is called crème d'amandes. However, a liqueur called crème de noyau – "noyau" being the French for the stone in which the almond-like kernel of a fruit is encased – will contain no actual almonds, only an approximation of the flavour.

These are all brandy-based drinks in which the chopped nuts are

HOW TO SERVE
These drinks are quite commonly taken with crushed ice as a digestif in France. Alternatively, they may be iced, slightly watered – about the same amount of water as liqueur – and drunk as aperitifs. The tradition in France is for a sweet appetizer (with the obvious exception of champagne), as distinct from the drier British taste.

FRANGELICO
*A branded liqueur
done up to look
like a monk*

NOCINO
*A strong walnut
liqueur from Italy*

steeped in a clear grape spirit and the resulting liqueur is clarified and bottled in a colourless state. The exception is crème de noyau, which more often than not has a faint pinkish hue if it has been made from cherry stones. They are all sweet, with fairly syrupy textures, and make invaluable additions to the cocktail repertoire. Italy produces a range of nut-based liqueurs, too. There is the distinctive almond-flavoured Disaronno Amaretto, and also a walnut liqueur called Nocino. In the 1980s, a product called Frangelico was released. It was a delicate straw-coloured liqueur flavoured with hazelnuts and herbs, then dressed up in a faintly ridiculous dark brown bottle designed to look like a monk. The large brown plastic top represented his cowl, and around the gathered-in waist, a length of white cord was knotted. It looked like a particularly embarrassing tourist souvenir, but the liqueur itself turned out to be delicious, not too sweet, and with an intriguing range of flavours.

EAU DE NOIX
A rare French
walnut liqueur

MIXING

Pink Almond: Shake a measure of Scotch with half a measure each of crème de noyau, Kirsch, fresh lemon juice and orgeat (a non-alcoholic almond syrup) with ice, and strain into a cocktail glass. (If you can't get orgeat, double the quantity of noyau.)

Walnut Whip: Shake equal measures of cognac, crème de noix and thick cream with ice and strain into a cocktail glass.

Mad Monk (below): Shake a measure each of gin and Frangelico with the juice of half a lemon and ice. Strain into a wine glass and add a squirt of soda.

HOW THEY ARE MADE

The nuts are crumbled up and left to infuse with the base spirit before sweetening and filtration. They are bottled at the average liqueur strength, around 25%. In the case of the crème de noix of Gascony, the walnuts are beaten off the trees while still green, the spirit is sweetened with honey and subjected to a further distillation. For crème de noyau, fruit stones are the infusion agent. They are usually either cherry or apricot, but peach and even plum may also be used.

TASTE GOOD WITH

They work well with nutty desserts – anything using almond paste or praline – but also in a chocolate mousse, or drunk alongside a piece of rich, dark fruitcake. Frangelico served chilled makes an unlikely table-fellow for a piece of mature Stilton.

FLAVOURINGS

Almonds
Walnuts
Hazelnuts
Fruit stones
Honey (in the case of some crème de noix)

PARFAIT AMOUR

THE LONG ASSOCIATION of drinking with seduction is celebrated in the name of purple Parfait Amour, "perfect love". In the 18th century particularly, the use of alcohol in amorous pursuits had less to do with getting your intended too stupefied to know what they were doing, than with stimulating the erotic impulses with artful concoctions of spices and flowers mixed with the alcohol.

Parfait Amour liqueur is really the only surviving link to that noble tradition. It is almost certainly Dutch in origin; its name, as with all such potions,

FLAVOURINGS
Lemons or other citrus fruits (such as the larger, shapeless citron of Corsica)
Cloves
Cinnamon
Coriander seeds
Violets

HOW TO SERVE
It is best to serve Parfait Amour unmixed, or else blended with something colourless such as lemonade, in order not to interfere with your beloved's enjoyment of the colour. It tastes better chilled, although you may feel that an excessively cold drink may numb the erogenous zones, which wouldn't do at all.

PARFAIT AMOUR
Indelibly associated with romance

MIXING
Eagle's Dream: Whizz up a measure and a half of gin, a measure of Parfait Amour, the juice of half a lemon, half a teaspoon of caster sugar and the white of an egg with smashed ice in a liquidizer, and strain into a large wine glass.

is French because that was considered the romantic language par excellence. As its (added) colour would lead you to expect, it is subtly scented with violets, but the flavour owes more to fruits and spices than flowers, which marks it out quite distinctly from the colourless crème de violette. The main components are citrus fruits – usually lemons – and a mixture of cloves and other spices.

The drink enjoyed great popularity during the cocktail boom in the 1920s. Apart from anything else, no other liqueur is quite the same colour. There was once a red version of it too, but somehow purple has come to be more inextricably associated with passion. Today, Parfait Amour is made not only by the Dutch liqueur specialists Bols, but by certain French companies as well.

HOW IT IS MADE
The various aromatizing elements are macerated in grape spirit, which may then be re-distilled, and the purple colour is achieved by means of a vegetable dye.

TASTES GOOD WITH
What else but a box of violet creams?

PASTIS

Pastis is one of the most important traditional drinks of Europe, despite having only minority status in Britain and the other northern countries. Around the Mediterranean fringe of Europe, from southeast France to the Greek islands, in its various derivatives, pastis functions in the same thirst-quenching way as beer does further north. It is important in terms of the quantity consumed locally, and is of great cultural significance too. It is an in-between-times drink rather than just an aperitif; it's a drink for lazy afternoons watching *boules* being played in the village square. There is also the tradition of illicit home distillation.

Drinkers the world

RICARD
*The famous
pastis
of southern
France*

OTHER NAMES
France: pastis *Greece*: ouzo *Spain*: ojen

MIXING
Monkey Gland: Shake two measures of gin with a measure of fresh orange juice and three dashes each of pastis and grenadine and plenty of ice, and strain into a large wine glass.

over have, on first contact with pastis, usually been fascinated by its most famous property – namely, that it clouds up when mixed with water. This attribute, indeed, is what gives the drink its name, *pastis* being an old southern French dialect word meaning muddled, hazy or unclear.

PERNOD AND ABSINTHE
The very close similarities of pastis to anis have been noted elsewhere (see Anis). Depending on which authority you consult, the principal flavouring element in pastis is either liquorice or aniseed – perhaps more often the former – but there are other herbal ingredients in it as well. A neutral, highly rectified alcohol base, generally of vegetable origin, provides the background for the aromatizing agents, which are steeped in it before essence of liquorice or anise is added and the whole mélange is sweetened and diluted.

Aniseed has been known as a digestive aid in medicine since the time of the Egyptians, which is why, to this day, many over-the-counter

p 64

stomach-settling remedies contain a hint of its flavour. (Oxyboldene, a popular French brand, is a case in point.) The history of pastis is somewhat entangled, however, with a similar type of drink that came to be seen as anything but health-giving. By the beginning of the 20th century, the name of absinthe was mud.

Apart from home distillates, and excepting individual brands, the only category of drink that has ever become extinct is absinthe. It was considerably stronger than much of today's commercial pastis, but what really doomed it was that it contained wormwood in concentrations that were held responsible for poisoning the brains of those who habitually drank it. During the late 19th century, absinthe became known as the house drink of decadent Parisian artists, Symbolist poets and others, many of whom died the kinds of squalid deaths associated with laudanum use during the English Romantic period 60 and 70 years earlier.

When absinthe was given its marching orders in France by a governmental decree of 1915, other countries soon followed suit. One of its chief manufacturers – the firm of Henri Pernod, which had been making it for over a century – then turned to making a similar product without wormwood at lower alcoholic strength, and using anise as its main flavouring agent. In effect, Pernod was the sanitized version of absinthe. In the 1990s, however, absinthe was re-legalized in many European countries

HOW TO SERVE

Pastis should ideally be served in a small, thick-bottomed glass with about the equivalent amount of water. The water should be very cold, so as to obviate the need for ice. Those with slightly sweeter tastes may add sugar to it. The best way to do this is to balance a perforated spoon or metal tea-strainer with a sugar-cube on it across the top of the glass and then pour the water over it. (This was the traditional way to sweeten absinthe.)

MIXING

Yellow Parrot: Shake equal measure of pastis, yellow Chartreuse and apricot brandy with ice, and strain into a cocktail glass over crushed ice.

PRODUCT (1805) OF FRANCE

PERNOD

PARIS

LONDON-PARIS-NEW YORK-SYDNEY-TOKYO

70 cl   40% vol.

PERNOD
Ricard's
northern
French
counterpart

(though not France). It is now restored to its former dark green, mind-blowing glory, often bottled at around 70% ABV.

Pernod is perhaps the most familiar pastis on the market today. The other main French brand, Ricard, is now part of the same group, although they are made at opposite ends of France. Berger is the other company of note making this sort of product. In northern European countries, where there is often an ambivalence about the flavour of aniseed or liquorice in a drink, Pernod and Ricard have been much favoured as bases for a fruit-juice mixer, but the only unimpeachably authentic way to drink them in their native regions, particularly around the town of Marseilles, is diluted with a small quantity of water.

As to absinthe, the question is: Is it really dangerous enough to have merited its disastrous reputation? Some claim to have had mildly hallucinogenic experiences on it, on account of the psychoactive wormwood it contains, but these may be the more suggestible type. A theory has gained currency that it was really only banned because it was highly alcoholic (in which case the hallowed Chartreuse might have been expected to find itself in more difficulties than it has). A scientific writer, Harold McGee, points out that wormwood contains a toxic oil called thujone, which was almost certainly linked to the formation of lesions on the cerebral cortex of the recklessly heavy user. You pays your money…

SPAIN

The Spanish equivalent is *ojen* (pronounced "oh-hen"). It is named after the town where it is made and is sold in two versions: sweet and dry.

GREECE

After pastis, the most familiar relative of this family of drinks is Greek ouzo, much beloved of holidaymakers on the Peloponnese and the islands, perhaps even more so than retsina. The flavouring agent is anise and, like pastis, the drink turns milky-white when water is added. It is drunk in much the same way, except perhaps with somewhat more water than is common in France, and generally as an aperitif. The bottled strength is around 35–40% ABV, again similar to pastis.

FLAVOURINGS

Herbs – possibly including coriander, camomile, parsley, veronica (which was once used in France as a substitute for tea), even spinach!

HOW TO SERVE

Ouzo should be served cold in a small, thick-bottomed glass, either on its own, with about the equivalent amount of water, or with an ice cube or two.

OUZO
The drink of
the sunny
Greek
islands

MIXING

Cocktails that include pastis tend to be among the most dramatic in the repertoire. Many of these contain no non-alcoholic ingredients. That is because a relatively small amount of pastis will have plenty to say for itself in even the most ferocious of mixes, concoctions that would drown the presence of many of the more delicate liqueurs.

Block and Fall: Stir together a measure each of cognac and Cointreau with half a measure each of pastis and calvados, over ice, in a tumbler.

Hurricane: Shake a measure and a half of cognac with half a measure each of pastis and vodka and ice, then strain into a cocktail glass.

Ojen Cocktail: Shake a double measure of dry ojen with a teaspoon of sugar, half a measure of water, a dash of orange bitters and ice, and strain into a small tumbler.

HOW THEY ARE MADE

The various herbs and plants are usually infused in a straight, highly purified vegetable spirit base and essence of anise or liquorice added. Further blending with rectified alcohol is followed by sweetening, and the drink is bottled at an average 35% ABV.

TASTES GOOD WITH

The combination of aromatizers in pastis is a particularly successful one with fish, either for marinating or adding to a sauce. Try marinating chunks of tuna in olive oil, pastis and dill and then grilling them on skewers.

PIMM'S *Orange on Gin*

Forever associated with the English summer, Pimm's No. 1 Cup is a proprietary version of a fruit cup created by the eponymous Mr Pimm in the 1820s. James Pimm originally devised his recipe in order to mark out his own establishment in the City of London from the run of common-or-garden oyster bars – oysters being not much more than ten a penny in those days – which traditionally served stout ale to wash the bivalves down.

He did such a roaring trade with his fruit cup that Pimm began to market it ready-mixed in 1859, the asking price for a bottle being a stiffish three shillings. Since that time, Pimm's has gone through a number of owners, including – at the turn of the century – the then Lord Mayor of London, Sir Horatio Davies. Popular throughout the British Empire during colonial times, it came to enjoy a sudden vogue in France and Italy after the war.

In the early years of the 20th century, Pimm's was elaborated into six different versions, each based on a different spirit. The market has since whittled these down to just two, Pimm's Vodka Cup and the original – still sold as No. 1 Cup, and based on London gin, with an unmixed strength of 25% ABV. Pimm's has suffered somewhat from being seen as too fiddly to prepare. Its present owner, one of Britain's biggest drinks companies, has tried to combat that by launching little cans of pre-mixed Pimm's.

TASTES GOOD WITH

Classic English picnic foods – cucumber sandwiches, hard-boiled quail's eggs, crackers with cream cheese and crudités – are all made the more splendid with plenty of Pimm's. Take a big jug and throw in half a bottle of Pimm's and a litre of lemonade.

HOW TO SERVE

A generous measure of Pimm's No. 1 should be poured over ice in a tall glass. (In Mr Pimm's oyster bar, they knocked it back by the pint). It is then topped up with lemonade or soda, and garnished with slices of orange, lemon and lime, a wedge of apple and a dangling twist of pared cucumber rind. If you can find fresh borage, use some of its smaller leaves instead of the cucumber. Float a little bundle of mint leaves on top. If that sounds too much of a fandango, just throw in a slice of lemon and get on with it.

FLAVOURINGS

All highly secret of course, but it contains fruit extracts – notably orange – and at least one other alcoholic ingredient, perhaps Curaçao. Who knows?

PIMM'S
The quintessential flavour of an English summer

POIRE WILLIAM

POIRE WILLIAM IS NOT to be confused with true pear brandy, which is a colourless spirit, eau de vie de poire, made in Alsace and Switzerland. The big liqueur companies nearly all make a sweet pear-flavoured liqueur, traditionally lightly coloured and made by the usual method of infusing crushed fruit in neutral grape spirit. Some may have a brief period of cask-ageing, but most don't.

One of the curiosities of Poire William – which is so named after the particular variety of pear used – is that, while its aroma is very strong and evocative, the flavour is often disappointingly mild. This is true of pears generally. The Williams is a gorgeously aromatic fruit when fully ripe but, used in cooking, its flavour often all but vanishes, which isn't at all true of the best apple varieties. As such, I find the liqueur has to be used in fairly enthusiastic quantities in a cocktail in order to get the best out of it.

Pear-flavoured liqueurs are made in France (about the best brand is Marie Brizard), Italy (which has Pera Segnana), Germany and Switzerland. A novelty product is Poire Prisonnière, which comes with a whole pear in the bottle. I remember as a student seeing one in a shop window in Venice and debating with a friend how on earth they managed to get the pear in. We eventually concluded they must somehow hand-blow the bottle around the fruit. So much for youthful

ingenuity. The pears are in fact *grown* in the bottles, which are attached to the tree, so that each fruit has its own private greenhouse. Before the bottles are filled with the liqueur, the pears are pricked in order to release their juices.

TASTES GOOD WITH
Poire William is excellent poured over certain fresh fruits, notably pink grapefruit segments, pineapple or, of course, pear.

FLAVOURING
Williams pears

MIXING
Old William (from G. Marcialis and F. Zingales's *Cocktail Book*): Pour a double measure of Poire William over ice in a tumbler. Add a half-measure each of maraschino and fresh orange and lemon juices, and mix thoroughly. Decorate with orange and lemon slices.

*POIRE WILLIAM
Delicately flavoured French pear liqueur*

*POIRE PRISONNIERE
The pear is painstakingly grown in the bottle*

HOW TO SERVE
Served well-chilled, or perhaps with a single piece of ice, it makes a good aperitif. Alternatively, add a splash of lemonade.

PUNSCH

PUNSCH IS MORE FAMILIARLY known in English-speaking countries as Swedish punch, although even then it isn't a drink many people have come across. Its lineage can be traced back to the 18th century, when Sweden's ocean-going trading vessels began doing business in the East Indies. Among the commodities they brought back was some of the arak that is the traditional spirit of those regions. Some arak is rice-based, some a distillate of sugar-cane, and therefore more like rum.

In its raw state, it wasn't much to northern European tastes, and so a few drink companies took to blending it with grape brandy and various wines and cordials, in effect creating a kind of powerful punch in the process. Like a traditional punch, the mixture is also highly spiced – just what the doctor ordered in the depths of the grim Scandinavian winter.

The original punch was a British colonial invention, but by the 18th century, a vogue for it had spread not only to

PUNSCH
The real thing – a cask-aged punsch from Sweden

OTHER NAMES
Britain: Swedish punch

MIXING
Diki-Diki: Shake a double measure of calvados, half a measure each of punsch and grapefruit juice, with ice, and strain into a cocktail glass.
Grand Slam (below): Mix a double measure of punsch with a measure each of dry white and sweet red vermouth, with ice, in a jug, and then strain over crushed ice in a wine glass.

Scandinavia but into France as well. Rum was a favoured base ingredient, variously boosted with hot tea, lemon juice and sweet spices such as cinnamon. Punch was, in every way, the grand-daddy of the cocktail.

In an echo of the British habit, Swedish punsch was usually served hot, at least until the end of the last century. Since that time, the universal fashion for alcoholic drinks to be served cold has meant it is now drunk straight or even iced.

HOW IT IS MADE
These days, punsch is exclusively a rum-based drink, to which other forms of alcohol – including wine – are added, together with a quantity of fragrant spices, such as cinnamon and cloves. It is sweetened and then aged for several months in cask.

TASTES GOOD WITH
Punsch works reasonably well with little salty nibbles made with strong cheese.

FLAVOURINGS
Sweet spices, such as cinnamon and cloves

HOW TO SERVE
To relive the old days, warm the punsch gently (without letting it boil) in a small saucepan and serve it in big, heatproof, wine glasses.

RATAFIA

unfermented juice w/ alcohol

RATAFIA WAS, CENTURIES AGO, a forerunner of the liqueur, in that it involved steeping fruits or nuts in a sweetened spirit base. That wouldn't in itself earn it a separate entry in this guide, were it not for the fact that the term ratafia has come to be applied mainly now to a type of aperitif made in the brandy-producing areas of France. The brandy is mixed with fresh fruit juice.

Ratafia is not a geographical name. It derives from the old French practice of concluding any formal agreement, such a legal contract or business transaction, with a shared drink – a "ratifier", if you like. The original phrase is Latin: *rata fiat* ("let the deal be settled").

There are also ratafias made in wine areas – particularly Burgundy and Champagne – in which the naturally sweet grape juice is mixed in with some of the regional wine. The most celebrated ratafia, however, is Pineau des Charentes, made in the Cognac region from grape juice fortified with cognac. It can't be considered a fortified wine, though, for

the very good reason that the grape juice has not undergone fermentation. It comes in white and rosé versions, and always has the sweetness of ripe grape juice about it.

In Armagnac, not to be outdone, they make their own version of this drink by exactly the same method. Called Floc de Gascogne, its production – like that of armagnac itself – is on a much more modest commercial footing than its Charentais counterpart.

There is also a variant of this type of ratafia made in the Calvados region of Normandy, in which fresh apple juice is fortified with apple brandy. It is called pommeau, and is a considerably more palatable proposition (to the author's taste at least) than either Pineau or Floc.

HOW IT IS MADE
By adding grape brandy to unfermented grape juice, or conversely apple brandy to apple juice, in each case to an average bottled strength of around 17% ABV.

TASTES GOOD WITH
Ratafia works quite well as an accompaniment to a slice of aromatic melon – better than most wine, at any rate.

PINEAU DES CHARENTES
The ratafia of the Cognac region

POMMEAU
An apple ratafia from Normandy

SAMBUCA

AN ITALIAN LIQUEUR that became quite fashionable beyond its home region of Rome in the 1970s and 80s, Sambuca Romana is a clear, moderately sweet, quite fiery drink, flavoured with elderberries and aniseed. Its name is derived from the botanical name for elderberry, *Sambucus nigra*. There are other herbs and roots in it too, but these are the two predominant flavours.

In the days when every drink had to be dignified with its own particular serving ritual, it was decreed that Sambuca was to be garnished with coffee beans and set alight. Aficionados of the custom differed quite sharply as to whether the correct number of beans was two or three. Such detail scarcely mattered since what mostly preoccupied the drinker was how to swallow it without singeing the nose.

To earn your Sambuca stripes, you have to blow out the flame on a glassful and then swallow the drink in one, like an oyster. In Rome, they will ask you whether you want it *con la mosca*, literally "with a fly" (i.e. with the coffee beans). There, they are not merely for garnish. If you say *si*, you will be expected to crunch the beans up as you drink.

SABRA
This is Israel's entry in the spirits and liqueurs stakes – a svelte concoction flavoured with a clever mélange of Jaffa orange and chocolate. Despite the bitterness contributed by the orange peels, the resulting drink is exceptionally sweet. Try mixing it with cognac and ice to throw it into relief.

MIXING
Matinée (from Michael Walker's *Cinzano Cocktail Book*): Shake a measure of gin, half a measure each of Sambuca and thick cream, half an egg white and a dash of fresh lime juice with plenty of ice, and strain into a cocktail glass. Sprinkle with finely grated nutmeg.

TASTES GOOD WITH
A chilled glass of Sambuca makes a good accompaniment to a genuine Italian *torta*, one of those heavenly sticky cakes of dried fruits, almonds and lemon zest.

SAMBUCA
A fiery liqueur in more ways than one

FLAVOURINGS
Elderberries
Aniseed

HOW TO SERVE
If you are going to try the flaming Sambuca trick, it helps to serve the liqueur in a narrow glass like an old-fashioned sherry schooner, because the flame will take more easily on a smaller surface.

SLOE GIN

LOE GIN, AND its French equivalent *prunelle*, rely for their flavour and colour on a type of small bitter-tasting plum, the fruit of a shrub called the blackthorn. English sloe gin, as marketed by companies such as Hawker's, is nothing more than sweetened gin in which sloes have been steeped and then strained out once they have stained the spirit a deep red. The fruits contribute a strong, rather medicinal taste to the drink.

Prunelle, from the French word for the fruit, is not red but green, and is made by macerating the fruit kernels in a grape spirit base. Although the colour may be added, it does reflect the greenish flesh of the fruit.

Liqueur companies such as Garnier and Cusenier (theirs is called Prunellia) make it, and it is especially popular in Anjou, in the

FLAVOURING
The fruit of the wild blackthorn bush

OTHER NAMES
France: Prunelle/Prunellia

western part of the Loire valley. They also make eau de vie from sloes in Burgundy and Alsace.

The plant itself is a wild shrub that grows quite plentifully throughout Europe, its little sour fruits only ripening properly in early winter. Sloe gin is still quite widely made at home in country areas of England, but only with commercial gin, of course.

HOW IT IS MADE

Sloe gin is easy to knock up at home if you have access to the fruits. The best ratio is about half-a-pound of sugar to a pound of the fruit, but if the fruit is very sour, you may want to increase the sweetening by a couple of ounces. The fruit should be partly squashed or pierced to encourage absorption of the flavour. Top up your bottle with gin (or vodka, if you prefer, but gin makes a more interesting marriage of flavours). Leave it sealed for at least three months, shaking it up from time to time, and then strain the spirit off the solids.

TASTES GOOD WITH

Like cranberries or rowanberries, sloes make a good, tart jelly for garnishing strong gamey meats. Perhaps a slug of sloe gin in the sauce or gravy would help matters along.

HOW TO SERVE
Sloe gin is best served as it comes and at room temperature. A marketing push for a brand of sloe gin a few years ago suggested adding a teaspoon or two of it to a glass of sparkling wine, which isn't a bad idea – especially if the sparkling wine is a bit rough.

SLOE GIN
A sloe gin from one of the big names in gin

SOUTHERN COMFORT

THE FOREMOST AMERICAN liqueur is Southern Comfort, a fruitier counterpart to the Scotch-based liqueurs. Naturally American whiskey is used as its starting point. As so often in the world of proprietary liqueurs, the exact composition of Southern Comfort is a closely guarded commercial secret, but what we do know is that the fruit flavouring it contains is peach.

Its origins probably lie in the mixing of bourbon with peach juice as a traditional cocktail in the southern states. Back in Mississippi, down in New Orleans (as the song goes), there was once a mixed drink called Sazerac. A recipe for it is given in the *Savoy Cocktail Book*. It consists of a shot of rye

SOUTHERN
COMFORT
A fruity whiskey
liqueur of the
Deep South

MIXING

Southern Peach: Shake a measure each of Southern Comfort, peach brandy and thick cream with a dash of Angostura and plenty of ice, and strain into a tumbler. Decorate with a wedge of peach.

FLAVOURING
Peaches

whiskey, with a sprinkling of peach bitters, a lump of sugar and a dash of absinthe. So traditional is it that a New Orleans company has been producing a pre-mixed version of it since around the middle of the 19th century.

Peaches themselves are grown in great quantities in the southern states; the Georgia peach is one of America's proudest agricultural products. The practice of blending the peach juice with whiskey in the bars of New Orleans undoubtedly also played its part in influencing the creation of Southern Comfort.

Today, the company that owns the brand is the same one that has the leading Tennessee whiskey brand, Jack Daniel's. The Southern Comfort distillery is located in St Louis, in the state of Missouri. The bottled strength is high – 40% ABV – which is perhaps one of the reasons it appealed so much to the late great rock legend Janis Joplin.

TASTES GOOD WITH

Southern Comfort makes a good substitute for bourbon poured over the traditional light fruitcake at Thanksgiving or Christmas. Quantities should be extremely generous, though: a whole bottleful is not unknown.

HOW TO SERVE
Southern Comfort is intended to be meditatively sipped, like other fine American whiskeys, but you could try taming its fire and emphasizing its fruitiness with a mixer of peach nectar. It's also fine with orange juice on the rocks.

no recipes for *Orange* *Love potion!*

STREGA

THE NAME STREGA, a popular proprietary liqueur produced in Italy, is Italian for "witch". It is so called because it is supposedly based on a witches' brew, an aphrodisiac love-potion guaranteed to unite any pair of lovers who drink it in eternal togetherness. You have been warned.

It is a bright yellow concoction full of all sorts of complex flavours. The fruit base is a citrus blend and it reputedly also contains around six dozen different botanical herbs, making it not dissimilar in style to the yellow version of Chartreuse. It has

MIXING

Golden Tang (from Michael Walker's *Cinzano Cocktail Book*): Shake a double measure of vodka, a measure of Strega, and half a measure each of crème de banane and fresh orange juice with ice, and strain into a large wine glass. (Alternatively, double the quantities all round and strain into a tall glass.)

the same kind of syrupy texture, too, and is considered an especially good digestif.

Although the colour resembles that other Italian liqueur speciality, Galliano, Strega's flavour is quite different, more obviously herbal and with a stronger citrus element.

TASTES GOOD WITH

As an accompaniment to freshly cracked nuts at the end of a meal, Strega works particularly well.

STREGA
This Italian liqueur is full of complex flavours

SUZE

IF I HAD TO NOMINATE one other product to make up a perfect trinity of aperitifs with champagne and pale dry sherry, it would unhesitatingly be Suze. Some may consider that Suze, and the various related Swiss and German products, should technically be considered under "Bitters", but they are not always direct distillates; some are actually wine-based. What they do all have in common is that they rely for their impact on gentian.

Gentian is a wild mountain plant found in the Alps and the mountains of the Jura, in France. It has large yellow flowers, but it is principally valued for its roots, which can grow up to a yard long and have one of the most uncompromisingly bitter flavours found anywhere in the plant world. It was once the quinine of its day, before that plant was brought back from the Americas in the 17th century. Like quinine, gentian has had a distinguished history in the pharmacist's repertoire; it was thought to be particularly good for ailments of the liver.

The Suze brand is owned by pastis manufacturers Pernod-Ricard, and it has a very

OTHER NAMES

France: Gentiane *Germany*: Enzian

MIXING

Drought: Shake equal measures of gin and Suze with a small splash of fresh orange juice, and strain into a cocktail glass. (This is an unimaginably dry mixture, and a particular energizer to the appetite.)

delicate primrose colour. It is based on wine, and its flavour is so dry and bitter, even when mixed with a little water or served on ice, that it acts as an extraordinarily powerful appetite-rouser.

Other similar products may be labelled Gentiane in France and Switzerland, or Enzian in Germany. The German products tend to be direct distillates of the gentian root, though, rather than wine-based.

HOW IT IS MADE

In the case of Suze and similar products, an extract of gentian is steeped in a white wine base, which imparts a little faint colour to the liquid. It is then clarified and bottled at fortified wine strength.

TASTES GOOD WITH

Suze is great served with any bitter nibbles, and is extremely appetizing with the more pungent varieties of green olive.

HOW TO SERVE

Pour a measure of Suze into a tumbler with either the merest splash of very cold water or a single cube of ice just to freshen it up.

FLAVOURING

Gentian root

GENTIANE

An alternative French brand of gentian aperitif.

SUZE
Well worth a journey to France to taste

TIA MARIA

JAMAICA'S CONTRIBUTION to the world of liqueurs, Tia Maria, has turned into one of the best-loved of all such products in both America and Europe. It is a suave, deep brown coffee-flavoured drink that proves itself highly versatile on the cocktail circuit as well as for after-dinner sipping.

It is based, not surprisingly, on good dark Jamaican rum of at least five-year-old standard and flavoured with the beans of the highly prized coffee variety, Blue Mountain. In addition to the coffee, the palate is further deepened by the addition of local spices too. Although the liqueur is sweet, noticeably sweeter than its Mexican counterpart Kahlúa, for example, the aromatic components in it prevent it from being cloying. This makes it one of the few such drinks that is actually quite acceptable to savour on its own.

Not the least reason for its popularity in Europe was the craze for the cocktail Black Russian, usually taken with Coca-Cola, in

FLAVOURINGS
Coffee
Spices

TIA MARIA
The world's most
famous coffee liqueur

MIXING
Sunburn: Shake equal measures of cognac and Tia Maria, half a measure each of fresh orange and lemon juices and ice, and strain into a cocktail glass.

Proportions of the classic **Black Russian** (below) vary according to taste. Two parts vodka to one part Tia Maria on ice, with no mixer, makes a very adult drink.

which it provides a luxurious note of richness to what is otherwise a fairly prosaic mix.

HOW IT IS MADE
Coffee beans and spices are infused in a base of cask-aged rum, which is then lightly sweetened. It is bottled at just under 27% ABV.

TASTES GOOD WITH
Tia Maria is brilliant for lacing chocolate desserts, and of course makes a good liqueur coffee – particularly when the coffee used is Blue Mountain.

HOW TO SERVE
On the rocks is a pleasant way to serve Tia Maria as a digestif. Otherwise, it is one of the few liqueurs to make a truly appetizing mix with cola. Some like it with orange juice, but the resulting muddy colour is somewhat unlovely.

TRAPPISTINE
Another of the few remaining liqueurs made by religious orders, Trappistine is made at the convent of the Abbaye de Grâce de Dieu in the eastern French *département* of Doubs, not far from the Swiss border. A naturally pallid, yellowy-green colour, it is based on armagnac and contains macerations of many wild herbs.

VAN *der* HUM

V AN DER HUM IS SOUTH AFRICA'S equivalent
of Curaçao, made by several producers in
the Cape, including the giant national wine
consortium KWV. The whimsical name literally
translates as "What's-his-Name". Its base is
Cape brandy, of which there is a large annual
production, and the citrus fruit used is a
tangerine-like orange variety locally known as
naartjies. Much in the way of Curaçao, the peels
of the orange are infused in the brandy and
supplemented with a herb or spice element. The
precise formula may vary from one producer to
the next, but nutmeg is a favoured addition.

Rather like Mandarine Napoléon, the drink
derives from the practice of steeping citrus
peels in the local brandy. Such a concoction
would have been widely produced domestically
by early Cape settlers, and the formula came to
be replicated on a commercial scale. It is a
reliable and attractive
liqueur, its pale gold
colour and
pronounced bitter
orange scent adding
to its appeal. The
bottled strength is
generally 25%-plus.

VAN DER HUM
South Africa's
answer to orange
Curaçao

MIXING
Sundowner: Shake a measure and a half
of South African brandy or cognac and a
measure of Van der Hum with half a
measure each of fresh orange and lemon
juices and ice. Strain into a cocktail glass.

LA VIEILLE CURE

The correct translation of this liqueur's
name is "The Old Rectory", not – as it
would seem – "The Old Cure". The
mistranslation would be right on at least one
score, though. It was once a golden potion
made by the monastic order at the abbey of
Cenons, near Bordeaux. It used over
50 different curative wild herbs macerated
in blended brandies, and was very much a
typical medieval alcohol remedy, first
conceived in the days when distillation
went hand in hand with the pharmacist's art.
The flavour has been compared to that of
Bénédictine. To enjoy it to the full,
La Vieille Cure should be served neat
and un-iced in small liqueur glasses.
In the 1980s, the production passed into the
hands of one of the large French drinks
companies of the region, but the liqueur's
manufacture should not be confused with
the wine-producing château of the same
name in Bordeaux.

VERVEINE

Verveine du Vélay, to give it its full title,
is another of those liqueurs that models
itself stylistically on Chartreuse, to the extent
that it comes in green and yellow, with the
green the stronger. It is a brandy-based
herbal concoction made near Puy,
in the Auvergne region of central France.
Verveine is the French for verbena, a
flowering herb whose leaves have been used
in folk medicine for centuries as a
restorative for the liver and also for neuro-
logical complaints. Its bitter flavour is
apparent in the liqueur named after it
(though there are other herbs in it too),
the sharpness gentled with a little honey.

FLAVOURINGS
Naartjie peels
Nutmeg and other spice
and herb aromatizers

HOW TO SERVE
Traditionally, Van der
Hum is quite heavily
sweetened by the
manufacturer. For those
who prefer a drier
drink, the customary
thing is to mix it half-
and-half with brandy.
Some companies bottle
it ready-mixed as
Brandy-Hum – the Cape
equivalent of B & B.

FORTIFIED WINES

THE DRINK PRODUCTS in this final section are, technically speaking, wines. If they were wines pure and simple, however, they would have no place in a book dealing with spirits and liqueurs. These wines have one important difference from ordinary table wines, though. They have all been fortified, and what they are fortified with is spirit, grape spirit more often than not. In that respect, none of these types of wine could have existed before the discovery of distillation.

In most cases, the creation of the classic fortified wines was a chance discovery occasioned in the course of trying to find ways of preserving ordinary wines. It wasn't that some bright spark in Portugal once thought, "Let's add some brandy to our wines and see what they taste like". The addition of spirit was intended to keep wines from spoiling on the long and often arduous sea voyages they had to undergo to their customers abroad.

In the days when the chemistry of fermentation was much less thoroughly understood than it is now, wine was often shipped, in the barrel, in a microbiologically unstable state. It may have been that its fermentation had only been interrupted by a sudden drop in the cellar temperature, as opposed to having run its natural course. When such wines arrived

at their destinations, it was often found that they begun re-fermenting or, worse, that they would re-ferment *after* being bottled.

The yeasts that ferment in grape juice and result in the production of alcohol can only continue to do their work as long as there is enough natural sugar in the liquid for them to feed on, and as long as the amount of alcohol generated doesn't exceed a certain level – usually estimated in the range of 16–17% by volume (ABV). After that, they die off, and the wine becomes stable. If you add a healthy dose of brandy or other spirit to wine that has apparently finished fermenting (or to one that is still in the process of fermenting, for that matter), you raise the alcohol level to such a degree that the yeasts are killed off.

In addition to then having a stable

Left: The essential flor (yeast cells) growing on the surface of a barrel of fino sherry.

Above: For tasting, sherry is still taken from the barrels in the traditional way using a long handled venecia.

Left: Neat rows of vines and fermentation tanks bake in the hot sun in the Douro valley at Pinhao, Portugal.

wine on your hands, you also of course have a product that is a fair bit higher in alcohol than most ordinary wines. The normal strength of unfortified table wines is in the region of 11–13% ABV. Some German and Italian wines make a virtue of being particularly low in alcohol (as little as 5%, perhaps), while certain Italian and Californian wines made from grapes that have grown in raging hot climates may climb up to around 15%. But 15% is the *starting* point for fortified wines, and they can be fortified up to 22%, putting them not far off the strength of the average liqueur.

Each of the world's classic fortified wines (they originated in southern Europe, but are now made in most winemaking countries) has its own particular method of production. The majority are made from white grapes, the most

notable exception being port, most of which is red. They tend to be sweet, but don't have to be – fino and manzanilla sherry are the driest of the dry. Most of them contain only wine and grape spirit, but in the case of vermouth and related products, a whole bunch of aromatizing ingredients (familiar to us from some of the herbal liqueurs) creates a style that is halfway between a fortified wine and a liqueur.

Fortified wines may once have seemed a good way of using up a sub-standard harvest, either through the distillation of grapes to make the fortifying agent, or in masking a poor wine's faults by adding spirit to it. By the time the 19th century dawned, however, most of these wines were seen as premium products – vintage port and Madeira particularly were as highly acclaimed as claret and burgundy.

Above: At one time, on the Douro River, Porto, Portugal, small boats were used to bring barrels of port from high in the valley.

Until about the time of the Second World War, they were held in special regard by the British, who have always had a taste for strong and fiery wines. Since that time a progressive decline has taken place as international tastes in wine have tended to the dry and light end of the spectrum, and away from the sort of sinew-stiffening brew to be sipped by the fireside on winter nights.

Despite that, there will always be a place for the traditional fortified wines. In a world where table wine is often accused of being infected by a bland homogeneity of taste, the fortifieds are, in their several ways, unashamedly unique styles of wine.

MADEIRA *Portugal rules Kitchen Wine*

OF ALL THE CLASSIC fortified wines of southern Europe, Madeira is the one with the most singular history. It comes from the island of the same name in the Atlantic Ocean; a volcanic outcrop, Madeira is actually slightly nearer to the coast of North Africa than it is to Portugal of which it is an autonomously governed region.

The evolution of this wine belongs to the days of the trading ships that plied the East India routes in the late 1600s. Madeira's geographical position made it a natural port of call for north European vessels on their way to Africa and the East Indies, and so they would load up with wine at the port of Funchal, the island capital. It gradually came to be noticed that, whereas many table wines would be badly spoiled by the combination of violent

shaking and the torrid heat in which they travelled the oceans, Madeiras were eerily improved by the experience.

The shippers were so sure of the benefits the sea voyage conferred on the wine that they began to send wines that were only destined for the European markets all the way to Indonesia and back. Some went the other way, and a great connoisseurship of Madeira grew up in the newly independent United States. Until virtually the end of the 19th century, this is how the most highly prized Madeiras were all made.

Eventually, it simply wasn't financially practical to keep treating Madeira to a round-the-world cruise, and so the conditions it endured at sea – the tortuous heat, especially – were recreated in the wineries or "lodges" where the wines originated. Some Madeira is heated simply

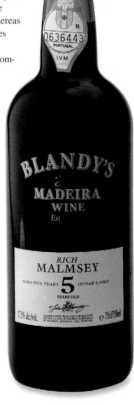

RICH MALMSEY This is the sweetest style of Madeira

VERDELHO The second driest style – this 5-year-old Madeira is only very slightly sweet

MIXING

It was common in America once to substitute sweet Madeira for the brandy in a **Prairie Oyster**, that most challenging of hangover cures, involving a raw egg yolk, salt and cayenne pepper and a dash of Worcestershire sauce.

Boston (below): Shake equal measures of dry Madeira and bourbon with half a teaspoon of caster sugar and yet another egg yolk. Strain into a small wine glass and sprinkle with grated nutmeg.

HOW IT IS MADE

A light, white base wine is made from any of the four main varieties, perhaps supplemented with some juice from the local red grape Tinta Negra Mole (though it is theoretically of declining importance). For the sweeter styles, Bual and Malmsey, the fermentation may be interrupted early on by the addition of grape spirit, meaning that some natural sugar remains in them, while the drier wines (Sercial and Verdelho) are fermented until more of the sugar has been consumed before being fortified. The wines are then subjected to heat during the cask-ageing, either by one of the heating systems known as an *estufa* (stove), or else by just being left in the hottest part of the lodge, in which case it may be known as a *vinho canteiro*.

TASTES GOOD WITH

The driest styles present the answer to that age-old problem of what to drink with soup. They are particularly good with clear, meaty consommé. As you proceed to the richer end of the scale, drink them with mince pies, Christmas cake and other dense fruitcake mixes or, of course, Madeira cake.

by being left under the roof of the lodge to bake in the heat of the tropical sun. Some is stored in rooms where fat central heating pipes run around the walls throughout the summer swelter, and even the lowest grades are matured in vats that have hot-water pipes running through them.

There are four basic styles of Madeira, named after the grape varieties that go into them. The palest and driest style is Sercial. Then comes Verdelho, a little sweeter and darker, then Bual, and finally Malmsey (the last is an English corruption of the Portuguese name Malvasia). The wines are also graded according to how long they have been aged. This may be given as a minimum age on the label (5-year-old, 10-year-old and so on), or one of the accepted descriptive terms may be used. "Reserve" 5 equates roughly to 5-year-old, "Special 10 Reserve" to 10, "Extra Reserve" to 15. Some Madeira is vintage-dated, meaning it is the unblended produce of the stated year's harvest.

SERCIAL
The palest and driest style of Madeira

MARSALA

SICILY'S VERY OWN fortified wine is named after the town of Marsala, in the province of Trapani at the western end of the island. Like many of the fortified wines of southern Europe, it has an English connection. It was effectively invented by a wine merchant, John Woodhouse, in 1773, in direct imitation of the sherry and Madeira in which he was something of a specialist. In the rough-and-ready way of the time, he simply added a quantity of ordinary brandy to the traditional white wines of western Sicily, and found on shipping them that the result was a reasonably close approximation of the already established fortified wines.

Woodhouse founded a commercial operation on the island at the end of the 18th century, and won valuable orders

from the Royal Navy among others. Marsala was carried on Nelson's ships during the hostilities with France, and the wine's reputation quickly spread. Although the early trade was dominated by English merchants, Italians themselves eventually got in on the act. The first significant house of Italian origin was Florio, founded by an entrepreneur from the mainland in 1832.

It is fair to say that Marsala's development since that period has been one of slow decline as a result of conflicting theories about how it should be made, and the widespread use of irrigation in the vineyards where it is grown. Irrigation can result in grapes of lower sugar concentration, which means that alternative methods of sweetening the wine have had to be found.

The rules and regulations governing the production of Marsala

TERRE ARSE
A vintage-dated
Marsala from
Florio

SECCO
The driest style
of Marsala

HOW TO SERVE

Dry and medium-dry Marsala, of which there is a regrettably small amount, should be served chilled in generously sized sherry glasses as an aperitif. The sweetest styles should be served at room temperature as digestifs or with certain types of old, dry cheese.

were only finally codified in 1969, and are considerably more flexible than those controlling the manufacture of the other famous fortified wines. Perhaps the least satisfactory aspect of them is the nature of the sweetening agents that may be added. It can be either a fortified grape juice, or just grape juice whose sweetness has been concentrated by cooking. This latter ingredient, known in Italian as *mosto cotto*, is not in itself alcoholic. The best Marsalas have natural sweetness from ripe grapes, which is retained through interrupted fermentation.

Marsala is classified by age – Fine is one year old, Superiore two, Superiore Riserva four, Vergine five, Stravecchio ten – and by sweetness. Dry is labelled "secco", medium-dry "semisecco" and the sweetest "dolce". It also comes in three colours. The better grades are both shades of tawny, either amber (*ambra*) or golden (*oro*), but there is a red version too (*rubino*). Producers of note include de Bartoli, Pellegrino and Rallo.

HOW IT IS MADE

Light white wines from local grape varieties Grillo, Inzolia and Catarratto are turned into Marsala by one of three methods. They can be fortified with grape spirit in the traditional way, or sweetened and strengthened with either alcohol-boosted juice from ultra-sweet, late-ripened grapes or with cooked grape juice concentrate. Concentrate is only permitted in the Ambra Marsala. The wines are then cask-aged for varying periods.

TASTES GOOD WITH

Marsala has come to be seen as even more of a kitchen ingredient than Madeira. It is indispensable as the alcohol element in both zabaglione and tiramisù, while the scallopini of veal, beloved of Italian trattorias the world over, are often sauced with a sticky brown reduction of Marsala.

DOLCE
This is best suited for classic Italian desserts

FINE
Fine Marsala is the youngest style

RISERVA
Superiore Riserva Marsala is four years old

MUSCAT *and* MOSCATEL

SWEET FORTIFIED WINES are made from Muscat all over the world. It is easy to think Muscat is a single grape variety, but it is in fact a grape family. Some of its offshoots are of the highest pedigree, notably a type the French call Muscat Blanc à Petits Grains. Others, such as Muscat of Alexandria and Muscat Ottonel, are of humbler extraction, and give corresponding-ly less exciting wines. Moscatel is the name the family assumes on the Iberian peninsula.

This is a quick global tour of the styles of sweet wine the Muscat relatives make. All should be served chilled as dessert wines or on their own. They tend to be in the range of 15–18% ABV, except for the first category, Australian Muscats, which reach up to 20%.

AUSTRALIAN LIQUEUR MUSCATS

These are hugely rich, strong, fortified Muscats made in and around the town of Rutherglen, in the north-western corner of the Australian state of Victoria. They are produced by a method that seems to combine a little of all the ways of making fortified wine. The grapes are left to overripen and shrivel on the vine, so that they are halfway to becoming raisins. After pressing, they ferment part-way, but the fermentation is arrested by fortification with grape spirit, keeping massive quantities of natural sugar in the wine. The cask-ageing they then receive combines elements of the *solera* system used in Spanish brandy and sherry, and the action of searing sunshine, as in *canteiro* Madeiras. Among the more notable producers are Stanton & Killeen, Mick Morris and Chambers.

VIN DOUX NATUREL MUSCATS

A group of Muscat wines made in southern France are made by virtually the same method as port. Their collective name, *vins doux naturels*, means "naturally sweet wines". The grapes are picked very ripe and the normal process of fermentation is stopped by adding a powerful grape spirit, so the natural grapey sweetness of Muscat is retained. There are six appellations for this type of wine, the most famous of which comes from the southern Rhône valley – Muscat de Beaumes de Venise. Best producers are Domaine Durban and Domaine de Coyeux.

Four of the others are located down in the Languedoc. They are Muscat de Frontignan, de Lunel, de Mireval and de St Jean de Minervois. The sixth, Muscat de Rivesaltes, is grown even further south, in Roussillon, near the Spanish border. De Rivesaltes does not have to be made from the noblest Muscat, though, and the quality varies hugely between producers.

SETUBAL MOSCATEL

This is a highly traditional fortified wine based on the Muscat of Alexandria grape, together with a couple of its more obscure cousins. It is made on the Setúbal peninsula in western Portugal, southeast of Lisbon, and was recognized

MUSCAT DE BEAUMES DE VENISE
Domaine de Coyeux is one of the best producers of Muscat

as a regionally demarcated wine in the first decade of the 20th century. The process is the same as for the French *vins doux naturels*, except that after fortification, the grape skins are allowed to macerate in the finished wine for several months. Some Setúbal Moscatel is released after five years or so when its colour is already a vivid orange from the wood. Other wines are aged for a couple of decades, deepening to burnished mahogany until they are a treacle-thick essence of pure Muscat flavour. The most significant producer is José Maria da Fonseca.

MOSCATEL DE VALENCIA

Around Valencia, on the eastern coast of Spain, they make what the French would call a *vin de liqueur*, that is, a wine that hasn't

SETÚBAL MOSCATEL
A 20-year-old Moscatel from Portugal's Setúbal

really fermented as such but for which the grapes have merely been pressed and then fortified with grape spirit. (In that respect, they could be considered similar to the ratafias made in the brandy regions of France.) Moscatels de Valencia are not made from the most distinguished Muscat variety and are more often than not seen in screw-top bottles. When very fresh and very well chilled, these can be pretty refreshing drinks, particularly in the stunning heat of a Spanish summer.

JEREPIGO

Jerepigo is the South African version of Moscatel de Valencia, except that it most emphatically does use the aristocratic Muscat Blanc à Petits Grains variety, here known – just to confuse everybody – as Muscadel or Muskadel. Otherwise, the production is the same, with grape spirit being added to the very sweet, freshly pressed grape juice. Vintages of Jerepigo (the name is Portuguese in origin) are occasionally released at around 15 years old, and are found to retain much of their initial freshness.

MOSCATEL DE VALENCIA
A highly ornate bottle for what is in fact a very simple drink

JEREPIGO
An old vintage of South Africa's answer to fortified Moscatel.

PORT

PORT IS THE ONLY one of the major fortified wines to be based on a red wine. True, there is such a thing as white port, but it only accounts for a fraction of the production. Port hails from only one delimited area, the Douro valley in northern Portugal. So popular has it traditionally been as a style of wine that many non-European wine-making countries have been trying their hands at port lookalikes since the 19th century. The difference today is that, in the countries of the European Union at least, they are no longer allowed to be called port.

The drink originated during one of the frequent periods of hostilities between the English and the French in the 1600s, as a consequence of which the English authorities declared a punitive tax levy on goods imported from France. This hit the wine trade hard. Wine shippers had to look to Portugal, England's oldest European ally, with whom there were preferential trade tariffs, to supply their customers. Journeying inland along the river Douro, the English merchants happened upon the fierce red wines of the region and found them pretty much to the domestic taste. As was common practice at the time, they fortified them with a little brandy for the sea voyage.

Thus was port born. Originally, it was of course a dry wine, since these were fully fermented wines that were being augmented with brandy. However, it only took the chance discovery of the effects of fortification

COCKBURN'S
1991
A vintage port from one of the English shippers

GRAHAM'S
1989 LBV
Port from a single year matured in the shipper's cellars

FOOD w/ PORT
134
180
184
182
178
248

HOW TO SERVE
Good port should be served in wine-glass quantities, not in silly little liqueur glasses, unchilled except in the case of white port. Older wines that have thrown a sediment may need to be decanted.

Port in a Storm (from Michael Walker's *Cinzano Cocktail Book*): Mix two measures of light red wine, a measure and a half of port and half a measure of cognac in a jug with plenty of ice and pour into a large wine glass, ice and all.

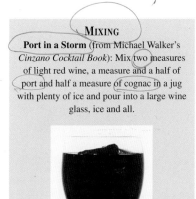

on an extremely ripe, sweet wine to remodel port in the image with which we are familiar today. To preserve that sweetness, the wines would have their normal fermentation interrupted (or "muted") with brandy, so that some of the grape sugars would remain unconsumed by the yeasts.

Eventually, it was considered that using a simple local grape spirit was cheaper than buying fine cognac for the fortification. Also, port was coming to be seen as a fine wine in its own right, and so it was desirable that the fortifying agent should be as neutral as possible, in order to allow the characteristics of the underlying wine to be shown off.

Port styles have since multiplied almost *ad infinitum*. At the top of the quality tree are the vintage ports, wines of a single year that must be bottled within two years of the harvest and are intended for long ageing. Late-bottled vintage (LBV) is also the product of a single year, but, one that has been kept in cask in the shipper's premises for longer – around six years usually – in order to be more mature on bottling, and readier to drink on purchase. Vintage Character port is an everyday blended product and nothing special, while the fine old tawny ports are often aged for many years in barrel so that their initial full-blooded red fades to an autumnal brown.

Other countries producing good port-style fortified wines are Australia (where the favoured grape variety is the spicy Shiraz), South Africa and the United States. There is a very good Greek fortified red called Mavrodaphne that makes an agreeable alternative to the more basic offerings of the Douro.

HOW IT IS MADE

The fermentation of Douro wines is stopped part-way through by the addition of grape spirit, to produce a sweet, strong, liquorous wine. Various periods of cask-ageing are given to the various grades. The bottled strength is in the region of 18-20%, but can be as high as 22%.

TASTES GOOD WITH

Port is excellent with nuts and with mature, strong hard cheeses, such as Cheddar, but less good with its traditional partner, Stilton.

QUINTA DO CRASTO
An LBV from a small Portuguese producer

TAYLOR'S 20 YEARS OLD
Twenty years is the average age of the blend

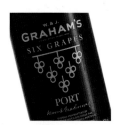

GRAHAM'S SIX GRAPES
A fairly basic ruby port

COCKBURN'S FINE RUBY
This is the lowest port designation

QUADY'S
A port-style fortified wine from the USA

SHERRY

FOOD: 162
170
192

ALTHOUGH FORTIFIED WINES bearing the name of sherry have been produced around the world for well over a century, true sherry comes only from a demarcated region in the southern Spanish province of Andalucía. There are three main centres of production – Jerez de la Frontera, Puerto de Santa María and Sanlúcar de Barrameda. The last is the traditional home of a type of pale, delicate dry sherry called manzanilla.

The production process for sherry is one of the most complicated of any fortified wine. When the new white wine is made, it

OTHER NAMES
Spain: Jerez *France*: Xérès

is fermented until fully dry, and then transferred into large butts. Some sherries, the ones that are destined to end up as the pale dry style known as fino (or manzanilla), develop a film of yeast culture called *flor* on the surface of the wine. In some barrels, the layer of *flor* dies out because it has consumed all the remaining nutrients in the wine, whereupon it breaks up and sinks to the bottom of the butt.

TIO PEPE
Muy Seco is the
very driest style
of sherry

HARVEYS
BRISTOL CREAM
A big-selling brown
cream sherry

HOW TO SERVE
Fino and manzanilla, and the sweetened pale sherries, should be served very well chilled, preferably from a freshly opened bottle. In Spain, they think nothing of drinking a bottle of dry sherry as we would a table wine. The other styles should be served at room temperature. Finos are brilliant aperitifs, old olorosos best at the other end of the meal.

With the subsequent greater exposure to the air, the colour of the wine deepens through oxidation, and the style known as amontillado results.

Some wines develop no *flor* at all and go on to turn a deep, woody brown colour. These are oloroso sherries. The fortification of the wine varies according to the style. Fino may be fortified to only 15% ABV, whereas oloroso is generally bottled at around 20%. At this stage, all of the wines are naturally dry, and some – the true connoisseur's sherries – will be bottled in that condition after ageing in cask.

Many commercial sherries, however, are made sweet by the addition of a quantity of *mistela*, the juice of raisined grapes to which grape spirit has been added. The best sweet sherries are sweetened with PX, which stands for Pedro Ximénez, the name of a grape variety whose berries are left to dry in the sun until loss of moisture has concentrated their sugars to an almost unbelievable degree. Some houses bottle some of their PX separately as a speciality product.

Other countries that produce sherry-style wines are Australia (which makes about the best outside Jerez), the United States, South Africa and Cyprus. Within Spain itself, there are two other regions near Jerez that produce similar fortified wines in the same range of styles, but they are not as distinguished as sherry. One is Montilla-Morilés, the other the virtually forgotten Condado de Huelva.

Spain's other great, now sadly nearly extinct, fortified wine is Málaga, made around the Mediterranean port of that name. Its finest wines are deep brown, caramel-sweet creations of great power, once hugely popular in Britain, now forsaken by fashion.

TASTES GOOD WITH

Dry sherries are good with salted nuts such as almonds, with piquant nibbles such as olives and salty fish like anchovies, and with Serrano ham or its Mediterranean equivalents. The sweet old olorosos are wonderful with rich, dark fruitcake and hard Spanish sheep's milk cheeses such as Manchego.

EMVA CREAM
A Cypriot wine, no longer labelled as "sherry"

VERMOUTH

VERMOUTH IS AS FAR removed from the natural produce of the vine as it is possible for a fortified wine to get. Not only is it strengthened with spirit, but it is also heavily aromatized with herbs and botanical ingredients in order to make a distinctive type of drink that is usually intended for drinking – either mixed or unmixed – as an aperitif. There is no particular connoisseurship of vermouth, as there is for aged sherries and vintage ports. This is an everyday product made to a consistent and unchanging recipe by each manufacturer.

The presence in vermouth of that cocktail of herbs and roots alerts us

to the fact that this was originally a medicinal drink. That said, the practice of adding herbs to wine goes back to ancient Greek times, when the extra ingredients may have been put in as much to disguise the taste of spoiled wine as for their curative powers. A popular early additive was wormwood, villain of the piece when absinthe was outlawed, yet much prized as a tonic for the stomach from classical antiquity through to medieval times and the beginnings of distillation in Europe.

As far as a drink identifiable as the precursor of modern vermouth is concerned, we have to travel back to the 1500s in order to find a merchant called d'Alessio selling a wormwood wine in Piedmont (now in northwest Italy). The inspiration had come from similar German products, probably produced on a domestic scale, and it is from the German word for wormwood, *Wermuth*, that the modern English word is derived. It was already popular in England by the middle years of the following century.

Two centres of vermouth production came to be established. One was in d'Alessio's part of Italy, close to the alpine hills that were a handy

HOW TO SERVE
A drop or two only of dry French vermouth is needed for the perfect dry Martini or Vodkatini.

All these drinks should be served as aperitifs or at the cocktail hour. Vermouth is not as fragile once opened as pale dry sherry tends to be. It doesn't have to be drunk up within a few days, and is able to withstand extremes of temperature far more hardily than the other light fortified wines.

MARTINI
EXTRA DRY
The top brand of vermouth internationally

wild source of the various botanical ingredients that went into the wine, and the other over the border in eastern and southeastern France. As the big commercial companies were founded, two distinct styles of vermouth emerged, one pale and dry with pronounced bitterness, the other red and sweet and not quite so bitter. The former was the style associated with France, the latter with Italy. So ingrained did these

NOILLY PRAT
A bone-dry
vermouth
produced in
the south of
France

MIXING

Lily: Shake equal measures of gin, Lillet and crème de noyau with a dash of fresh lemon juice and ice, and strain into a wine glass.
Perfect Cocktail (below): Shake exactly equal measures of gin, dry vermouth and sweet vermouth with ice, and strain into a cocktail glass. (Substitute Pernod for the gin and you have a **Duchess**.)

definitions become that, even now, drinkers still refer to "French" and "Italian" to mean dry and sweet respectively, when these may not necessarily be the geographical origins.

In fact, sweet and dry vermouths are made in both countries, and indeed elsewhere, including the United States. Brands vary according to the number and type of the herbal ingredients added, but the basic style remains the same from one batch to the next. Cloves, cinnamon, quinine, citrus peels, ginger, perhaps a touch of wormwood still (although the banning of absinthe sharply decreased the amount of wormwood that was considered acceptable in other drinks) are typical elements in the pot-pourri of aromatizers that go into the modern vermouths.

FLAVOURINGS

May include quinine, coriander seeds, cloves, juniper, ginger, dried orange and lemon peel, hyssop, camomile, raspberries, rose-petals, and so on.

As with many of the traditional liqueurs, the medicinal image of vermouth was – by the onset of the 20th century – something of an albatross around its neck, rather than a marketing opportunity. It was once again the cocktail era that rode to its rescue, finding multifarious uses for both styles of vermouth. After all, if the traditional dry Martini was destined to be the only use to which dry vermouth could be put behind the bar – one drop at a time – then not a great deal of it was ever going to be sold. Because it is quite as perfumed, in its way, as gin, vermouth proved hugely versatile in mixed drinks, and the demand for it

today – thanks in part to the big proprietary brands – remains reasonably steady.

The bulk-producing Italian firm of Martini e Rossi, based at Turin, is still the vermouth name that springs most readily to mind for consumers today. Other Italian producers are Riccadonna, Cinzano and Gancia. In France, the Marseillan producer Noilly Prat makes one of the more highly regarded dry vermouths, but also has a sweeter style. The region of Chambéry in eastern France has been awarded the *appellation contrôlée* for its vermouths, which include a strawberry-flavoured fruit version called Chambéryzette. As well as red and white styles

CINZANO BIANCO Hugely popular brand of sweet white vermouth

CARPANO PUNT E MES A deep red vermouth produced at Turin

of vermouth, there is a golden or amber variant, and a rosé.

Other similar branded products include Lillet of Bordeaux, owned by one of the classed-growth claret châteaux, which blends a proportion of fruit juice in with the wine base along with the customary herbs; the French Dubonnet, a red or white sweet vermouth also full of highly appetizing quinine bitterness; and Punt e Mes, a similar but dark-coloured Italian product that combines sweetening and bittering elements in intriguing balance.

DUBONNET
The red version mixes well with lemonade

MIXING

Bamboo: Shake two measures of dry sherry and three-quarters of a measure of sweet red vermouth with a dash of orange bitters and ice, pour into a large cocktail glass. Add one or two ice cubes if you like.

HOW IT IS MADE

A low-alcohol, mostly white wine is produced and may be allowed a short period of ageing. For the sweeter styles of vermouth, it then has a quantity of sugar syrup added to it before the fortification with spirit. This is usually grape spirit but may occasionally also be derived from vegetable sources such as sugar beet. The wine is then transferred into large barrels or tanks to which the dried aromatising ingredients have already been added. From time to time, the mixture is stirred up manually with wooden paddles. After absorption of the flavourings, the vermouth will be bottled at around 17% ABV. Some producers insist their vermouths will continue to age in the bottle for a couple of years if kept. There are no vintage vermouths.

TASTES GOOD WITH

Dry vermouths are particularly useful in the kitchen for adding to sauces to accompany fish. The herbal ingredients in the vermouth add an attractive savoury note to the dish. A seasoned reduction of Noilly Prat, lemon juice and single cream is a fine way to treat good white fish such as sole or turbot.

MIXING

Bentley: Shake generous equal measures of calvados and red Dubonnet with plenty of ice, and strain into a cocktail glass.
Midsummer Night: Shake equal measures of gin and Punt e Mes with a half-measure of cassis and ice. Strain into a cocktail glass.

NON-ALCOHOLIC MIXERS

ALTHOUGH MANY of the drinks talked about in this book are commonly drunk unmixed, such as single malt whiskies, aged brandies and rums, and the fortified wines, the great majority of them would not be consumed at all were it not for non-alcoholic mixers. Some of these are so familiar as to need no explanation; others may be more rarely used, but nonetheless constitute an important element in the mixed drink and cocktail repertoire.

WATER

The simplest of all mixers is the one that dilutes the strength of ardent spirits without altering the character of their basic flavour. Water is indispensable to whisky drinkers, who claim that it enhances rather than mutes the aromatic personalities of their favoured spirit. Water softens the olfactory impact of the alcohol while allowing the complexities of grain, peat and wood to announce themselves.

Pastis drinkers use plain water, too, for the cloudiness that gives the drinks their collective name can only be obtained by mixing. In all cases, good spring water or mineral water is preferable to heavily chlorinated tap – especially so in the case of Highland and Lowland malts.

FRUIT JUICES

Of all the fruit juices, orange is probably the most important for mixing with single spirit shots, most notably with the white spirits that don't muddy its colour. To the cocktail-maker, freshly squeezed lemon juice is undoubtedly the most versatile ingredient. The juice of lemons has the uncanny ability to accentuate the flavours of other fruits, almost in the manner of a seasoning (try tasting a fresh fruit purée with and without lemon juice to demonstrate this point), and so it complements the fruit-flavoured liqueurs very well. Additionally, its sourness mitigates the syrupy sweetness of many of the classic liqueurs. Lime juice is yet more sour and is used in drinks that should have a particularly biting tang. Pineapple makes a sweetly exotic element in some rum-based mixtures.

ORANGE JUICE

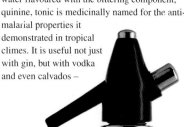

FRESHLY SQUEEZED LEMON JUICE

SPARKLING BEVERAGES

To achieve the diluting effects of water without changing flavour, and add a refreshing sparkle to a mixture, soda water is the required ingredient. At one time, no bar (or home for that matter) was complete without a soda-siphon. They were charged with tablets of sodium bicarbonate and dispensed a stream of bubbling water through a pressurized nozzle. Nowadays, there is effectively no difference between bottled or canned soda and carbonated mineral water.

TONIC WATER

Tonic water and gin go together like Fred Astaire and Ginger Rogers. A sweetened fizzy water flavoured with the bittering component, quinine, tonic is medicinally named for the anti-malarial properties it demonstrated in tropical climes. It is useful not just with gin, but with vodka and even calvados –

SODA-SIPHON

wherever the dryness of a drink can be made the more appetizing with bitterness.

Lemonade should not be thought of solely as a children's drink, as it provides a useful way of administering citric sourness and fizz to a long drink. The best lemonades for bar use are not as sweet as the kids may like them, and some are actually still, in which case you may just as well use lemon juice and a pinch of sugar.

LEMONADE

All cola is derived from the invention of Coca-Cola in the United States in the late 19th century by one John Pemberton. It was originally intended as a stimulating tonic drink, and included the ground nuts of the cola tree, along with crushed coca leaves. The latter are also the source of the drug cocaine, which came to be frowned on in the early years of this century, and so Coca-Cola removed them from the recipe.

COCA-COLA

Rum and neutral vodka seem to be the main spirits with which cola mixes most happily, coffee-flavoured Kahlúa and Tia Maria its closest liqueur companions.

Ginger ale or ginger beer also has its uses, with Scotch for example, but perhaps most famously with vodka as a Moscow Mule. Vodka-maker Smirnoff now makes a pre-mixed version of this drink.

SYRUPS

Cocktail-making would not be quite what it is without the availability of a range of flavoured non-alcoholic syrups to add complexity and interest to a drink. Of these, the most famous is grenadine, used to give a strong red colouring to otherwise clear mixtures, and to create the red-orange-yellow colour spectrum in the classic

Tequila Sunrise. Grenadine is made principally from the juice of the pomegranate, the peculiar Asiatic fruit that looks like a thick-skinned onion but, when cut, reveals a mass of jewel-like seeds within. It is thick, ruby-coloured and intensely sweet; some brands are made with a small alcohol quotient, but no more than about 3% ABV.

Orgeat is another little-seen syrup that was once used very widely in cocktails. Its flavouring element was almonds and it added that telltale taste of marzipan to a drink, even when used in very sparing quantities. Its name derives from the French word *orge*, meaning barley, which was once one of its ingredients.

Other syrups, flavoured with a whole greengrocer's shop of exotic ingredients, are now available. Pineapple, apricot, strawberry, banana, even kiwi-fruit are produced, and can add an appetizing dash of fruit flavour to a mixed drink, without the extra alcohol that liqueurs bring.

In addition to the flavoured syrups, it is also possible to buy a bottled neutral sugar syrup called gomme, but as it consists only of sugar and water, you may as well make your own.

GRENADINE
The principal flavour of this red syrup is pomegranate

GOMME
This is simply a straight sugar and water syrup

ORGEAT
An almond-flavoured syrup once widely used

GINGER BEER
A traditional English summer concoction, ginger beer works well as a mixer for basic Scotch, and with vodka for a Moscow Mule.

RECIPES

Cooking with alcohol is a traditional and exciting feature of the cuisine of many countries. This collection of new and traditional recipes uses the best seasonal produce, the rich culinary traditions of Europe, Asia and America, and just a splash or two of liquid nectar to develop and intensify the dishes' flavours. The alcohol used for the traditional dishes is indigenous to the places or regions in which they have arisen. For the many other recipes, unfamiliar combinations of food and alcohol have been brought together.

Over the years, cooks have been adding a little alcohol as an essential ingredient to many classic dishes. Here are time-honoured recipes, such as pepper steak with chive butter and brandy, crêpes Suzette with Cointreau and cognac, and zabaglione with Marsala. Explore the hidden potential of the wide variety of foods that are now available, and mix and match foods and alcohol to discover exciting combinations, such as scallops sautéed with green Chartreuse, or the thrilling flavours of roasted fennel with Pernod in a warm walnut salad.

The alcoholic drinks used in these recipes range from aperitifs and vermouths to spirits and liqueurs: those of universal appeal and renown include gin, brandy and Madeira, and there are fine regional drinks, such as Pernod, calvados and Noilly Prat.

Whether you are looking for recipes that are quick and easy, wanting to attempt a restaurant classic, or wish to try something more innovative and surprising, you will enjoy this bold and exciting approach to using spirits and liqueurs with food.

SOUPS AND STARTERS

A successful first course will invariably set the tone for the meal to follow
by stimulating the appetite without overwhelming it and by setting up an
anticipation of the succeeding flavours and textures. Choose from this
wide selection which includes: crisp, crunchy tempura vegetables served
with a piquant sherry dipping sauce, refreshing melon and cucumber
infused with the flavours of port and ginger, the surprising combination of
gin with salmon ceviche and brandied Roquefort tarts.

PUMPKIN SOUP *with* ANIS

Liquorice-flavoured anis adds a touch of excitement to this winter soup.

SERVES 4

675g/1¹/₂ lb *pumpkin*
30ml/2 tbsp *olive oil*
2 large *onions, sliced*
1 *garlic clove, crushed*
2 *fresh red chillies, seeded
and chopped*
5ml/1 tsp *curry paste*
750ml/1¹/₄ pints/3 cups *vegetable or
chicken stock*
15ml/1 tbsp *anis*
150ml/¹/₄ pint/²/₃ cup *single cream*
salt and ground black pepper
hot bread, to serve

COOK'S TIP

*Use hollowed-out small
squashes or pumpkins as individual
soup bowls.*

1 Peel the pumpkin, remove the seeds and chop the flesh roughly.

2 Heat the oil and fry the onions until golden. Stir in the garlic, chillies and curry paste. Cook for 1 minute, then add the chopped pumpkin and cook for 5 minutes more.

3 Pour over the stock and season with salt and pepper. Bring to the boil, lower the heat, cover and simmer for about 25 minutes.

4 Process until smooth in a blender or food processor, then return to the clean pan. Add the anis and reheat. Taste and season if necessary. Serve the soup in individual heated bowls, adding a spoonful of cream to each portion. Hot bread makes an ideal accompaniment.

FRENCH ONION SOUP *with* COGNAC

Cognac adds a delicious kick to this time-honoured, classic French soup.

SERVES 4

30ml/2 tbsp olive oil
25g/1oz/2 tbsp butter
3 onions (about 450g/1lb total
weight), sliced
5ml/1 tsp soft light brown sugar
2 garlic cloves, crushed
1.2 litres/2 pints/5 cups vegetable
or chicken stock
60ml/4 tbsp cognac
4 slices of French bread
15ml/1 tbsp Dijon mustard
115g/4oz/1 cup Gruyère
cheese, grated
salt and ground black pepper

COOK'S TIP
Don't rush the browning of the
onions. Their sweetness emerges
through long, gentle cooking.

1 Heat the oil and butter in a heavy-based saucepan and cook the onions very gently for 30 minutes until they are very soft. Sprinkle the brown sugar and garlic over and cook until the onions are golden brown.

2 Stir in the stock and cognac, with salt and pepper to taste. Bring to the boil, then lower the heat and simmer for 30 minutes.

3 Just before serving, toast the bread under a hot grill on one side only. Turn the slices over, spread them with the mustard and cover with the grated cheese. Grill until all the cheese has melted and is golden.

4 Spoon the soup into bowls and float the toasted bread on top. Serve at once.

ICED TOMATO *and* VODKA SOUP

This fresh-flavoured soup packs a punch like a frozen Bloody Mary.

SERVES 4

450g/1lb ripe, well-flavoured
  tomatoes, halved or
  roughly chopped
600ml/1 pint/2½ cups jellied beef
  stock or consommé
1 small red onion, halved or
  roughly chopped
2 celery sticks, cut into
  large pieces
1 garlic clove
15ml/1 tbsp tomato purée
10ml/2 tsp lemon juice
10ml/2 tsp Worcestershire sauce
handful of small basil leaves
30ml/2 tbsp vodka
salt and ground black pepper
crushed ice, 4 small celery sticks
  and sun-dried tomato bread,
  to serve

1 Put the tomatoes, jellied stock or consommé, onion, celery, garlic and tomato purée in a blender or food processor and process to a smooth purée.

2 Press the mixture through a strainer into a large bowl and stir in the lemon juice, Worcestershire sauce, basil leaves and vodka.

3 Add salt and pepper to taste. Cover and chill. Serve the soup with a little crushed ice and place a celery stick in each bowl. Sun-dried tomato bread is delicious with this soup.

COOK'S TIP

*Have more celery sticks and a jug of
iced water on the table for guests to
help themselves. The celery sticks can
be dipped into the soup.*

CHILLED VEGETABLE SOUP *with* PASTIS

Fennel, star anise and pastis give a delicate aniseed flavour to this sophisticated soup.

SERVES 6

175g/6oz leek, finely sliced
225g/8oz fennel, finely sliced
1 potato, diced
3 pieces of star anise, tied in a
  piece of muslin
300ml/¹/₂ pint/1¹/₄ cups single
  cream
10ml/2 tsp pastis
90ml/6 tbsp double cream or
  crème fraîche
salt and ground black pepper
chives, finely snipped, to garnish

1 Pour 900ml/1¹/₂ pints/3³/₄ cups boiling water into a saucepan, add the sliced leek and fennel, the diced potato and star anise and season to taste with salt and pepper. Bring to the boil and simmer for 25 minutes.

2 With a slotted spoon remove the star anise, then process the vegetables until smooth in a blender or food processor and place in a clean pan.

3 Stir in the single cream, bring to the boil, taste and and adjust the seasoning if necessary.

COOK'S TIP
To chill the soup quickly, stir in a spoonful of crushed ice.

4 Strain into a bowl, cover and leave until cold. To serve, stir in the pastis, pour into bowls, add a swirl of double cream or a spoonful of crème fraîche and garnish with snipped chives.

CHARENTAIS MELON *with* PORT

Very refreshing, the port forms a syrup when infused with the melon, ginger and cucumber.

SERVES 4

1 medium Charentais melon
60ml/4 tbsp port
15ml/1 tbsp chopped glacé ginger
$\frac{1}{2}$ cucumber, peeled, halved
   lengthways and seeded
mint leaves, to garnish

COOK'S TIP

To test whether melons are ripe, use your nose – ripe melons have a strong perfume. The blossom end will yield slightly to pressure.

1 Cut the melon in half and remove the seeds. Using a small spoon or melon baller, scoop the flesh into a bowl. Stir in the port and chopped ginger.

2 Cut the cucumber into long thin ribbon strips with a vegetable peeler. Stir into the melon mixture and chill before serving. Garnish with mint leaves.

BRANDIED CHICKEN LIVER PATE

The rich flavour of chicken livers in this delicious starter is enhanced by the addition of a little brandy.

SERVES 4–6

350g/12oz chicken livers
115g/4oz/$\frac{1}{2}$ cup butter
1 rindless streaky bacon
   rasher, chopped
1 shallot, chopped
2 garlic cloves, crushed
30ml/2 tbsp brandy
30ml/2 tbsp chopped fresh parsley
salt and ground black pepper
fresh bay leaves and peppercorns,
   to garnish
olive bread, to serve

1 Rinse, trim and roughly chop the chicken livers. Melt half the butter in a large frying pan. Add the chopped bacon, shallot and garlic and fry for 5 minutes. Add the chicken livers and fry gently for 5 minutes more.

COOK'S TIP

If properly sealed, the pâté will keep in the fridge for 3–4 days.

2 Stir in the brandy and chopped parsley, with salt and pepper to taste. Bring to the boil and cook for about 2 minutes, then remove from the heat and process in a blender or food processor until smooth.

3 Spoon the pâté into individual dishes. Melt the remaining butter and pour carefully over the surface of each pâté to seal. Garnish with bay leaves and peppercorns.

4 When cool, chill the pâté until firm. Serve with olive bread.

VEGETABLE TEMPURA *with* SHERRY DIPPING SAUCE

Battered vegetables in traditional Japanese style are always served with potent green horseradish, grated daikon and a dipping sauce.

SERVES 4

1 red pepper, seeded and cut into diamond shapes
2 courgettes, sliced
2 carrots, cut into batons
1 small daikon (mooli), sliced
8 button mushrooms, halved
handful of celery leaves
FOR THE BATTER
1 egg, lightly beaten
115g/4oz/1 cup plain flour
oil, for frying
grated daikon (mooli), garnished with shaped carrot slices and celery leaves, and wasabi (green horseradish), to serve
FOR THE DIPPING SAUCE
150ml/¼ pint/⅔ cup dashi
75ml/5 tbsp soy sauce
60ml/4 tbsp dry sherry
30ml/2 tbsp caster sugar

1 Spread the prepared vegetables on a clean dish towel or kitchen paper to make sure that they are completely dry.

2 To make the batter, put 300ml/½ pint/1¼ cups cold water into a bowl. Add the egg and sprinkle over the flour. Stir just until they are mixed – the batter should be lumpy.

3 Heat the oil until a little batter added to the frying pan sinks and then quickly comes back up to the surface. Dip the vegetables into the batter and fry a few pieces at a time until golden. Drain and keep hot while you cook the remainder.

4 Mix together the dipping sauce ingredients, stirring until the sugar has dissolved. Pour into individual bowls. Serve the tempura with the dipping sauce and wasabi. Offer a bowl of grated daikon, garnished with shaped carrot slices and celery leaves.

COOK'S TIP
Daikon (mooli) is a variety of white radish which looks rather like a large parsnip.

GOAT'S CHEESE *and* GIN CROSTINI *with* FRUIT

A gin marinade accentuates the flavour of goat's cheese and contrasts beautifully with the fruit salsa.

SERVES 4

8 slices of goat's cheese (chèvre)
15ml/1 tbsp gin
30ml/2 tbsp walnut oil
30ml/2 tbsp olive oil
4 slices of Italian or French
 bread
1 garlic clove, halved
2 spring onions, sliced
6 shelled walnut halves,
 roughly broken
15ml/1 tbsp chopped fresh parsley
salt and ground black pepper
tomatoes and mixed salad leaves,
 to serve
FOR THE SALSA
5 tomatoes, peeled, seeded
 and chopped
2 oranges, segmented
 and chopped
15ml/1 tbsp chopped fresh basil
30ml/2 tbsp olive oil
pinch of soft light brown sugar
basil sprig, to garnish

1 Put the goat's cheese slices into a shallow bowl, pour the gin, walnut oil and olive oil over, then leave in a cool place to marinate for 1 hour.

2 In a bowl, mix together all the ingredients for the salsa. Season to taste. Garnish with the basil sprig.

COOK'S TIP
Chèvre is French goat's milk cheese.
It is often cylindrical in shape, which
makes it perfect for this dish.

3 Toast the slices of bread on one side, then turn them over and rub the untoasted surfaces with the cut pieces of garlic. Brush with the marinade, sprinkle over the sliced spring onions and top with the slices of cheese.

4 Pour over any remaining marinade, sprinkle with pepper and cook the crostini under a hot grill until the cheese has browned. Scatter over the walnuts and parsley. Serve with the tomatoes, salad leaves and salsa.

SCALLOPS *with* PASTIS *on* VEGETABLE FRITTERS

The aniseed flavour of pastis combines wonderfully with shellfish.

SERVES 4

2 carrots
1 large courgette
1 parsnip
1 small potato
1 egg, lightly beaten
oil, for frying
2 shallots, chopped
1 green pepper, seeded
  and chopped
8 large scallops, halved
3 dill sprigs, chopped
15ml/1 tbsp pastis
150ml/¹/₄ pint/ ²/₃ cup chicken or
  fish stock
2.5ml/¹/₂ tsp lemon juice
salt and ground black pepper
dill sprigs, to garnish

VARIATION

Oysters can be cooked in the same way as these scallops.

1 Coarsely grate the carrots, courgette, parsnip and potato into a bowl. Bind the mixture with the egg.

2 Heat a little oil in a large frying pan and drop 3–4 heaped spoonfuls of the vegetable mixture into the pan. Flatten a little, then cook for 8–10 minutes until golden, turning once. Remove from the pan and keep them hot while cooking successive batches.

3 In another frying pan, heat a little oil and sauté the shallots and green pepper for 6–8 minutes.

4 Add the scallops, chopped dill, pastis, stock and lemon juice and poach for 2 minutes. Season to taste. Spoon the mixture on to the vegetable fritters, garnish with dill and serve immediately.

SALMON CEVICHE *with* GIN *and* LIME

Marinating in a mixture of gin and lime juice "cooks" fresh fish and gives it a marvellous flavour.

SERVES 4

675g/1¹/₂lb skinless salmon fillet
1 small red onion, thinly sliced
6 chives
6 fennel sprigs
3 parsley sprigs
2 limes
30ml/2 tbsp gin
45ml/3 tbsp olive oil
sea salt and ground black pepper
salad leaves, to serve

VARIATION

For a tasty alternative, marinate strips of very fresh sea bass, bream, halibut or cod.

1 Cut the salmon fillet into thin slices, removing any large bones with tweezers. Lay the pieces in a wide, shallow glass or pottery dish. Scatter over the onion slices, chives, fennel and parsley sprigs.

2 Using a canelle knife, remove a few fine strips of rind from the limes and reserve for the garnish. Cut off the remaining rind, avoiding the pith, and slice it roughly. Squeeze the lime juice into a jug and add the sliced rind, with the gin and olive oil. Add sea salt and black pepper to taste. Pour over the fish and mix gently.

3 Cover the dish and chill for 4 hours, stirring occasionally. Scatter over the reserved strips of lime rind just before serving with the salad leaves.

DUCK *and* CALVADOS TERRINE

A classic dish from Normandy, using the regional apple brandy.

SERVES 4

*500g/1¼lb boneless duck meat,
 coarsely chopped
225g/8oz belly pork, minced
2 shallots, chopped
grated rind and juice of 1 orange
30ml/2 tbsp calvados
10 rindless streaky bacon rashers
2 eggs, beaten
30ml/2 tbsp chopped fresh parsley
salt and ground black pepper
mixed salad and hot toast,
 to serve*

1 Grease and base-line a 900g/2lb loaf tin or ovenproof dish. Place the chopped duck meat in a bowl with the minced pork, shallots, orange rind and juice, calvados and seasoning. Mix well, cover and chill for 1–2 hours.

2 Stretch the bacon rashers with the back of a large knife and use them to line the loaf tin or dish, leaving any excess hanging over the edge.

3 Stir the eggs and parsley into the meat mixture, then spoon it into the prepared tin or dish. Smooth the surface, fold the bacon over, then cover with foil. Preheat the oven to 180°C/350°F/Gas 4.

COOK'S TIP
*Marinating the duck for a
few hours will develop the flavours.*

4 Stand the terrine in a roasting tin and pour in boiling water to come about two-thirds of the way up the sides of the tin or dish.

5 Bake for 1¼ hours, then remove the terrine from the water bath, lift off the foil and leave to cool. Cover with clean foil and a weight and chill for 3–4 hours until firm. Slice and serve with salad and hot toast.

BOURBON PANCAKES *with* ASPARAGUS *and* HAM

Double your delight by adding bourbon to the batter and the dressing for the asparagus and ham.

SERVES 4

50g/2oz/¹/₂ cup self-raising flour
2.5ml/¹/₂ tsp mustard powder
1 egg, beaten
60ml/4 tbsp milk
15ml/1 tbsp bourbon
8 cooked asparagus spears,
 to serve
8 slices of Parma ham, to serve
FOR THE DRESSING
45ml/3 tbsp olive oil
15ml/1 tbsp bourbon
salt and ground black pepper

1 Sift the flour and mustard powder into a bowl. Make a well in the centre and add the egg, milk and bourbon. Whisk the batter until smooth.

2 Heat a griddle or heavy-based frying pan. Grease it thoroughly. Drop spoonfuls of the batter on to the hot griddle to make four pancakes. Cook for 2–3 minutes until bubbles rise to the surface of each pancake and burst.

3 Turn the pancakes over with a palette knife and cook for 2–3 minutes more, until golden brown. Remove and keep hot while making four more pancakes in the same way.

COOK'S TIP
For evenly shaped pancakes pour the batter into greased muffin rings.

4 Mix the dressing ingredients together in a bowl. Taste and adjust the seasoning if necessary.

5 Place two pancakes on each plate. Put an asparagus spear on top of each pancake, drape decoratively with a slice of Parma ham and spoon over a little of the dressing.

QUAIL'S EGG *and* VERMOUTH TARTLETS

Eggs hard-boiled in this way have an attractive marbled surface rather like Chinese hundred-year-old eggs.

SERVES 4

10 quail's eggs
30ml/2 tbsp soy sauce
30ml/2 tbsp mustard seeds
15ml/1 tbsp green tea leaves
6 filo pastry sheets
50g/2oz/¹/₄ cup butter, melted
1 small avocado
45ml/3 tbsp dry white vermouth
30ml/2 tbsp mayonnaise
10ml/2 tsp fresh lime juice
salt and ground black pepper
paprika, for dusting
lamb's lettuce, to serve

1 Put the quail's eggs into a saucepan. Pour over cold water to cover. Add the soy sauce, mustard seeds and tea leaves. Bring to the boil, then lower the heat and simmer for 3 minutes.

2 Remove the pan from the heat and lift out the eggs with a slotted spoon. Gently tap them on a firm surface so that the shells crack all over. Put the eggs back into the liquid and leave in a cool place for 8 hours or overnight.

COOK'S TIP
Pack cooked shelled eggs into wide-necked sterilized jars and cover with dry sherry or vermouth. Seal, label, store in a cool place. Use within six weeks.

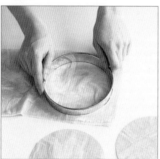

3 Preheat the oven to 190°C/375°F/ Gas 5. Grease four 10cm/4in tartlet cases. Brush each sheet of filo pastry with a little melted butter and stack the six sheets on top of each other. Stamp out four rounds with a 15cm/6in cutter.

4 Line the tartlet cases with the pastry and frill the edge of each. Put a crumpled piece of foil in each filo case and bake for 12–15 minutes until cooked and golden. Remove the foil and leave to cool.

5 Cut the avocado in half, remove the stone and scoop the flesh into a blender or food processor. Add the vermouth, mayonnaise and lime juice, and season to taste with salt and pepper. Process until smooth.

6 Shell the quail's eggs and cut them in half. Pipe or spoon the avocado mixture into the pastry cases and arrange the halved eggs on top. Dust the eggs with a little paprika and serve at once, with the lamb's lettuce.

Brandied Roquefort Tarts

Light puff pastry rounds topped with the irresistible combination of brandy and Roquefort cheese.

Makes 6

150g/5oz Roquefort cheese
30ml/2 tbsp brandy
30ml/2 tbsp olive oil
2 red onions (about 225g/8oz
total weight), thinly sliced
225g/8oz puff pastry, thawed
if frozen
beaten egg or milk, to glaze
6 walnut halves, chopped
30ml/2 tbsp snipped fresh chives
salt and ground black pepper
chive knots, to garnish
salad leaves, diced cucumber and
thin tomato wedges, to serve

1 Crumble the Roquefort into a small bowl, pour the brandy over and leave to marinate for 1 hour. Meanwhile, heat the oil in a frying pan and gently fry the onions for 20 minutes, stirring occasionally. Set the pan aside.

2 Preheat the oven to 220°C/425°F/ Gas 7. Grease a baking sheet. Roll out the pastry on a floured surface and stamp out six rounds with a 10cm/4in fluted cutter. Put the rounds on the baking sheet and prick them with a fork.

3 Brush the edges of the pastry with a little beaten egg or milk. Add the walnuts and chives to the onion mixture, with salt and pepper to taste. Divide the mixture among the pastry shapes, leaving the edges clear.

4 Spoon the brandied cheese mixture on top of the pastries and bake for 12–15 minutes until golden. Serve warm, garnished with chive knots, on a bed of salad leaves, diced cucumber and thin tomato wedges.

Cook's Tip
To make the chive knots, simply tie chives together in threes, with a central knot. Blanch the chives briefly if they are not very pliable.

FISH AND SEAFOOD

Fish is fashionable and healthy. Flat fish, round fish, shellfish in their many varieties lend themselves to speedy and stylish dishes. If your inclination is for shellfish, green Chartreuse adds the tastes and aromas of brandy and herbs to a creamy scallop dish, whilst mussels with dry sherry are given Thai flavours with a spiced coconut sauce. A stew can sound very mundane, that is unless it is one made with carp, trout and eel, laced with a little Marc de Bourgogne.

LOBSTER NEWBURG *with* MADEIRA

A traditional shellfish dish in which the lobster is sautéed in a rich cream sauce flavoured with Madeira.

SERVES 4

*2 cooked lobsters, about
 675g/1¹/₂lb each
25g/1oz/2 tbsp butter
150ml/¹/₄ pint/²/₃ cup Madeira
45ml/3 tbsp fish stock
250ml/8fl oz/1 cup double cream
3 egg yolks
1.5ml/¹/₄ tsp grated nutmeg
salt and ground black pepper
chopped fresh parsley, parsley
 sprigs and lemon wedges,
 to garnish*

1 Preheat the oven to 200°C/400°F/
Gas 6. Crack the lobster claws and legs,
remove the cooked meat and chop it in
neat chunks.

2 With a sharp knife, cut down the back
of each lobster from head to tail and
open it out. Remove and discard the
thread-like intestinal canal and the grey-
ish green sac from each lobster.

3 Carefully lift the meat from the shells,
then cut the lobster meat into thick
slices. Wash and dry the shells and set
them aside for serving.

4 Melt the butter in a large pan and fry
the lobster meat for 3 minutes over a
medium heat, stirring gently with a
wooden spoon.

5 Pour over the Madeira and fish stock,
then cook slowly until they are almost
absorbed. Lower the heat to a bare simmer. Mix the cream, egg yolks and
grated nutmeg in a small bowl. Add salt
and pepper to taste.

6 Gradually stir the cream mixture into
the pan. Cook for 3–4 minutes over a
low heat, stirring constantly until the
sauce thickens. Taste for seasoning. Be
careful not to let the mixture boil, or it
will curdle.

7 Spoon the lobster and sauce into the
half shells, garnish with chopped
parsley, parsley sprigs and lemon
wedges, and serve.

VARIATION
*Use this delicious sauce with cooked
crab, king prawns or langoustine
instead of lobster, if you prefer.*

KING PRAWNS *with* NOILLY PRAT

This French vermouth, redolent with herbs, is the perfect accompaniment for Mediterranean flavours.

SERVES 4

*20 raw king prawns, heads
  removed*
¹/₂ cucumber
25g/1oz/2 tbsp butter
15ml/1 tbsp olive oil
1 small shallot, finely chopped
*25g/1oz/¹/₄ cup drained sun-dried
  tomatoes in oil, chopped*
60ml/4 tbsp vegetable stock
30ml/2 tbsp Noilly Prat
150ml/¹/₄ pint/²/₃ cup double cream
*15ml/1 tbsp chopped fennel
  leaves*
45ml/3 tbsp golden salmon roe
salt and ground white pepper
fennel leaves, to garnish

COOK'S TIPS

*Try using sun-dried peppers instead
of the tomatoes. The salmon roe adds
a delicious flavour, but isn't essential
– omit it if you prefer.*

1 Peel the prawns, leaving the tail section on. Cut each prawn down the back and remove the black intestine. Rinse, then dry with kitchen paper.

2 Peel the cucumber, cut it in half lengthways and then scoop out the seeds. Slice the cucumber thickly into crescents.

3 Heat the butter and oil in a large frying pan or wok, add the chopped shallot and fry until softened.

4 Add the sun-dried tomatoes, vegetable stock, Noilly Prat and prawns. Cook over a low heat for 8–10 minutes.

5 Cook the cucumber crescents in a small pan of boiling salted water for 3 minutes, then drain.

6 Stir the cream and chopped fennel leaves into the prawns and cook until the sauce thickens. Season to taste with salt and pepper and stir in the cooked cucumber and the salmon roe. Reheat and serve, garnished with fennel leaves.

CRAB *and* PRAWN FILO TART *with* PASTIS

Pastis and shellfish are good companions and make a perfectly delicious filo tart.

SERVES 4–6

2 eggs, beaten
150ml/¼ pint/⅔ cup milk
30ml/2 tbsp pastis 64891
200g/7oz crab meat
200g/7oz cooked prawns, peeled
 and deveined
225g/8oz/1 cup curd cheese
115g/4oz/2 cups mushrooms,
 chopped
10 filo pastry sheets
50g/2oz/¼ cup butter, melted
salt and ground black pepper
50g/2oz/⅔ cup Parmesan cheese
 shavings, to garnish

COOK'S TIP
Work quickly with filo pastry as it
soon becomes dry and brittle.
Cover any filo not actually being
used with a damp, clean dish towel.

1 Preheat the oven to 190°C/375°F/ Gas 5. Grease a deep 18cm/7in flan tin. Mix together the eggs, milk, pastis, crab meat, prawns, curd cheese and mushrooms in a bowl. Season to taste with salt and pepper.

2 Line the flan tin with filo pastry, placing the sheets at alternate angles and brushing each one with a little of the melted butter. Leave the excess pastry hanging over the sides of the tin.

3 Spoon the filling into the filo-lined tin. Fold the excess pastry over, crumpling it slightly to make a decorative edge. Brush with melted butter. Bake the tart for 35–40 minutes. Scatter the Parmesan cheese over. Cut into wedges to serve.

SARDINES *with* APPLE RINGS *and* CIDER BRANDY

Fast-fried sardines and apple rings in a sweet-and-sour sauce.

SERVES 4

a few fresh tarragon sprigs
900g/2lb large sardines, gutted
  and with heads removed
1 egg white
30ml/2 tbsp cold water
50g/2oz/scant ¹/₂ cup cornmeal
oil, for frying
2 apples, cored and sliced
30ml/2 tbsp soft light
  brown sugar
pinch of ground cloves
15ml/1 tbsp balsamic vinegar
45ml/3 tbsp cider brandy
150ml/¹/₄ pint/²/₃ cup vegetable
  stock
salt and ground black pepper

COOK'S TIP
*Finely crushed taco shells, water
biscuits or oatmeal all make tasty
coatings for oily fish.*

1 Tuck a small piece of tarragon inside each sardine. Set a few tarragon sprigs aside for the garnish.

2 In a small bowl, lightly whisk the egg white with the cold water. Dip each sardine in turn in the egg white, then coat with the cornmeal.

3 Heat the oil in a large frying pan and fry the sardines until crisp and golden on both sides. Lift them out of the pan and keep hot.

4 Add more oil to the pan if necessary and fry the apple slices until crisp and golden. Remove with a slotted spoon and keep hot.

5 Stir the brown sugar, cloves, balsamic vinegar, cider brandy and stock into the pan. Bring to the boil and bubble for 2 minutes, then season to taste with salt and pepper. Add the sardines and apple rings, spoon the sauce over and serve immediately, garnished with the reserved tarragon sprigs.

TUNA *with* OLIVES, CORIANDER *and* NOILLY PRAT

Rather like a hot tuna salad with a pungent vermouth-flavoured sauce.

SERVES 4

45ml/3 tbsp Noilly Prat
3 canned anchovy fillets, drained
30ml/2 tbsp lemon juice
115g/4oz/¹/₂ cup butter, diced
1 garlic clove, roughly chopped
175g/6oz/1¹/₂ cups stoned
  black olives
4 tuna steaks, about 115–175g/
  4–6oz each
oil, for shallow frying
350g/12oz red cherry tomatoes,
  halved
3 courgettes, diagonally sliced
olive oil, for brushing
45ml/3 tbsp chopped fresh
  coriander
dressed salad leaves, to serve

1 Pour the Noilly Prat into a blender or food processor. Add the anchovies, lemon juice, butter, garlic and half the black olives. Process to a rough purée.

2 Sear the tuna in hot oil over a high heat for 1 minute on each side. Keep hot.

3 Brush the cherry tomatoes and courgette slices with a little olive oil. Spread out in a grill pan and grill until golden, turning occasionally.

4 Meanwhile, pour the olive purée into the frying pan. Bring to the boil and cook for 2 minutes, stirring constantly. Add the remaining olives and chopped coriander. Serve the tuna steaks with a little of the sauce poured over, accompanied by the vegetables and salad leaves.

COOK'S TIP
*Tuna is cooked very quickly
so that it browns on the outside,
yet is still moist and rare inside.*

THAI MUSSELS *with* DRY SHERRY

Superb, spiced seafood – East meets West in the fiery, sherry-flavoured coconut sauce.

SERVES 4

1.5kg/3–3¹/₂lb fresh mussels
45ml/3 tbsp dry sherry
45ml/3 tbsp Thai fish stock
400ml/14fl oz/1²/₃ cups coconut
 milk
150ml/¹/₄ pint/²/₃ cup water
30ml/2 tbsp olive oil
1 onion, chopped
2 garlic cloves, crushed
1 piece of lemon grass, sliced
30ml/2 tbsp tomato purée
10ml/2 tsp Thai curry paste
15ml/1 tbsp grated fresh
 root ginger
1 fresh red chilli, seeded
 and sliced
15ml/1 tbsp cornflour
60ml/4 tbsp chopped fresh
 coriander
salt and ground black pepper
French bread, to serve

1 Wash and scrub the mussels. Pull off any bits of "beard". Discard any open shells that do not close when tapped.

2 Put the mussels into a large, deep pan. Pour in the sherry, fish stock, coconut milk and water. Bring to the boil, cover tightly and cook for 5 minutes or until the shells have opened.

3 Using a slotted spoon, transfer the cooked mussels to a large bowl, discarding any that remain closed. Keep the mussels hot. Strain the cooking juices into a jug and set them aside.

4 Heat the oil in another pan and fry the onion and garlic for 5 minutes, stirring occasionally until softened.

COOK'S TIP
If the lemon grass is dry and "woody", then leave it whole and bruise lightly. Remove the bruised stalk from the sauce before serving.

5 Stir in the lemon grass, tomato purée, curry paste, ginger and chilli. Pour in the reserved cooking juices and season with pepper. Bring to the boil, lower the heat and simmer for 5 minutes.

6 Blend the cornflour to a smooth paste with a little water and stir into the pan. Bring to the boil, stirring constantly, then season to taste. Pour the sauce over the cooked mussels. Sprinkle with the chopped coriander and serve with sliced French bread.

PAN-FRIED SQUID *with* OUZO

Ouzo gives the flavours of aniseed and herbs to this rustic dish.

SERVES 4

500g/1¼lb prepared squid
30ml/2 tbsp olive oil
30ml/2 tbsp sesame seeds
15ml/1 tbsp green peppercorns
2 garlic cloves, crushed
6 spring onions, sliced
25g/1oz drained canned
  anchovies, chopped
1 piece of lemon grass, sliced
15ml/1 tbsp chopped fresh parsley
15ml/1 tbsp chopped fresh basil
150ml/¼ pint/⅔ cup fish stock
10ml/2 tsp lemon juice
10ml/2 tsp ouzo
75g/3oz/¾ cup mangetouts
salt
basil sprigs, to garnish
4 cooked poppadoms, to serve

1 Cut the squid into strips, rinse under cold water and dry with kitchen paper.

2 Heat the oil in a pan and toast the sesame seeds with the green peppercorns for a few seconds.

3 Add the garlic, spring onions and squid. Toss to coat in the sesame mix.

4 Stir in the anchovies, lemon grass, chopped parsley and basil. Pour in the stock, lemon juice and ouzo and simmer for about 12 minutes. Add the mangetouts and cook for 2 minutes more. Season to taste with salt and spoon on to the cooked poppadoms. Garnish with basil sprigs.

COOK'S TIP
If you find the flavour of the anchovies a little strong, soak them in cold milk to cover for 30 minutes, then drain and use.

MONKFISH BROCHETTES WITH BOURBON MARINADE

The bourbon marinade adds moisture and flavour to this firm fish, making it ideal for a barbecue.

SERVES 4

500g/1¼lb monkfish, cubed
2 large green peppers, halved
* and seeded*
olive oil, for brushing
3 tomatoes, peeled, seeded
* and chopped*
30ml/2 tbsp chopped fresh basil,
* plus basil sprigs, to garnish*
salt and ground black pepper
FOR THE MARINADE
30ml/2 tbsp white wine vinegar
30ml/2 tbsp bourbon
15ml/1 tbsp olive oil
45ml/3 tbsp chopped fresh dill
15ml/1 tbsp mustard seeds
15ml/1 tbsp clear honey

1 Mix the ingredients for the marinade in a shallow dish large enough to hold all the monkfish cubes in a single layer. Add the fish and stir to coat. Cover and chill for at least 1 hour.

2 Lift the fish out of the marinade and thread on to metal skewers. Set aside half the marinade for basting and pour the rest into a small pan.

3 Place the fish brochettes and pepper halves on a rack over a grill pan, or on the barbecue. Brush the brochettes with marinade and the peppers with olive oil. Grill or barbecue until the fish is golden and the peppers have browned, basting occasionally.

4 Meanwhile, add the chopped tomatoes and chopped basil to the marinade in the pan. Bring to the boil. Cook for 2 minutes and season to taste with salt and pepper. Spoon into the pepper halves and serve with the brochettes, garnished with basil sprigs.

ROASTED COD *in an* ALMOND CRUST *with* ANISETTE

An aniseed–and–lime–flavoured French dressing is delicious with cod.

SERVES 4

30ml/2 tbsp plain flour
4 cod fillets, about 115–175g/
* 4–6oz each*
50g/2oz/1 cup fresh brown
* breadcrumbs*
50g/2oz/½ cup grated Cheddar
* cheese*
50g/2oz/½ cup flaked almonds,
* roughly chopped*
2 eggs, beaten
pared lime rind, to garnish
salt and ground black pepper
FOR THE DRESSING
60ml/4 tbsp olive oil
15ml/1 tbsp anisette
5ml/1 tsp fresh lime juice

1 Preheat the oven to 200°C/400°F/ Gas 6. Grease a baking sheet. Put the flour into a plastic bag and season with salt and pepper. Add each cod fillet in turn and shake until evenly coated.

2 Mix the breadcrumbs, cheese and almonds in a shallow dish. Add a little salt and pepper. Pour the eggs into a similar dish. Coat the floured fish in egg and then the crumb mixture. Repeat the process.

3 Arrange the fish on the greased baking sheet and bake for 20 minutes until golden.

4 Meanwhile, make the dressing. Put the oil, anisette and lime juice in a screw-topped jar. Add salt and pepper to taste, close the jar tightly and shake to mix. Garnish the fish with curls of finely pared lime rind and serve with the dressing.

COOK'S TIP

The cheese, almond and crumb mixture can also be used as a stuffing.

RED SNAPPER *with* CHILLI, GIN *and* GINGER SAUCE

Gin and ginger add piquancy and spice to a fine fish dish that tastes every bit as good as it looks.

SERVES 4

1.5kg/3–3½lb red snapper,
  cleaned
30ml/2 tbsp sunflower oil
1 onion, chopped
2 garlic cloves, crushed
50g/2oz/½ cup button mushrooms,
  sliced
5ml/1 tsp ground coriander
15ml/1 tbsp chopped fresh parsley
30ml/2 tbsp grated fresh
  root ginger
2 fresh red chillies, seeded
  and sliced
15ml/1 tbsp cornflour
45ml/3 tbsp gin
300ml/½ pint/1¼ cups chicken or
  vegetable stock
salt and ground black pepper

FOR THE GARNISH

15ml/1 tbsp sunflower oil
6 garlic cloves, sliced
1 lettuce heart, finely shredded
1 bunch fresh coriander, tied
  with red raffia

1 Preheat the oven to 190°C/375°F/ Gas 5. Grease a flameproof dish large enough to hold the fish. Make several diagonal cuts on one side of the fish.

2 Heat the oil in a frying pan and fry the onion, garlic and mushrooms for 2–3 minutes. Stir in the ground corian-der and chopped parsley. Season with salt and pepper.

3 Spoon the filling into the cavity, then lift the snapper into the dish. Pour in enough cold water to cover the bottom of the dish. Sprinkle the ginger and chillies over, then cover and bake for 30–40 minutes, basting from time to time. Remove the cover for the last 10 minutes.

4 Carefully lift the snapper on to a serving dish and keep hot. Tip the cooking juices into a pan.

5 Blend the cornflour and gin in a cup and stir into the cooking juices. Pour in the stock. Bring to the boil and cook gently for 3–4 minutes or until thick-ened, stirring all the time. Taste for seasoning then pour into a sauce-boat.

6 Make the garnish. Heat the oil in a small pan and stir-fry the sliced garlic and shredded lettuce over a high heat until crisp. Spoon alongside the snapper. Place the coriander bouquet on the other side. Serve with the sauce.

TROUT *and* SOLE PARCELS *with* VERMOUTH

Contrasting fish, sandwiched with a peppery watercress filling, are served with a simple sauce spiked with vermouth.

SERVES 4

1 bunch watercress
1 courgette, grated
5ml/1 tsp Tabasco sauce
grated rind and juice of 1 lemon
450g/1lb trout fillets, skinned
450g/1lb sole fillets, skinned
50g/2oz/¼ cup butter
150ml/¼ pint/⅔ cup fish stock
120ml/4fl oz/½ cup dry
 white vermouth
salt and ground black pepper
fresh watercress sprigs,
 to garnish

1 Preheat the oven to 200°C/400°F/ Gas 6. Strip the watercress leaves from the thick stalks and chop them finely. Place them in a bowl with the grated courgette, Tabasco sauce, lemon rind and juice. Season with salt and pepper to taste.

2 Season the trout and sole fillets on both sides. Cover each sole fillet in turn with the watercress mixture. Top with the trout fillets.

3 Tie the fish "sandwiches" into neat parcels. Put the fish into a shallow flameproof dish and dot with the butter.

COOK'S TIP
If the fish fillets are uneven sizes, trim the larger piece. Finely chop the trimmings and add to the stuffing.

4 Pour the stock and vermouth over, cover and bake for 20 minutes until the fish is tender. Carefully lift the fish parcels on to a serving platter and keep them hot.

5 Transfer the flameproof dish to the hob and cook the stock mixture until it has reduced by half. Pour the sauce over the fish, garnish with watercress and serve.

SCALLOPS SAUTEED *with* GREEN CHARTREUSE

One of the oldest French liqueurs, green Chartreuse gives the flavours of brandy and herbs to this creamy shellfish dish.

SERVES 4
75g/3oz/6 tbsp butter
1 leek, white part only, cut into
 julienne strips
1 carrot, cut into julienne strips
30ml/2 tbsp green Chartreuse
50ml/2fl oz/¼ cup single cream
20 scallops
salt and ground black pepper
chervil sprigs, to garnish

1 Heat 25g/1oz/2 tbsp of the butter in a pan, add the julienne strips of leek and carrot and season to taste with salt and pepper. Cook over a low heat for about 12 minutes until soft but not coloured.

2 Remove the pan from the heat, add the green Chartreuse and stir. Flambé if you wish.

VARIATION
Use the delicious creamy base with crab, lobster or salmon fillets.

3 Stir in the single cream and cook gently until the sauce has reduced a little. Taste and adjust the seasoning if necessary.

4 Meanwhile, heat the remaining butter and, when foaming, add the scallops. Sauté for a few minutes until just cooked. To serve, put the vegetable and cream mixture on to serving plates, top with the scallops and garnish with chervil.

HADDOCK RIBBONS *en* PAPILLOTE *with* WHISKY

Open these parchment parcels to release the heady aroma of warm whisky.

SERVES 4

50g/2oz/¹/₄ cup butter, melted
500g/1¹/₄lb haddock fillet, skinned
3 spring onions, thinly sliced
2 garlic cloves, crushed
15ml/1 tbsp drained bottled
  capers
115g/4oz drained canned palm
  hearts, sliced
2 large tomatoes, seeded
  and sliced
30ml/2 tbsp whisky Jack Daniels
15ml/1 tbsp white wine vinegar
15ml/1 tbsp chopped fresh parsley
salt and ground black pepper
char-grilled peppers, onions and
  mangetouts, to serve

1 Preheat the oven to 220°C/425°F/
Gas 7. Cut four 28cm/11in square
sheets of non-stick baking paper. Brush
each sheet with a little of the melted
butter. Cut the haddock into thin ribbon
strips and put some in the middle of
each paper square.

3 Mix the whisky, wine vinegar and
parsley in a small bowl. Add salt and
pepper to taste. Whisk well, then spoon
over the fish.

4 Fold the paper over the fish, making a
pleat in the top, then twist the ends to
seal. Put the paper cases on a baking
sheet and bake for 10–12 minutes until
the paper has turned brown and the
cases have puffed up. Lift on to serving
plates and serve at once, with the
peppers, onions and mangetouts.

2 Top each square with a quarter of the
spring onions, garlic, capers, palm
hearts and tomatoes.

VARIATION
Use shellfish, cod or trout instead
of the haddock, and artichoke
hearts instead of palm hearts.

FRENCH FISH STEW *with* MARC *de* BOURGOGNE

A traditional recipe using freshwater fish and Marc de Bourgogne.

SERVES 6

*1.5kg/3–3¹/₂lb freshwater fish, such
   as carp, trout and skinned eel*
45ml/3 tbsp plain flour
50g/2oz/4 tbsp butter
*225g/8oz smoked bacon, cut
   into lardons*
4 shallots, very finely chopped
225g/8oz small onions
*225g/8oz/3 cups mushrooms,
   chopped*
*120ml/4fl oz/¹/₂cup Marc de
   Bourgogne*
1 litre/1³/₄ pints/4 cups red wine
*300ml/¹/₂ pint/1¹/₄ cups veal or
   chicken stock*
1 garlic clove, crushed
1 bouquet garni
salt and ground black pepper
chopped fresh parsley, to garnish
garlic bread, to serve

1 Clean the carp and trout, remove the heads and fins, fillet the flesh and cut into slices. Cut the eel into chunks.

2 Put half of the flour into a plastic bag, season with salt and pepper, add the fish pieces and shake to coat.

3 In a large pan, melt the butter over a medium high heat and brown the fish pieces on both sides. Remove from the pan and set aside.

4 Add the lardons, shallots and onions to the pan and cook over a low heat for a further 10 minutes until golden. Stir in the chopped mushrooms and cook a further 5 minutes.

COOK'S TIPS

Marc de Bourgogne is a Marc brandy from Burgundy. If it is not available use another brandy. If carp is not available, use extra trout, or substitute another fish, such as red mullet, John Dory or bream.

5 Pour in the Marc de Bourgogne, stir and flambé (optional). Add the red wine and simmer for a few minutes.

6 Stir in the stock, garlic and bouquet garni, bring to the boil and simmer for 5 minutes. Add the fish and simmer until cooked.

7 With a slotted spoon, remove the fish and keep hot. In a small bowl, blend the remaining flour with a little cold water and stir into the pan. Bring to the boil and cook for 5 minutes, then return the fish to the pan. Serve garnished with chopped parsley and accompanied by garlic bread.

COD STEAKS *with a* CREAMY SHERRY SAUCE

A molasses marinade gives these cod steaks a dusky colour that contrasts well with the creamy sherry sauce, studded with pink and green peppercorns.

SERVES 4

30ml/2 tbsp molasses
5ml/1 tsp salt
30ml/2 tbsp chopped fresh dill
30ml/2 tbsp lemon juice
4 cod steaks, about 115–175g/
  4–6oz each
50g/2oz/¼ cup butter
30ml/2 tbsp olive oil
3 shallots, chopped
150ml/¼ pint/⅔ cup fish stock
45ml/3 tbsp dry sherry
5ml/1 tsp pink peppercorns,
  lightly crushed
5ml/1 tsp green peppercorns,
  lightly crushed
3 potatoes, sliced
300ml/½ pint/1¼ cups crème
  fraîche
oil, for frying
3 carrots, thinly sliced
1 courgette, thinly sliced
1 slim parsnip, thinly sliced
salt and ground black pepper
lime wedges and fresh dill sprigs,
  to garnish

1 Mix the molasses, salt, chopped dill and lemon juice in a small bowl. Spread this mixture over both sides of the cod steaks. Put the fish in a shallow dish, cover and chill for 2 hours.

2 Heat the butter and olive oil in a frying pan. Add the shallots and cook until soft. Stir in the stock, sherry and both types of peppercorns. Cook for 2 minutes more.

3 Add the cod steaks to the pan and cook them for 10–12 minutes, turning once. Meanwhile, cook the potato slices in a saucepan of lightly salted boiling water for 5 minutes. Drain and set aside.

COOK'S TIP
Pink peppercorns are readily available from delicatessens. Use them with caution, however, as they can provoke an allergic reaction in susceptible individuals.

4 Lift the cooked fish out of the pan and keep hot. Stir the crème fraîche into the pan, season to taste with salt and pepper and reheat gently.

5 Deep-fry the potato slices in hot oil until golden. In a separate pan, stir-fry the carrots, courgette and parsnip in 30ml/2 tbsp hot oil for 1–2 minutes until crisp.

6 Divide the potatoes among four plates, add the stir-fried vegetables and top with the cod and sauce. Garnish with lime wedges and fresh dill sprigs.

HERB-STUFFED LEMON SOLE
with a SORREL *and* VERMOUTH SAUCE

Lemon sole tastes superb when served with a classic, light fluffy egg sauce delicately flavoured with vermouth.

SERVES 4

115g/4oz/½ cup butter
1 small onion, chopped
115g/4oz/1 cup mushrooms,
 chopped
50g/2oz/1 cup fresh brown
 breadcrumbs
30ml/2 tbsp chopped fresh
 lemon balm
4 skinless lemon sole fillets, halved
150ml/¼ pint/⅔ cup milk
50ml/2fl oz/¼ cup dry white
 vermouth   *p 120*
10ml/2 tsp lemon juice
2 egg yolks
handful of sorrel leaves, finely
 chopped
salt and ground black pepper

1 Preheat the oven to 190°C/375°F/
Gas 5. Melt 25g/1oz/2 tbsp of the butter
in a frying pan. Fry the onion and
mushrooms until the onion is golden
and the mushrooms have absorbed the
liquid. Add the breadcrumbs and lemon
balm and stir in salt and pepper to taste.

2 Place the pieces of sole skinned side
up on a board and spread some of the
filling on each. Roll up the fish pieces
carefully from head to tail and pack
them tightly in a shallow casserole.

3 Pour the milk over, cover and bake
for 15 minutes.

4 Bring a saucepan of water to simmering point. In a separate pan, heat the
vermouth until it has reduced by half.

COOK'S TIP
*If the sauce separates, whisk in
another egg yolk.*

5 Pour the vermouth into a heatproof
bowl, set it over the pan of water, add
the lemon juice and egg yolks and
whisk until fluffy.

6 Remove from the heat and continue to
whisk while adding the remaining butter, a piece at a time. Stir in the
chopped sorrel, season to taste with salt
and pepper and spoon over the fish.
Garnish with whole sorrel leaves.

MEAT, POULTRY AND GAME

Alcohol is a traditional accompaniment to meat, poultry and game. A rich
Madeira sauce makes a perfect match for ham or gammon, while an
armagnac-based sauce is served with lamb, and the rich tastes of pheasant
with juniper and port make heart-warming fare. Classic or contemporary,
all these dishes will make for elegant entertaining.

PEPPER STEAK *with* CHIVE BUTTER *and* BRANDY

A classic dish which never disappoints.

SERVES 4

4 fillet or sirloin beef steaks,
* about 115–175g/4–6oz each*
45ml/3 tbsp olive oil
15ml/1 tbsp black and white
* peppercorns, coarsely crushed*
1 garlic clove, halved
50g/2oz/¼ cup butter
30ml/2 tbsp brandy
250ml/8fl oz/1 cup jellied
* beef stock*
salt and ground black pepper
tied chive bundles, to garnish
FOR THE CHIVE BUTTER
50g/2oz/¼ cup butter
45ml/3 tbsp snipped fresh chives

1 Make the chive butter. Beat the butter until soft, add the chives and season with salt and pepper. Beat until well mixed, then shape into a roll, wrap in foil and chill.

2 Brush the steaks with a little olive oil and press crushed peppercorns on to both sides.

3 Rub the cut surface of the garlic over a frying pan. Melt the butter in the remaining oil. When hot, add the steaks and fry quickly, allowing 3½–4 minutes on each side for medium-rare. Lift out with tongs and keep hot.

4 Add the brandy and stock to the pan, boil rapidly until reduced by half, then season with salt and pepper to taste. Slice the chive butter and put a piece on top of each steak. Garnish each steak with a chive bundle and serve with a simple vegetable accompaniment, such as boiled new potatoes.

> **COOK'S TIP**
> *Flavoured butters freeze well.*

HAM *with* MADEIRA SAUCE

A rich bacon, celery and tomato sauce flavoured with Madeira is a perfect match for ham or gammon.

SERVES 4

30ml/2 tbsp sunflower oil
2 ham or gammon steaks, about
* 115–175g/4–6oz each, fat*
* snipped to prevent curling*
1 onion, sliced
175g/6oz/1½ cups button
* mushrooms*
175g/6oz raw beetroot, peeled
* and cut into thin sticks*
salt and ground black pepper
chopped fresh parsley, to garnish
FOR THE SAUCE
25g/1oz/2 tbsp butter
1 large onion, chopped
1 rindless streaky bacon
* rasher, chopped*
1 celery stick, diced
10ml/2 tsp plain flour
2 tomatoes, peeled and diced
15ml/1 tbsp tomato purée
300ml/½ pint/1¼ cups beef stock
15ml/1 tbsp chopped fresh parsley
30ml/2 tbsp Madeira

1 Make the sauce. Heat the butter and fry the onion, bacon and celery for 5–7 minutes until golden. Stir in the flour and cook until browned, then add the tomatoes, tomato purée, stock and parsley. Bring to the boil, then simmer for 15 minutes.

2 Strain the sauce into a bowl, stir in the Madeira and season to taste with salt and pepper.

3 Heat the oil in a frying pan and fry the ham or gammon steaks with the onion for about 10 minutes. Turn the steaks over, add the mushrooms and fry for about 10 minutes more, or until the steaks are fully cooked.

4 Meanwhile, cook the beetroot sticks in a pan of lightly salted boiling water for 5 minutes or until tender. Drain. Reheat the sauce, pour it over the steaks and serve with the mushrooms, onion and beetroot. Garnish with the parsley.

> **COOK'S TIP**
> *Straining the sauce through muslin or a very fine mesh will give a shiny, glossy finish.*

FIG-STUFFED PORK *with* BRANDY

Pork stuffed with dried fruit and spiked with brandy makes an ideal dinner-party dish.

SERVES 4

1 large pork fillet, about
  500g/1¼lb, trimmed
45ml/3 tbsp brandy
30ml/2 tbsp chopped fresh herbs,
  such as parsley, dill or chives
8 dried figs, halved
oil, for brushing
15ml/1 tbsp plain flour
300ml/½ pint/1¼ cups pork or
  chicken stock
salt and ground black pepper
fresh parsley sprigs, to garnish

1 Preheat the oven to 190°C/375°F/ Gas 5. Cut a deep slit along the length of the pork fillet; do not cut all the way through. Open out the pork. Brush with 15ml/1 tbsp of the brandy, sprinkle the herbs over and season with salt and pepper. Arrange the dried fig halves in a row on top.

2 Fold the meat over the filling and tie with raffia or string. Put the pork into a roasting tin, brush with oil, season with pepper and roast for 35 minutes.

3 Lift the meat from the roasting tin and keep it hot. Spoon off the excess fat, leaving the sediment and about 15ml/1 tbsp of the fat in the bottom of the tin. Place the tin on the hob over a medium heat.

COOK'S TIP
This recipe also works very well with dry sherry, Noilly Prat or Madeira.

4 Stir in the flour and cook for 1 minute, then whisk in the stock and remaining brandy. Cook until thickened, then boil for 2 minutes, whisking frequently. Season with salt and pepper to taste.

5 Slice the meat, garnish with parsley sprigs and serve with the gravy. Roast or sautéed potatoes and peas braised with lettuce would be ideal accompaniments.

PORK *with* SHERRY *and* COUSCOUS

A lightly spiced dish with a good balance of flavours between the pork and sherry.

SERVES 4

30ml/2 tbsp plain flour
500g/1¼lb boneless pork, diced
45ml/3 tbsp olive oil
1 large onion, chopped
2 garlic cloves, crushed
45ml/3 tbsp tomato purée
225g/8oz can chopped tomatoes
30ml/2 tbsp lemon juice
600ml/1 pint/2½ cups pork or
  chicken stock
115g/4oz/1 cup cooked chick-peas
30ml/2 tbsp dry sherry
25g/1oz/3 tbsp raisins
175g/6oz/1½ cups couscous
50g/2oz/¼ cup butter, melted
45ml/3 tbsp chopped fresh parsley
salt and ground black pepper

1 Put the flour into a plastic bag and season with salt and pepper. Add the pork and toss to coat. Heat the oil in a flameproof casserole and fry the onion until soft. Add the pork and cook, stirring occasionally, until golden.

2 Stir in the garlic, tomato purée, tomatoes, lemon juice and stock. Season with salt and pepper. Bring to the boil, lower the heat, cover and simmer for 45 minutes.

3 Stir in the chick-peas, sherry and raisins. Cook for 15 minutes more.

4 Line a steamer with scalded muslin and sprinkle in the couscous. Put the steamer over the stew, cover and cook for 30 minutes. Tip the cooked couscous into a bowl, stir in the melted butter and parsley and fluff up with a fork. Serve with the stew.

COOK'S TIP

Moistened couscous can be heated
in a pan or put into a covered
ovenproof dish and baked for
20 minutes. Flavour with herbs,
nuts or chopped dried fruits,
such as apricots.

GRILLED LAMB ESPAGNOLE *with* SHERRY

Espagnole is a traditional brown sauce, rich in flavour. Given the name, sherry is an obvious addition.

SERVES 4

2 large carrots, chopped
2 parsnips, chopped
50g/2oz/¼ cup butter
15ml/1 tbsp chopped fresh parsley
8 lamb cutlets
30ml/2 tbsp sunflower oil
1 large onion, sliced into rings
salt and ground black pepper
parsley sprigs, to garnish
FOR THE SAUCE
50g/2oz/¼ cup butter
1 small onion, chopped
2 rindless streaky bacon
  rashers, chopped
1 celery stick, sliced
1 small carrot, sliced
50g/2oz/½ cup plain flour
600ml/1 pint/2½ cups beef stock
30ml/2 tbsp tomato purée
1 bouquet garni
60ml/4 tbsp dry sherry

1 Make the sauce. Melt the butter in a saucepan and fry the onion and bacon over a medium heat for 5 minutes. Add the celery and carrot and cook for about 10 minutes until browned.

COOK'S TIP
This sauce freezes very well.

2 Stir in the flour. When it starts to brown, stir in the stock and tomato purée. Add the bouquet garni. Bring to the boil, lower the heat and simmer for 25 minutes. Press through a sieve into a bowl. Stir in the sherry, with salt and pepper to taste. Keep warm.

3 Cook the carrots and parsnips in a saucepan of boiling salted water until tender. Drain, mash, stir in the butter and parsley and season to taste. Keep warm.

4 Brush the lamb cutlets lightly with a little of the oil and season with pepper. Cook under a hot grill for 2–3 minutes on each side.

5 Meanwhile, heat the remaining oil and fry the onion rings until very crisp and golden. Spoon a portion of mashed carrots and parsnips on to each plate, place two cutlets on top and add some crisp onion rings. Pour over some of the sauce and garnish with parsley sprigs.

NOISETTES OF LAMB *with* TARRAGON *and* ARMAGNAC

A generous splash of armagnac brings out the best in this simple meat dish.

SERVES 4

15ml/1 tbsp vegetable oil
25g/1oz/2 tbsp butter
12 noisettes of lamb
45ml/3 tbsp armagnac
45ml/3 tbsp dry white wine
300ml/¹/₂ pint/1¹/₄ cups lamb stock
10ml/2 tsp chopped fresh
 tarragon
salt and ground black pepper
tarragon sprigs, to garnish

VARIATION
Untie the noisettes before cooking, stuff with chopped fresh herbs, smoked oysters or olive paste, then retie.

1 Heat the oil and half the butter in a frying pan. Season the noisettes of lamb with salt and pepper and fry over a high heat until cooked, and browned on both sides. Remove the noisettes from the pan and keep warm.

2 Remove the pan from the heat, pour off the excess oil, add the armagnac and flambé (optional). Add the white wine and heat until reduced by three-quarters of its original volume.

3 Stir in the lamb stock and chopped tarragon. Bring to the boil and simmer for 3–4 minutes. Stir in the remaining butter and season if necessary. Serve the noisettes with the sauce and garnish with tarragon sprigs.

PAUPIETTES *of* VEAL *with* ARMAGNAC

Ham-stuffed veal parcels are partnered with a mouth-watering armagnac sauce.

SERVES 6

6 veal escalopes, flattened
50g/2oz/4 tbsp butter
225g/8oz small onions, peeled
225g/8oz button mushrooms
10ml/2 tsp tomato purée
3 large tomatoes, quartered,
  and seeded
45ml/3 tbsp armagnac
150ml/¹/₄ pint/²/₃ cup dry
  white wine
400ml/14fl oz/1²/₃ cups veal stock
2 garlic cloves, crushed
1 bouquet garni
salt and ground black pepper
FOR THE STUFFING
15ml/1 tbsp butter
1 shallot, finely chopped
115g/4oz/1¹/₂ cups mushrooms,
  finely chopped
45ml/3 tbsp armagnac
30ml/2 tbsp crème fraîche
115g/4oz/²/₃ cup finely chopped
  cooked ham
175g/6oz sausagemeat

1 To make the stuffing, melt the butter in a pan, add the shallot and mushrooms and cook for 4–5 minutes. Pour in the armagnac and simmer for 3–4 minutes. Stir in the crème fraîche, bring to the boil, then remove the pan from the heat and leave to cool. When cold, add the ham and sausagemeat and season with salt and pepper.

2 Lay the veal escalopes out on a clean surface and top with some of the stuffing. Fold and roll the escalopes over the filling to give a rectangular shape and tie with string or strong thread.

3 In a pan, melt the butter and brown the paupiettes on all sides, then remove and keep warm. Add the small onions to the pan and brown, stir in the mushrooms and cook for a further 2–3 minutes.

4 Stir in the tomato purée and the tomato quarters, pour in the armagnac and flambé (optional). Add the white wine, stock, garlic cloves, bouquet garni and veal paupiettes. Bring to the boil, cover and simmer for 45 minutes.

5 Remove the paupiettes, untie them and keep warm. Strain the liquid into a clean pan and, if necessary, boil to reduce, then season to taste. Serve the paupiettes of veal with the sauce.

VARIATION
Turkey or large chicken escalopes could be substituted successfully for the veal.

VEAL ESCALOPES *en* PAPILLOTE *with* KUMMEL

Delicate herb-and-mushroom-topped veal slices are enhanced with caraway-flavoured kümmel.

SERVES 4

15ml/1 tbsp butter
4 veal escalopes, flattened
15ml/1 tbsp kümmel
salt and ground black pepper
cooked asparagus, to serve
FOR THE STUFFING
25g/1oz/2 tbsp butter
1 shallot, finely chopped
225g/8oz/3 cups mushrooms,
  chopped
15ml/1 tbsp mixed herbs, chopped
15ml/1 tbsp crème fraîche
1.5ml/¼ tsp caraway seeds

1 To make the stuffing, heat the butter in a frying pan, add the shallot and cook for 5 minutes. Stir in the chopped mushrooms and herbs, season to taste with salt and pepper and cook for a further 5 minutes or until all the juices have evaporated.

2 Stir in the crème fraîche and caraway seeds and leave to cool.

COOK'S TIP

To flatten the escalopes, place between sheets of non-stick baking paper and beat gently with the end of a wooden rolling pin.

3 Preheat the oven to 220°C/425°F/ Gas 7 and cut four pieces of non-stick baking paper the size of a dinner plate. Melt the butter and fry the veal escalopes until browned, then remove the pan from the heat.

4 Place a veal escalope on each piece of non-stick baking paper, cover with some of the stuffing and add a splash of kümmel.

5 Fold the baking paper over the filling and seal the edges to form a parcel. Lift them on to a baking sheet and bake 10–15 minutes. Serve immediately with lightly cooked asparagus.

WHISKY CHICKEN *with* ONION MARMALADE

A whisky, honey and sesame seed paste enhances the flavour of chicken.

SERVES 4

25g/1oz/4 tbsp sesame seeds,
* crushed*
2 garlic cloves, crushed
pinch of paprika
30ml/2 tbsp oil
30ml/2 tbsp whisky
30ml/2 tbsp clear honey
4 chicken portions
salt and ground black pepper
FOR THE MARMALADE
30ml/2 tbsp oil
2 large onions, finely sliced
1 green pepper, seeded and sliced
150ml/¹/₄ pint/ ²/₃ cup vegetable
* stock*

1 Preheat the oven to 190°C/375°F/
Gas 5. In a small bowl, make a paste
with the sesame seeds, garlic, paprika,
oil, whisky and honey. Season with salt
and pepper. Add a little water if the
paste is too thick.

2 Make several cuts in the chicken
portions and arrange them in an ovenproof dish. Spread the paste over. Roast
for 40 minutes or until cooked.

3 Meanwhile, make the marmalade.
Heat the oil in a frying pan and fry the
onion slices over a medium-high heat
for 15 minutes. Add the green pepper
and fry for 5 minutes more. Stir in the
stock, season with salt and pepper and
cook gently, stirring occasionally, for
about 20 minutes. Serve warm with the
cooked chicken.

VARIATION
Instead of making cuts in the
chicken portions ease the skin away
from the flesh and push the paste
underneath. This keeps the flesh
wonderfully moist.

CHICKEN *with* WILD MUSHROOMS *and* VERMOUTH

Tender chicken slices are folded into a rich soured cream sauce spiked with vermouth.

SERVES 4

30ml/2 tbsp oil
1 leek, finely chopped
4 chicken breasts, sliced
225g/8oz/2 cups wild mushrooms,
* sliced if large*
15ml/1 tbsp brandy
pinch of grated nutmeg
1.5ml/¹/₄ tsp chopped fresh thyme
150ml/¹/₄ pint/ ²/₃ cup dry white
* vermouth*
150ml/¹/₄ pint/ ²/₃ cup chicken
* stock*
6 green olives, stoned and
* quartered*
150ml/¹/₄ pint/ ²/₃ cup soured
* cream*
salt and ground black pepper
thyme sprigs and croûtons,
* to garnish*

1 Heat the oil and fry the chopped leek
until softened but not browned. Add the
chicken slices and mushrooms. Fry, stirring occasionally, until just beginning to
brown.

COOK'S TIP
Chinese dried mushrooms work well
in this dish. Soak them for an hour
in cold water before use.

2 Pour over the brandy and ignite.
When the flames have died down, stir
in the nutmeg, thyme, vermouth and
stock, with salt and pepper to taste.

3 Bring to the boil, lower the heat and
simmer for 5 minutes. Stir in the olives
and most of the soured cream. Reheat
gently, but do not let the mixture boil.
Garnish with the remaining soured
cream, the thyme sprigs and croûtons.

VINE-LEAF WRAPPED TURKEY *with* NOILLY PRAT

Pretty vine-leaf parcels conceal a delicious wild rice and pine nut stuffing flavoured with Noilly Prat.

SERVES 4

*115g/4oz drained vine leaves
 in brine
4 turkey escalopes, about
 115–175g/4–6oz each
300ml/¹/₂ pint/1¹/₄ cups chicken
 stock
salt and ground black pepper*
FOR THE STUFFING
*30ml/2 tbsp sunflower oil
3 shallots, chopped
75g/3oz/³/₄ cup cooked wild rice
4 tomatoes, peeled and chopped
45ml/3 tbsp Noilly Prat
25g/1oz/¹/₃ cup pine nuts, chopped*

1 Preheat the oven to 190°C/375°F/
Gas 5. Rinse the vine leaves a few
times in cold water and drain.

2 Make the stuffing. Heat the oil in a
frying pan. Fry the chopped shallots
until soft. Remove the pan from the
heat and stir in the cooked rice,
tomatoes, Noilly Prat and pine nuts.
Season with salt and pepper to taste.

3 Put the escalopes between sheets of
clear film and flatten with a rolling pin.

4 Spread out the meat and top each
escalope with a quarter of the stuffing.
Roll the meat over the filling.

COOK'S TIP

*Use fresh young vine leaves if you are
lucky enough to find them. Trim the
stalks, then plunge them into boiling
salted water for 20–30 seconds until
they have just wilted. Refresh in cold
water and pat dry on kitchen paper.*

5 Overlap a quarter of the vine leaves to
make a rectangle. Centre a turkey roll
on top, roll up neatly and tie with raffia
or string. Repeat with the
remaining leaves and turkey rolls.

6 Pack the rolls snugly in an ovenproof
dish, pour over the stock and bake for
40 minutes. Skim any surface fat from
the stock and serve with the parcels.

DUCK BREASTS *with* CALVADOS

A plum and calvados purée is the perfect accompaniment for glazed duck breasts with chicory.

SERVES 4

15ml/1 tbsp lemon juice
4 heads of chicory
4 duck breasts, about 115–175g/
*   4–6oz each*
15ml/1 tbsp clear honey
5ml/1 tsp sunflower oil
salt and ground black pepper
FOR THE PURÉE
1 cooking apple, peeled, cored
*   and sliced*
175g/6oz plums, halved
*   and stoned*
15ml/1 tbsp soft light
*   brown sugar*
150ml/¼ pint/⅔ cup vegetable
*   stock*
45ml/3 tbsp calvados
10ml/2 tsp sherry vinegar

1 Preheat the oven to 220°C/425°F/
Gas 7. Make the purée. Put the apple,
plums, sugar and stock into a saucepan.
Bring to the boil, lower the heat and
simmer for 10 minutes until the fruit is
very soft. Press the fruit through a
strainer into a bowl.

2 Stir the lemon juice into a saucepan
of lightly salted water and bring to the
boil. Cut the heads of chicory lengthways into quarters and add to the pan.
Cook for 3 minutes, then drain and
set aside.

3 Score the duck breasts, brush with
honey and sprinkle with a little salt.
Transfer to a baking sheet and bake for
6–9 minutes, depending on weight.

COOK'S TIP
Adding lemon juice to the water used
for cooking the chicory helps to
prevent discoloration.

4 Brush the chicory pieces with oil and
place them alongside the duck. Bake for
6 minutes more.

5 Stir the calvados and vinegar into the
purée and season to taste with salt and
pepper. Arrange the chicory pieces on a
platter. Slice the duck breasts and fan
them out on top of the chicory. Spoon
the purée over and serve at once.

WOOD PIGEON *and* CHESTNUT CASSEROLE *with* PORT

Relish the flavours of autumn in this delicious casserole.

SERVES 4

30ml/2 tbsp oil
4 pigeons, halved
1 onion, chopped
6 rindless streaky bacon
  rashers, chopped
25g/1oz/2 tbsp plain flour
400ml/14fl oz/1²/₃ cups game or
  chicken stock
150ml/¹/₄ pint/²/₃ cup orange
  juice
30ml/2 tbsp port
225g/8oz/2 cups shelled chestnuts
25g/1oz/2 tbsp butter
2 oranges, sliced
salt and ground black pepper
watercress sprigs, to garnish

1 Preheat the oven to 180°C/350°F/ Gas 4. Heat the oil in a shallow flame-proof casserole and sauté the pigeons until browned. Using a slotted spoon, transfer them to a bowl.

2 Add the chopped onion and bacon to the pan and sauté until golden. Stir in the flour and cook for 1 minute until it begins to brown. Pour in the stock, orange juice and port, with salt and pepper to taste. Bring to the boil, stirring constantly, then return the pigeons to the casserole. Cover, place in the oven and cook for 30 minutes.

3 Stir in the chestnuts, return the casserole to the oven and cook for 30 minutes more.

COOK'S TIP
To shell fresh chestnuts, make a cross with a sharp knife on each nut. Cook in a hot oven for 15 minutes, until the shells crack, then peel.

4 Just before serving, melt the butter in a frying pan. Fry the orange slices until golden on both sides. Garnish the pigeon casserole with the orange slices and watercress sprigs. Serve at once.

POUSSINS *with* BULGUR WHEAT *and* VERMOUTH

Vermouth is a valuable asset in the kitchen. It appears twice in this recipe, first flavouring the bulgur wheat stuffing and then in the glaze for the poussins.

SERVES 4

50g/2oz/¹/₃ cup bulgur wheat
150ml/¹/₄ pint/²/₃ cup dry white
  vermouth
60ml/4 tbsp olive oil
1 large onion, finely chopped
2 carrots, finely chopped
75g/3oz/1 cup pine nuts, chopped
5ml/1 tsp celery seeds
4 poussins
3 red onions, quartered
4 baby aubergines, halved
4 patty pan squashes
12 baby carrots
45ml/3 tbsp corn syrup
salt and ground black pepper

1 Preheat the oven to 200°C/400°F/ Gas 6. Put the bulgur wheat in a heat-proof bowl, pour over half the vermouth and cover with boiling water. Set aside.

2 Heat half the oil in a large, shallow frying pan. Fry the onion and carrots for 10 minutes, then remove the pan from the heat and stir in the pine nuts, celery seeds and well-drained bulgur wheat.

3 Stuff the poussins with the bulgur wheat mixture. Place them in a roasting tin, brush with oil and sprinkle with salt and pepper. Roast for 45–55 minutes until cooked.

COOK'S TIP

Corn syrup is an American product, available in both light and dark versions. If you are unable to locate it, use golden syrup.

---

4 Meanwhile, spread out the red onions, aubergines, patty pans and baby carrots in a single layer on a baking sheet.

5 Mix the corn syrup with the remaining vermouth and oil in a small bowl. Season with salt and pepper. Brush the corn syrup mixture over the vegetables and roast for 35–45 minutes until golden. Cut each poussin in half and serve with the roasted vegetables.

GAME PIE *with* PORT

A good game pie is one of the triumphs of traditional British cooking, and this is one of the best. Cut the hot water crust to reveal a rich filling, flavoured with port and juniper berries.

SERVES 8–10

450g/1lb/4 cups plain flour
10ml/2 tsp salt
175g/6oz/³⁄₄ cup lard or white vegetable fat
175ml/6fl oz/³⁄₄ cup milk, or milk and water
beaten egg, to glaze
10ml/2 tsp powdered gelatine
30ml/2 tbsp cold water
salt and ground black pepper
mixed salad, to serve
FOR THE FILLING
675g/1¹⁄₂ lb lean boneless game, such as pheasant, grouse, partridge and rabbit, diced
115g/4oz rindless streaky bacon rashers, chopped
115g/4oz minced pork
30ml/2 tbsp port
10ml/2 tsp grated orange rind
2 juniper berries, crushed — GIN !
2.5ml/¹⁄₂ tsp dried sage

1 Preheat the oven to 200°C/400°F/ Gas 6. Grease a 20cm/8in springform cake tin. Sift the flour and salt into a bowl and make a well in the centre.

2 In a saucepan, melt the lard or white vegetable fat in the milk or milk and water. Bring to the boil, pour into the well in the flour, and mix with a wooden spoon until cool enough to handle. Knead until smooth, then wrap in clear film and leave to cool.

3 Mix the game, bacon and pork in a bowl. Add the port, orange rind, juniper berries and sage. Season with plenty of salt and pepper.

4 Roll out two-thirds of the dough and fit it into the tin, taking care not to stretch it. Do not trim the edge.

5 Fill the pastry case with the meat mixture and smooth the surface. Brush the edge of the pastry with beaten egg. Roll the remaining pastry into a round to fit the top of the pie. Make a hole in the middle to allow steam to escape. Fit the lid in place and seal, trim and crimp the edge.

6 Decorate the lid with pastry shapes cut from the trimmings. Brush the lid with beaten egg, add the shapes and brush again.

400°F

7 Bake the pie for 30 minutes, then lower the oven temperature to 180°C/350°F/Gas 4 and bake for 1¹⁄₄ hours, covering the pie with foil if the pastry starts to over-brown. About 20 minutes before the end of the cooking time, remove the sides of the tin. Quickly brush the sides of the pie with beaten egg and return it to the oven.

8 Sprinkle the gelatine over the water in a heatproof bowl. When spongy, stir over simmering water until dissolved. Pour through a funnel into the pie and leave to cool. Serve the pie in generous slices, with mixed salad.

COOK'S TIP
If you are short of time, shortcrust pastry can be used instead of the hot water crust pastry.

RABBIT *with* PUY LENTILS *and* PORT

Port gives this rustic dish from France a wonderfully warm and rich flavour.

SERVES 4

15ml/1 tbsp plain flour
450g/1lb diced boneless rabbit
15ml/1 tbsp olive oil
2 onions, sliced
1 garlic clove, crushed
225g/8oz/2 cups mushrooms,
  sliced
45ml/3 tbsp port
400ml/14fl oz/1²⁄₃ cups chicken or
  vegetable stock
5ml/1 tsp red wine vinegar
30ml/2 tbsp chopped fresh
  parsley, plus extra to garnish
15ml/1 tbsp tomato purée
175g/6oz/³⁄₄ cup puy lentils
12 slices French bread
30ml/2 tbsp olive purée
15g/¹⁄₂ oz/1 tbsp butter
salt and ground black pepper

1 Preheat the oven to 180°C/350°F/
Gas 4. Put the flour into a plastic bag,
season with salt and pepper and add
the rabbit. Shake until all the pieces
are evenly coated.

2 Heat the oil in a flameproof casserole
and fry the rabbit until browned.

3 Stir in the sliced onions, garlic and
mushrooms. Add the port, stock,
vinegar, parsley and tomato purée. Stir
well, then bring the mixture to the boil.

4 Cover the casserole with a lid,
transfer it to the oven and cook for
40 minutes. Meanwhile, bring a
saucepan of lightly salted water to the
boil. Add the lentils and cook for
35 minutes until tender.

5 Spread the French bread with the olive
purée. Drain the lentils, stir them into
the casserole and put the bread on top,
with the topping uppermost. Dot with
butter. Return the casserole to the oven
and cook, uncovered, for 10 minutes.
Serve garnished with chopped parsley.

COOK'S TIP
*The lentils do not need to be soaked
before use, but should be picked over
so that any grit can be removed.*

VENISON STEAKS *with* DRAMBUIE *and* CELERIAC

There's a taste of the Highlands in this stylish dish, which is quick and simple to make.

SERVES 4

4 venison steaks,
  115–175g/4–6oz each
1 small celeriac, thinly sliced
oil, for deep-fat frying
25g/1oz/2 tbsp plain flour
300ml/½ pint/1¼ cups game or
  chicken stock
salt and ground black pepper
FOR THE MARINADE
45ml/3 tbsp Drambuie
45ml/3 tbsp oil
30ml/2 tbsp apple juice
1 bay leaf
2 fresh thyme sprigs, plus extra
  thyme sprigs to garnish
2 juniper berries, crushed

1 Make the marinade by mixing the Drambuie, oil, apple juice, bay leaf, thyme sprigs and juniper berries in a large bowl. Stir in salt and pepper to taste. Add the venison steaks, turning to coat them in the mixture. Cover and chill for 3 hours or overnight.

2 Fry the celeriac slices in hot oil until crisp. Remove with a slotted spoon and drain on kitchen paper.

3 Lift the steaks out of the marinade and dry them with kitchen paper. Carefully pour off most of the oil from the frying pan, leaving just enough to shallow fry the steaks. Add them to the pan and fry for 4 minutes on each side. Transfer the cooked steaks to a platter and keep them hot.

4 Strain the marinade into a jug and blend with the flour to a smooth paste. Stir into the pan with the stock and season with salt and pepper. Bring to the boil, stirring constantly, and cook for 2 minutes. Pour the sauce over the venison steaks, garnish with thyme and serve with the celeriac crisps.

COOK'S TIP
Farmed venison steaks are young, so can be cooked very quickly. Wild venison can be considerably older and should be simmered in the marinade for 45 minutes.

PHEASANT *with* JUNIPER *and* PORT

*A warming winter casserole, flavoured with juniper and thyme, that brings together
the rich tastes of game and port.*

SERVES 4

2 pheasants
8 rindless smoked bacon rashers
30ml/2 tbsp sunflower oil
2 celery sticks, sliced
12 pickling onions
3 carrots, sliced
8 bay leaves
8 fresh thyme sprigs
2.5ml/½ tsp juniper berries
60ml/4 tbsp port
600ml/1 pint/2½ cups game stock
15ml/1 tbsp cornflour mixed to a
  paste with water
30ml/2 tbsp redcurrant jelly
salt and ground black pepper

2 Heat the oil in a shallow flameproof
casserole and fry the pheasant portions
until browned. Lift out with tongs on to
a plate. Add the celery, onions and
carrots to the casserole, with more oil if
needed, and cook for 5–7 minutes until
golden, stirring occasionally.

4 Add the juniper berries to the
casserole, pour the port and stock over
and season the pheasant portions to
taste with salt and pepper.

1 Preheat the oven to 190°C/375°F/
Gas 5. Cut each pheasant into four
pieces. Wrap each portion in a rasher of
smoked bacon and tie on neatly with
strong thread.

3 Push a bay leaf and a sprig of thyme
under the thread on each pheasant
portion and arrange them on top of the
vegetables.

5 Cover the casserole and place in the
oven. Cook for 1 hour, then remove the
casserole from the oven and stir in the
cornflour paste and redcurrant jelly.
Return the covered casserole to the
oven and cook for about 15 minutes
more or until the pheasant is tender and
the sauce has thickened slightly. Serve
from the casserole.

COOK'S TIP

*Pheasant is a very lean meat, so
wrapping it with strips of bacon before
cooking helps to keep it moist and
prevents it from drying out.*

VEGETABLES AND VEGETARIAN DISHES

Crisp and refreshing or full-flavoured and satisfying, vegetable dishes are never, or certainly never should be, dull. Serve these dishes as an accompaniment or in a larger portion as a main course. Calvados gives some French finesse to spiced cabbage, and Pernod adds a delicate aniseed flavour to a tomato and dill sauce for spring vegetables.

CARAMELIZED ONIONS *with* MADEIRA SAUCE

Like other fortified wines, Madeira gives a smooth rich flavour to sauces, and is particularly good with onions.

SERVES 4

450g/1lb button onions, peeled
150ml/¹/4 pint/²/3 cup chicken stock
30ml/2 tbsp soft light
  brown sugar
50g/2oz/¹/4 cup butter
salt and ground black pepper
fresh herb leaves, to garnish
FOR THE SAUCE
15g/¹/2oz/1 tbsp butter
15ml/1 tbsp plain flour
250ml/8fl oz/1 cup vegetable or
  chicken stock
30ml/2 tbsp Madeira
30ml/2 tbsp single cream

1 Place the onions in a single layer in a large pan. Pour over the stock – it should just cover. Bring to the boil, lower the heat and simmer for 15 minutes until the onions are just tender, adding extra stock or water if necessary. Remove the pan from the heat and add the sugar and butter. Mix well, season with salt and pepper, then return the pan to the heat and cook until the onions are a rich golden colour.

2 Meanwhile, make the sauce. Melt the butter in a saucepan, stir in the flour and cook for 2 minutes. Gradually add the stock, stirring until the sauce boils and thickens.

3 Add the Madeira and simmer for 5 minutes. Stir in the cream and reheat gently. Add salt and pepper to taste. Serve the onions with the sauce, garnished with fresh herb leaves.

ASPARAGUS *with* VERMOUTH SAUCE

Coating grilled young asparagus spears with a vermouth and parsley sauce creates a sensational side dish or starter.

SERVES 4

20 asparagus spears
5ml/1 tsp olive oil
50g/2oz/²/3 cup grated Parmesan
  cheese
salt and ground black pepper
FOR THE SAUCE
45ml/3 tbsp dry white vermouth
250ml/8fl oz/1 cup jellied
  chicken stock
15ml/1 tbsp chopped fresh parsley
25g/1oz/2 tbsp chilled butter,
  cubed

1 Brush the asparagus spears with olive oil and season to taste with salt and pepper. Place on a grill rack, sprinkle with the Parmesan and grill slowly until the asparagus is cooked.

2 Meanwhile, pour the vermouth and stock into a saucepan. Boil over a high heat until reduced by half. Stir in the parsley and season with salt and pepper.

3 Lower the heat and stir in the chilled butter cubes, two at a time. Continue to stir over a gentle heat until all the butter has melted and the sauce has thickened. Arrange the asparagus spears in a serving dish, pour the sauce over and serve at once.

COOK'S TIP

A Noilly Prat or dry sherry sauce is also good with asparagus.

PEPPER *and* COURGETTE RISOTTO *with* VERMOUTH

All it takes is time and patience to create this superb risotto, flavoured with vermouth and Parmesan.

SERVES 4

30ml/2 tbsp olive oil
1 onion, chopped
2 garlic cloves, crushed
1 litre/1³/4 pints/4 cups chicken or
  vegetable stock
250g/9oz risotto rice (arborio)
2 courgettes, chopped
1 green pepper, seeded and
  chopped
50g/2oz/¹/4 cup grated Parmesan
  cheese
30ml/2 tbsp dry white vermouth
salt and ground black pepper
Parmesan shavings, to serve

1 Heat the oil in a large frying pan. Fry the onion until soft, then add the garlic and cook for 1 minute more.

2 Pour the stock into a saucepan. Bring it to the boil over a high heat, then lower the heat slightly until the stock is barely simmering.

3 Stir the rice into the onion mixture. Add salt and pepper to taste and cook for 2 minutes. Ladle in about 150ml/ ¹/4 pint/²/3 cup of the hot stock and stir over a low to medium heat until the rice has absorbed it.

COOK'S TIP

Use a non-stick pan for this dish. Don't try to hurry the process: it is vital that each batch of stock is absorbed before the next is added.

4 Tip the courgettes and pepper into the pan, add the same amount of stock and once again cook until it has been absorbed. Stir frequently. Repeat this process until the rice has absorbed all the stock and the risotto is creamy. The process should take about 20 minutes.

5 Stir in the cheese and vermouth, reheat briefly and serve, topped with Parmesan shavings.

PUFF PASTRY BOXES *filled with* SPRING VEGETABLES *in* PERNOD SAUCE

Pernod is the perfect companion for the tender taste of early vegetables in crisp cases.

SERVES 4

225g/8oz puff pastry, thawed
  if frozen
15ml/1 tbsp grated Parmesan
  cheese
15ml/1 tbsp chopped fresh parsley
beaten egg, to glaze
175g/6oz podded broad beans
115g/4oz baby carrots, scraped
4 baby leeks, cleaned
75g/3oz/generous ¹/₂ cup peas,
  thawed if frozen
50g/2oz mangetouts, trimmed
salt and ground black pepper
fresh dill sprigs, to garnish
FOR THE SAUCE
200g/7oz can chopped tomatoes
25g/1oz/2 tbsp butter
25g/1oz/2 tbsp plain flour
pinch of sugar
45ml/3 tbsp chopped fresh dill
300ml/¹/₂ pint/1¹/₄ cups water
15ml/1 tbsp Pernod

1 Preheat the oven to 220°C/425°F/ Gas 7. Lightly grease a baking sheet. Roll out the pastry very thinly. Sprinkle the cheese and parsley over, fold and roll once more and cut out four 7.5 x 10cm/3¹/₂ x 4in rectangles.

2 Lift the rectangles on to the baking sheet. With a sharp knife, cut an inner rectangle about 1cm/¹/₂in from the edge of the pastry, cutting halfway through. Score criss-cross lines on top of the inner rectangle, brush with egg and bake for 12–15 minutes until golden.

3 Meanwhile, make the sauce. Press the tomatoes through a sieve into a pan, add the remaining ingredients and bring to the boil, stirring all the time. Lower the heat and simmer until required. Season to taste with salt and pepper.

4 Cook the broad beans in a pan of lightly salted boiling water for about 8 minutes. Add the carrots, leeks and peas, cook a further 5 minutes, then add the mangetouts. Cook for 1 minute. Drain all the vegetables very well.

5 Using a knife, remove the notched squares from the pastry boxes. Set them aside to use as lids. Spoon the vegetables into the pastry cases, pour the sauce over, pop the pastry lids on top and serve garnished with dill.

COOK'S TIP
If there is time, chill the pastry shapes for 20 minutes before baking.

MIXED LEAF *and* PARMESAN SALAD *with* SHERRY

Croûtons flavoured with sherry and oil add crunch to this salad.

SERVES 4

4 eggs
2 garlic cloves, crushed
90ml/6 tbsp olive oil
4 slices thick-cut white bread,
  crusts removed
15ml/1 tbsp lemon juice
15ml/1 tbsp dry sherry
90ml/6 tbsp mayonnaise
175g/6oz mixed salad leaves
75g/3oz/³/₄ cup coarsely grated
  Parmesan cheese
salt and ground black pepper

COOK'S TIP

To make a more substantial main meal salad, add some cooked smoked chicken or fish.

---

1 Hard-boil the eggs and remove the shells. When cool, cut them into quarters. Mix the crushed garlic with 45ml/3 tbsp of the olive oil in a bowl.

2 Make the croûtons. Cut the bread into cubes. Quickly toss the bread in the garlic oil, then tip into a hot frying pan. Fry until golden, then drain thoroughly on kitchen paper.

3 Combine the remaining oil, lemon juice, sherry and mayonnaise in a small bowl. Season with salt and pepper and mix well.

4 Place the salad leaves in the bottom of a bowl. Arrange the eggs, croûtons and Parmesan on top, then pour the dressing over. Serve as soon as possible, while the croûtons are still crisp.

ROASTED FENNEL *with* PERNOD *and* WALNUT SALAD

Pernod enhances the aniseed flavour of fennel, and makes an excellent warm salad dressing.

SERVES 4

1.5ml/¹/₄ tsp butter
4 fennel bulbs, trimmed
60ml/4 tbsp Pernod
30ml/2 tbsp olive oil
10ml/2 tsp soft light brown sugar
salt and ground black pepper
FOR THE SALAD
30ml/2 tbsp olive oil
50g/2oz/¹/₂ cup walnut halves,
  broken
2.5ml/¹/₂ tsp mustard seeds
15ml/1 tbsp Pernod
3 handfuls of salad leaves
1 bunch radishes, with small
  leaves left on

VARIATION

This recipe is also very good with celery or chicory.

---

1 Preheat the oven to 190°C/375°F/ Gas 5. Use the butter to grease a large, shallow casserole. Cook the fennel bulbs in a saucepan of lightly salted boiling water until tender and drain.

2 Cut each fennel bulb lengthways in quarters. Arrange them in a single layer in the casserole. Pour the Pernod and oil over, sprinkle the sugar over and season with salt and pepper. Cover and bake for about 30 minutes, basting from time to time.

3 To make the salad, warm the oil in a small pan. Remove from the heat and stir in the walnuts and mustard seeds. Return the pan to the heat, cover and heat until the mustard seeds start to pop. Mix in the Pernod.

4 Arrange the salad leaves and radishes (some whole, some sliced) on a platter. Pour the warm dressing over. Top with the roasted fennel and serve at once.

DRUNKEN MUSHROOMS *with* BRANDY

Mixed mushrooms in a creamy brandy sauce, served on a bed of open-cap mushrooms, makes a delicious treat.

SERVES 4

300ml/¹/₂ pint/1¹/₄ cups double cream
1 garlic clove, crushed
30ml/2 tbsp mustard seeds
15ml/1 tbsp drained green peppercorns in brine
5ml/1 tsp Worcestershire sauce
450g/1lb/6 cups mixed mushrooms, such as button, oyster, chanterelle, shiitake or brown cap, sliced or halved if large
30ml/2 tbsp coarse-grain mustard
30ml/2 tbsp brandy
15ml/1 tbsp olive oil
12 small open-cap mushrooms
salt and ground black pepper
flat leaf parsley, to garnish

1 Combine the cream, crushed garlic, mustard seeds, green peppercorns and Worcestershire sauce in a saucepan. Bring to the boil.

2 Stir in the mixed mushrooms. Cook for 10 minutes, or until the mushrooms are tender and the sauce has thickened.

COOK'S TIP
Use whisky, gin or vermouth instead of the brandy in the sauce.

3 Stir the mustard and brandy into the sauce. Season to taste. Keep warm over a very low heat.

4 Brush the open-cap mushrooms with oil, then cook in a hot frying pan, turning once, until browned. Divide among four plates and spoon the creamy mushrooms and their sauce on top. Garnish with flat leaf parsley and serve.

SWEET POTATOES *with* SHERRY *and* CITRUS TOMATO SALSA

*Treat vegetarian guests to a dish that's as delicious as it is different. Sweet potatoes in a spicy
sherry dressing are served with a fresh-tasting citrus salsa.*

SERVES 4

500g/1¼lb sweet potatoes, diced
45ml/3 tbsp olive oil
5ml/1 tsp mustard seeds
5ml/1 tsp cumin seeds
1.5ml/¼ tsp fennel seeds
30ml/2 tbsp dry sherry
4 small radicchio leaves
salt and ground black pepper
fresh basil sprigs, to garnish
FOR THE SALSA
2 oranges
1–2 tomatoes
1 spring onion
handful of fresh basil leaves
30ml/2 tbsp olive oil
pinch of sugar

1 Cook the sweet potatoes in a
saucepan of lightly salted boiling water
for 6 minutes. Drain and set aside.

2 Heat the olive oil in a large frying
pan. Add the mustard, cumin and fennel
seeds and cook for 3–4 seconds until
they pop. Stir in the sherry.

3 Add the sweet potatoes, turning to
coat them thoroughly, then fry for
10–15 minutes, stirring frequently.
Season to taste with salt and pepper.

4 To make the salsa, peel the oranges
with a sharp knife, then segment and
chop them. Peel, seed and chop the
tomatoes, and slice the spring onion.
Shred the basil leaves.

5 Mix the salsa ingredients in a bowl,
season with salt and pepper, spoon on
to the radicchio leaves and serve with
the potatoes. Garnish with basil.

COOK'S TIP

*If you prefer, boil the sweet potatoes
with the skins on, then peel and dice.*

VEGETABLE ROSTI *with* WHISKY

Based on Swiss potato rösti, but with extra vegetables and a cheese and mushroom filling,
this has a hint of whisky.

SERVES 4

3 medium carrots, grated
1 celeriac (about 275g/10oz),
  grated
1 large potato, grated
2 medium parsnips, grated
45ml/3 tbsp chopped fresh parsley
115g/4oz/1½ cups mushrooms,
  chopped
50g/2oz/½ cup grated Cheddar
  cheese
30ml/2 tbsp whisky
50g/2oz/¼ cup butter
30ml/2 tbsp olive oil
salt and ground black pepper
flat leaf parsley and cherry
  tomatoes, to garnish

1 Mix the grated vegetables with the chopped parsley in a large bowl. Season with salt and pepper. In another bowl, combine the mushrooms, grated cheese and whisky.

2 Heat the butter and most of the oil in a large non-stick frying pan that can safely be used under the grill. Add half the grated vegetables and press down in an even layer. Cover with the cheese mixture and top with the remaining grated vegetables. Press down firmly.

3 Cook over a high heat for 5 minutes, then cover, lower the heat and cook for about 10 minutes more or until the vegetables are soft. Brush the top with the remaining oil and cook under a hot grill until golden. Serve in generous wedges, garnished with the parsley and cherry tomatoes.

COOK'S TIPS
Instead of cooking the rösti on top of the stove, press the mixture into an ovenproof dish and cook in a hot oven for 40 minutes. If you like, make individual rösti to serve with roast meats or fish.

SESAME SEED TOFU *with* AUBERGINES *and* BRANDY

Tofu is a marvellous ingredient. With little taste of its own, it readily absorbs other flavours.
Marinated and fried, it makes a fine topping for aubergines.

SERVES 4

1.5ml/¼tsp Chinese five-spice
  powder
1 garlic clove, crushed
30ml/2 tbsp sesame seeds
10ml/2 tsp soy sauce
350g/12oz firm tofu, cut into
  large cubes
2 aubergines, halved lengthways
oil, for shallow frying
1 carrot, cut into julienne strips
2 spring onions, sliced
30ml/2 tbsp brandy
salt and ground black pepper
chopped fresh coriander,
  to garnish   Cilantro

1 Combine the five-spice powder, garlic, sesame seeds and soy sauce in a bowl. Add the cubed tofu. Stir until thoroughly coated, then cover and chill for 2 hours.

2 Brush the aubergines with a little oil and cook under a hot grill until cooked and golden.

3 Meanwhile, heat the oil in a frying pan and cook the tofu until crisp and golden. Transfer to a plate. Add more oil to the pan if necessary and stir-fry the carrot strips and spring onions for 2 minutes.

4 Add the brandy and seasoning, bring to the boil and return the tofu cubes to the pan. Toss until heated through. Place half a grilled aubergine on each plate and pile the tofu mixture on top. Garnish with coriander and serve.   Cilantro

VEGETABLE TERRINE *with* BRANDY

A feast for the eye and the palate – that's this luscious layer of brandy-flavoured custard and colourful vegetables.

SERVES 4

1 red pepper, seeded and
  quartered
1 green pepper, seeded and
  quartered
75g/3oz/generous ½ cup fresh or
  frozen peas
6 fresh green asparagus spears
2 carrots, cut into batons
150ml/¼ pint/⅔ cup milk
150ml/¼ pint/⅔ cup double cream
6 eggs, beaten
15ml/1 tbsp brandy
175g/6oz/¾ cup curd cheese
15ml/1 tbsp chopped fresh parsley
salt and ground black pepper
salad leaves, cucumber slices and
  halved tomatoes, to serve

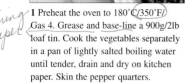

1 Preheat the oven to 180°C/350°F/
Gas 4. Grease and base-line a 900g/2lb
loaf tin. Cook the vegetables separately
in a pan of lightly salted boiling water
until tender, drain and dry on kitchen
paper. Skin the pepper quarters.

lining paper

2 In a bowl, combine the milk, cream,
eggs, brandy, curd cheese and parsley.
Mix well and season.

3 Arrange some of the vegetables in the
bottom of the loaf tin, trimming them to
fit if necessary. Spoon some of the
cheese mixture over. Continue layering
the vegetables and the cheese mixture,
ending with a layer of peppers.

COOK'S TIP

*This is a very soft mixture, so it must
be cold before you try to turn it out.
It also makes a good filling for
a deep pastry case.*

4 Cover the tin with foil and stand it in
a roasting tin. Pour in boiling water to
come halfway up the sides of the tin.

5 Bake for 45 minutes or until the
custard is just firm. Leave the terrine in
the tin until cold, then remove it from
the roasting tin and invert on to a plate.
Lift off the lining paper and cut the
terrine into neat slices. Serve with the
salad leaves, cucumber slices and
halved tomatoes.

POLENTA TRIANGLES *with* SPICED RED CABBAGE

Smooth and dry, calvados is widely used in French cookery, especially in its native Normandy.
It is particularly good with apples and red cabbage.

SERVES 4

25g/1oz/2 tbsp butter
15ml/1 tbsp olive oil
1 onion, sliced
1 garlic clove, crushed
1 red cabbage, shredded (about
  450g/1lb/5 cups)
250ml/8fl oz/1 cup vegetable or
  chicken stock
45ml/3 tbsp red wine vinegar
45ml/3 tbsp clear honey
15ml/1 tbsp lemon juice
pinch of ground cloves
2 cooking apples
30ml/2 tbsp calvados
salt and ground black pepper
flat leaf parsley, to garnish
FOR THE POLENTA
475ml/16fl oz/2 cups water
5ml/1 tsp salt
175g/6oz/1 cup polenta
50g/2oz/¼ cup butter, diced
30ml/2 tbsp grated Parmesan
  cheese
45ml/3 tbsp chopped fresh herbs
olive oil, for brushing
25g/1oz/¼ cup pine nuts, crushed

1 Start by making the polenta. Bring the water to the boil in a large pan. Add the salt, pour in the polenta and cook for about 8 minutes, stirring constantly with a wooden spoon, until the mixture resembles thick porridge. Do not let it stick to the bottom of the pan.

COOK'S TIPS
Alternatively, you can brush the polenta with oil and grill or barbecue it, turning once.
Spiced red cabbage tastes better the next day, when the flavours have had a chance to develop further.

2 Remove the polenta from the heat and stir in the butter, Parmesan cheese and herbs. Spread the polenta about 1cm/½in thick on a flat plate, cover with foil or clear film and chill.

3 Preheat the oven to 190°C/375°F/ Gas 5. Heat the butter and olive oil in a large frying pan. Fry the onion until golden, then add all the remaining ingredients, except the apples and calvados. Bring to the boil, lower the heat, cover and simmer for 40 minutes. Stir the mixture occasionally and add a little water if it becomes too dry.

4 Peel, core and chop the apples. Stir them into the red cabbage mixture, then pour over the calvados and add salt and pepper to taste. Simmer for 15 minutes.

5 Grease a baking sheet. Cut the polenta into triangles and arrange on the baking sheet. Brush with oil, sprinkle over the nuts and bake for 15–20 minutes until golden brown. Arrange around the rim of a heated serving platter and pile the red cabbage in the centre. Garnish with the flat leaf parsley and serve.

DESSERTS, ICES AND CANDIES

Light and elegant or rich and smooth, desserts, ices and candies are the crowning glory of any meal. Try maraschino crème brûlée with its rich cherry liqueur soaked fruits covered with a rosewater-flavoured cream, delight in luscious hot Grand Marnier soufflés with bitter orange iced centres or choose tempting mocha truffles flavoured with Café Noir.

CREPES SUZETTE *with* COINTREAU *and* COGNAC

Thin pancakes filled with Cointreau-flavoured butter and flambéed with cognac may be a classic, but they remain as popular as ever.

SERVES 6

115g/4oz/1 cup plain flour
2.5ml/¹/₂ tsp salt
2 eggs, beaten
300ml/¹/₂ pint/1¹/₄ cups milk
oil, for frying
juice of 2 oranges
45ml/3 tbsp cognac
icing sugar, for dusting
strips of thinly pared orange
  rind, to decorate
FOR THE ORANGE BUTTER
175g/6oz/³/₄ cup unsalted butter
50g/2oz/¹/₄ cup granulated sugar
grated rind of 2 oranges
30ml/2 tbsp Cointreau

1 Start by making the orange butter. Cream the butter with the sugar in a bowl. Stir in the orange rind and Cointreau. Set aside while you make the pancake batter.

2 Make the pancakes. Sift the flour and salt into a bowl, make a well in the centre and add the eggs. Mix thoroughly. Gradually stir in the milk and beat to a smooth batter. Pour into a jug. Heat the oil in a pan, pour in a little batter and make a thin 15cm/6in pancake. Cook until the underside is golden, turn over and cook the other side. Slide out of the pan. Make at least five more pancakes with the remaining batter.

3 Spread the pancakes with half the orange butter and fold into quarters.

COOK'S TIP

Not traditional, but equally delicious, is to use rum in place of the Cointreau and cognac, and add sliced fresh pineapple and a little toasted coconut.

4 Heat the rest of the orange butter in a frying pan with the orange juice, add the folded pancakes and turn them to heat them through. Push the pancakes to one side of the pan and pour in the cognac. Heat, then carefully set alight. When the flames die down, spoon the sauce over the pancakes. Serve immediately, dusted with icing sugar and decorated with strips of orange rind.

HOT SOUFFLES *with* GRAND MARNIER ICE

Grand Marnier contributes the flavours of cognac and bitter oranges to these hot fluffy soufflés with their surprising iced centres.

SERVES 6

40g/1½oz/3 tbsp butter
40g/1½oz/3 tbsp plain flour
250ml/8fl oz/1 cup milk
40g/1½oz/3 tbsp caster sugar
30ml/2 tbsp Grand Marnier
5 eggs, separated
icing sugar, for dusting
FOR THE ICE CREAM
150ml/¼ pint/⅔ cup double cream
30ml/2 tbsp Grand Marnier
30ml/2 tbsp orange juice
10ml/2 tsp icing sugar

1 Make the ice cream. Mix the cream, Grand Marnier, orange juice and icing sugar in a small bowl. Spoon into a freezer container and freeze for 30 minutes, or until ice crystals begin to form round the edge. Stir well. Freeze until firm.

2 Using two spoons form the frozen Grand Marnier ice into six small ovals. Place on a plate and freeze until solid.

3 Preheat the oven to 200°C/400°F/ Gas 6. Lightly grease six individual soufflé dishes. Put the butter, flour and milk into a large pan. Bring to the boil, stirring constantly. Cook for 2 minutes, then remove from the heat. Cool slightly and beat in the sugar, Grand Marnier and egg yolks.

COOK'S TIP
The bowl and whisk used for whisking egg whites must be grease-free.

4 Whisk the egg whites in a large bowl until stiff. Using a metal spoon, fold them into the sauce mixture.

5 Spoon the mixture into the soufflé dishes, stand the dishes on a baking sheet and bake for 25–35 minutes until the soufflés are risen and browned. Very quickly dust with icing sugar, make a hole in the top of each soufflé and add a spoonful of Grand Marnier ice cream. Serve at once.

ZABAGLIONE

This gloriously creamy, classic Italian dessert is made with Marsala, a Sicilian fortified wine.

SERVES 4

2 sponge fingers, crumbled
90ml/6 tbsp Marsala
6 fresh apricots, stoned and
 sliced
5 egg yolks
50g/2oz/¼ cup caster sugar

VARIATION
Madeira can be used instead of Marsala, and crumbled ratafias instead of sponge fingers.

1 Divide the crumbled sponge fingers among four heatproof dessert glasses. Sprinkle over 15ml/1 tbsp of the Marsala. Set aside eight of the apricot slices for decoration and divide the rest among the glasses.

2 Put the egg yolks in a heatproof bowl. Whisk them lightly, then whisk in the sugar and remaining Marsala.

3 Put the bowl over a saucepan of barely simmering water and continue to whisk until the mixture is very thick and creamy. When you lift the whisk out of the bowl, the trail should lie on top of the mixture for 2–3 seconds.

4 Pour the zabaglione into the glasses and decorate with the reserved apricot slices. Serve while still warm.

POACHED MANDARINS *with* SHORTBREAD LEAVES

Whole mandarins macerated in a liqueur-flavoured syrup make a superb sweet, especially when served with melt-in-the-mouth shortbread biscuits.

SERVES 4

225g/8oz/generous 1 cup soft
 light brown sugar
750ml/1¼ pints/3 cups water
12 small mandarin oranges
45ml/3 tbsp Mandarin Napoléon
 liqueur
15ml/1 tbsp lemon juice
whipped double cream, to serve
FOR THE SHORTBREAD
50g/2oz/¼ cup butter, softened
75g/3oz/⅔ cup plain flour, sifted
25g/1oz/2 tbsp caster sugar, plus
 extra for sprinkling
5ml/1 tsp finely grated lemon rind

COOK'S TIP
Store the biscuits in an airtight tin. Add a few grains of rice to prevent them from softening.

---

1 Preheat the oven to 160°C/325°F/ Gas 3. Grease a baking sheet. Make the shortbread. Put the butter, flour, sugar and lemon rind in a large bowl and knead together until smooth and silky.

2 Roll out on a lightly floured surface to a thickness of 5mm/¼in. Cut out leaf shapes by hand or with a biscuit cutter. Lift on to the baking sheet and bake for 15 minutes. Sprinkle with caster sugar and leave to cool on the baking sheet for 5 minutes before removing.

3 Mix the brown sugar and water in a large saucepan. Heat until the sugar has dissolved, bring to the boil and simmer until reduced by half. Lower the heat so that the syrup barely simmers.

4 Peel the mandarins and remove any pith. Stir the liqueur and lemon juice into the syrup, add the mandarins, cover and cook gently for 40 minutes. Leave to cool. Serve with the shortbread leaves, and offer whipped double cream to those who want it.

SHERRY TRIFLE

There are many versions of sherry trifle, ranging from the everyday to the exquisite.
This one falls into the latter category.

SERVES 6–8

75g/3oz ratafia biscuits
90ml/6 tbsp raspberry jam
175ml/6fl oz/³⁄₄ cup sherry
175g/6oz/1 cup fresh raspberries
225g/8oz/2 cups seedless black
 grapes, halved
300ml/¹⁄₂ pint/1¹⁄₄ cups double
 cream, whipped
crystallized fruit and icing sugar,
 to decorate

FOR THE CUSTARD
25g/1oz/¹⁄₄ cup cornflour
600ml/1 pint/2¹⁄₂ cups milk
3 egg yolks
2.5ml/¹⁄₂ tsp vanilla essence
25g/1oz/2 tbsp caster sugar

VARIATION

Vary the fruit filling to make the most
of seasonal availability. Match the
fruit to the jam. If preferred, an
appropriate liqueur can be used
instead of sherry.

1 Make the custard. In a heatproof bowl, blend the cornflour with a little of the milk. Stir in the egg yolks, vanilla essence and sugar. Pour the remaining milk into a saucepan and bring to the boil. Pour the milk on to the cornflour mixture, stirring constantly.

2 Return to the heat and, continuing to stir, bring to the boil again, then lower the heat and simmer for 3 minutes. Remove from the heat, cover the surface with greaseproof paper and leave to cool.

3 Sandwich the ratafia biscuits together with the raspberry jam, then arrange them in a deep glass bowl and sprinkle over the sherry.

4 Spoon over half the custard. Level the surface and arrange the fruit on top. Cover with the remaining custard, ensuring that the layers are visible through the side of the bowl. Swirl or pipe the cream on top of the trifle and decorate with pieces of crystallized fruit. Dust with a little icing sugar just before serving.

GRAPEFRUIT *in* HONEY *and* WHISKY

A colourful fan of grapefruit segments in a sweet whisky sauce.

SERVES 4

1 pink-fleshed grapefruit
1 red-fleshed grapefruit
1 yellow-fleshed grapefruit
50g/2oz/¼ cup granulated sugar
60ml/4 tbsp clear honey
45ml/3 tbsp whisky
mint leaves, to decorate

1 Peel the grapefruits, removing all the pith, then cut them into segments.

2 Put the sugar and 150ml/¼ pint/⅔ cup water into a pan, bring to the boil, stirring, until the sugar has dissolved, then simmer for 10 minutes.

3 Heat the honey in a pan and boil until it becomes a slightly deeper colour or caramelizes. Remove from the heat, add the whisky, flambé (optional) and pour into the sugar syrup.

4 Bring to the boil and pour over the grapefruit segments. Cover and leave until cold. To serve, put the grapefruit segments on to serving plates, alternating the colours, pour over some of the syrup and decorate with mint.

VARIATION
The whisky can be replaced with brandy, Cointreau or Grand Marnier.

FRAMBOISE SABAYON *with* BLUEBERRIES *and* RASPBERRIES

This couldn't be simpler, but tastes superb.

SERVES 4

115g/4oz/1 cup fresh blueberries
175g/6oz/1 cup fresh raspberries
3 egg yolks
60ml/4 tbsp framboise
25g/1oz/2 tbsp caster sugar
extra sugar, for topping

VARIATION
In the winter, when fresh soft fruits are out of season (and expensive), try this with dried apricots macerated in brandy and topped with Greek-style yogurt.

1 Arrange the fresh blueberries and raspberries in wide flameproof soup bowls or on flameproof dessert plates.

2 Mix the egg yolks, framboise and sugar in a large heatproof bowl. Place the bowl over a pan of barely simmering water and whisk until thick and foamy. Preheat the grill.

3 Spoon the sauce over the fruits, sprinkle with a little sugar and flash briefly under the hot grill until the sugar caramelizes and turns golden.

AMARETTO ICE CREAM

Almond-flavoured liqueur gives this ice cream a wonderful depth of flavour.

SERVES 4–6

750ml/1¼ pints/3 cups vanilla ice
cream, softened
30ml/2 tbsp amaretto
15ml/1 tbsp orange juice
1.5ml/¼ tsp vanilla essence
thinly pared orange rind,
to decorate
FOR THE BRANDY SNAP BASKETS
50g/2oz/¼ cup butter
50g/2oz/¼ cup caster sugar
75g/3oz/¼ cup golden syrup
5ml/1 tsp ground ginger
grated rind and juice of 1 lemon
50g/2oz/½ cup plain flour

1 Preheat the oven to 180°C/350°F/ Gas 4. Line 3 baking sheets with non-stick baking paper.

2 Beat the ice cream until soft and creamy, then beat in the amaretto, orange juice and vanilla essence. Return to the tub, or similar container for freezing. Freeze until firm.

3 Put the butter, sugar, syrup and ground ginger into a saucepan. Heat gently, stirring constantly until the butter has melted, then turn off the heat and stir in the lemon rind and juice, then the flour.

4 The mixture hardens quickly, so only bake two biscuits at a time. Put spoonfuls of the mixture on to the baking sheets. Bake for 10-12 minutes until golden. Cool for a few seconds.

5 Lift each biscuit in turn with a palette knife and drape over a small orange or the outside of an upturned cup. Leave to cool and harden, then invert on to plates. Add scoops of amaretto ice cream, decorate with the orange rind.

COFFEE *and* KAHLUA MACADAMIA CREAMS *with* MERINGUE FINGERS

These rich, moulded creams have a wonderfully intense flavour, thanks to coffee liqueur.

SERVES 4–6

10ml/2 tsp powdered gelatine
45ml/3 tbsp water
350ml/12fl oz/1½ cups double cream
150ml/¼ pint/⅔ cup thick natural yogurt
15ml/1 tbsp strong black coffee
25g/1oz/¼ cup icing sugar
15ml/1 tbsp Kahlúa
50g/2oz/½ cup macadamia nuts, toasted and chopped
toasted macadamia nuts and chocolate coffee beans, to decorate
FOR THE MERINGUE FINGERS
1 egg white
50g/2oz/¼ cup caster sugar

1 Preheat the oven to 120°C/250°F/ Gas ½. Cover a baking sheet with non-stick baking paper. Make the meringue fingers. Whisk the egg white in a grease-free bowl until stiff and dry. Whisk in half the sugar until stiff, then fold in the remaining sugar.

2 Pipe or spoon finger shapes of meringue on to the baking sheet. Bake for 2½ hours or until crisp.

3 Meanwhile, make the creams. Sprinkle the gelatine over the water in a small heatproof bowl. When spongy, stir over simmering water until dissolved.

4 Combine the cream, yogurt, coffee, icing sugar and Kahlúa in a bowl. Stir in the dissolved gelatine mixture. Chill until on the point of setting, then stir in the nuts and spoon into small moulds. Chill until firm, unmould and decorate with nuts and chocolate coffee beans. Serve with the meringue fingers.

MARASCHINO CREME BRULEE

Crack the crunchy topping to discover rich cherry liqueur-soaked fruits under a creamy blanket.

SERVES 6

6 eggs, lightly beaten
300ml/½ pint/1¼ cups milk
300ml/½ pint/1¼ cups double cream, lightly whipped
50g/2oz/¼ cup caster sugar
5ml/1 tsp rosewater
50g/2oz/½ cup stoned fresh cherries, halved
50g/2oz/½ cup seedless grapes, halved
15ml/1 tbsp maraschino
75g/3oz/⅓ cup soft light brown sugar
whole fresh cherries, to serve

1 Mix the eggs and milk in a large heat-proof bowl. Place over a saucepan of barely simmering water and heat until the mixture thickens to a light custard.

2 Fold in the cream, sugar and rose-water. Remove the pan from the heat and leave to cool.

3 Divide the fruit among six flameproof dishes. Sprinkle the maraschino liqueur over the fruit and spoon the custard on top. Preheat the grill.

4 Sprinkle the sugar over the custard in an even layer. Stand the dishes under the grill until the sugar caramelizes. Serve hot or cold with whole cherries.

BOURBON BALLS

This American speciality laces biscuit and pecan truffles with bourbon.

MAKES ABOUT 25
175g/6oz Nice biscuits
115g/4oz/1 cup pecan nuts,
  chopped
30ml/2 tbsp cocoa powder
75g/3oz/³⁄₄ cup icing sugar,
  sifted
30ml/2 tbsp clear honey
120ml/4fl oz/¹⁄₂ cup bourbon

COOK'S TIP

Brandy snaps can be used instead of Nice biscuits and cognac or brandy in place of the bourbon.

---

1 Put the biscuits in a plastic bag and crush them finely with a rolling pin. Tip the crumbs into a bowl and add the chopped nuts, cocoa powder and half the icing sugar. Add the honey and bourbon. Stir until the mixture forms a stiff paste. Add a little more bourbon if necessary.

2 Shape the mixture into small balls, place on a plate and chill until firm.

3 Roll the balls in the remaining icing sugar, then chill for 15 minutes and roll again in sugar. Serve on a plate or pack into a presentation box.

MOCHA TRUFFLES *with* CAFE NOIR

The combination of coffee liqueur and chocolate is irresistible.

MAKES ABOUT 25
175g/6oz dark chocolate, broken
  into squares
50g/2oz/¹⁄₄ cup unsalted butter
10ml/2 tsp instant coffee granules
30ml/2 tbsp double cream
225g/8oz/4 cups Madeira cake
  crumbs
50g/2oz/¹⁄₂ cup ground almonds
30ml/2 tbsp Café Noir
cocoa powder, chocolate
  vermicelli or ground almonds,
  to coat

1 Put the chocolate in a heatproof bowl. Add the butter and instant coffee granules. Stand the bowl over a saucepan of hot water and heat gently until the chocolate and butter have melted and the coffee granules have dissolved. (Do not let the water boil, or let the bottom of the bowl touch the water or the chocolate will overheat.)

3 Chill the mixture until firm. Shape into small balls, roll in cocoa powder, chocolate vermicelli or ground almonds and place in foil petit four cases.

VARIATION

Omit the coffee granules and use cherry brandy instead of Café Noir. Hide a maraschino cherry in each truffle.

2 Remove from the heat and stir in the cream, cake crumbs, ground almonds and Café Noir.

COINTREAU CHOCOLATE COLETTES

Small chocolate cases, filled with swirled chocolate and Cointreau cream, make tempting treats.
Serve them with a glass of the liqueur at the end of a special meal.

MAKES 14

115g/4oz dark chocolate, broken
into squares
icing sugar, for dusting
FOR THE FILLING
65g/2½oz dark chocolate
25g/1oz/2 tbsp unsalted butter
30ml/2 tbsp Cointreau
60ml/4 tbsp double cream,
whipped

1 Put the chocolate in a heatproof bowl. Stand the bowl over a saucepan of hot water and heat gently until the chocolate has melted.

2 Brush the insides of 14 petit four cases with a thin coating of melted chocolate and leave to set. Repeat three or four times. When finally set, carefully peel off the paper cases.

3 Make the filling. Melt the chocolate and butter together in a heatproof bowl over a saucepan of hot water.

4 Remove from the heat. When cool (but still liquid), stir in the Cointreau and fold in the whipped double cream.

5 Chill this mixture until firm, then pipe into the chocolate cases. Dust with icing sugar.

COOK'S TIP

When making the chocolate cases,
it is better to build up thin layers
rather than make one thick layer, which
is more likely to break when you peel
away the paper.

MINI FLORENTINES *with* GRAND MARNIER

Orange liqueur adds a luxury note to these ever-popular nut and dried fruit biscuits.

MAKES ABOUT 24

50g/2oz/¹⁄₃ cup soft light
  brown sugar
15ml/1 tbsp clear honey
15ml/1 tbsp Grand Marnier
50g/2oz/4 tbsp butter
40g/1¹⁄₂oz/3 tbsp plain flour
25g/1oz/¹⁄₄ cup hazelnuts, roughly
  chopped
50g/2oz/¹⁄₂ cup flaked almonds,
  chopped
50g/2oz/¹⁄₄ cup glacé cherries,
  chopped
115g/4oz dark chocolate, melted,
  for coating

1 Preheat the oven to 180°C/350°F/
Gas 4. Line 3–4 baking sheets with
non-stick baking paper. Combine the
sugar, honey, Grand Marnier and butter
in a small pan and melt over a low heat.

2 Remove the pan from the heat and tip
in the flour, hazelnuts, almonds and
cherries. Stir well.

3 Spoon small heaps of the mixture on
to the baking sheets. Bake for about
10 minutes until golden brown. Leave
the biscuits on the baking sheets until
the edges begin to harden a little, then
remove and cool on a wire rack.

4 Spread the melted chocolate over one
side of each florentine. When it begins
to set, drag a fork through to give wavy
lines. Leave to set completely.

VARIATION
*For an extra decoration, pour melted
milk, plain or white chocolate into
a paper piping bag, snip off the end
and pipe zigzag lines over the plain
side of each florentine.*

TARTS AND PIES

Crisp, feather-light pastry and a medley of fruits and nuts can be transformed quite wonderfully into exciting and exotic pies and tarts. Coffee-flavoured pastry is the base for a rich, sticky filling of molasses and nuts laced with a dusky Highland measure of Drambuie. You will also find here a mouth-watering meringue pie made with plums and eau de vie de Mirabelle, a fruit brandy made from Mirabelle plums, and a rich, creamy custard tart flavoured with Marsala.

APPLE, RAISIN *and* MAPLE PIES *with* CALVADOS

Calvados accentuates the apple flavour of these individual puff pastry pies.

SERVES 4

350g/12oz puff pastry, thawed
if frozen
beaten egg or milk, to glaze
whipped cream, flavoured with
orange liqueur and sprinkled
with grated orange rind,
to serve
FOR THE FILLING
75g/3oz/¹/₂ cup soft light
brown sugar
30ml/2 tbsp lemon juice
45ml/3 tbsp maple syrup
150ml/¹/₄ pint/²/₃ cup water
45ml/3 tbsp calvados
6 small eating apples
75g/3oz/¹/₂ cup raisins

1 Preheat the oven to 200°C/400°F/ Gas 6. Make the filling. Combine the sugar, lemon juice, maple syrup and water in a saucepan. Heat gently until the sugar has dissolved, then bring to the boil and cook until reduced by half. Stir in the calvados.

2 Halve and core four of the apples and cut them into eighths. Add the apple wedges to the syrup and simmer for 5–8 minutes until just tender. Using a slotted spoon, lift the apple wedges out of the syrup and set them aside.

3 Peel, core and chop the remaining apples. Add them to the syrup with the raisins. Simmer until the mixture is very thick, then leave to cool.

4 Roll out the pastry on a lightly floured surface and stamp out eight 15cm/6in rounds with a fluted cutter. Use half the pastry rounds to line four 10cm/4in flan tins. Spoon in the raisin mixture and level the surface.

5 Arrange the apple wedges on top of the raisin mixture. Brush the edge of each pastry case with egg or milk and cover with a pastry lid. Trim, seal and flute the edges. Cut suitable shapes from pastry trimmings and use to decorate the pies. Brush the tops with beaten egg or milk, then bake for 30–35 minutes. Serve hot, with the flavoured cream.

COOK'S TIP
Flavoured cream is delicious with pies and tarts. Lightly whip double cream, add a spoonful or two of your favourite liqueur and sweeten to taste.

PLUM *and* EAU *de* VIE *de* MIRABELLE MERINGUE PIE

A fruit brandy made from Mirabelle plums intensifies the flavour of fresh fruits.

SERVES 6–8
175g/6oz/1½ cups plain flour
40g/1½oz/3 tbsp block
  margarine, diced
40g/1½oz/3 tbsp white cooking
  fat, diced
3 egg whites
75g/3oz/6 tbsp caster sugar
FOR THE FILLING
350g/12oz plums, stoned
  and sliced
10ml/2 tsp granulated sugar
60ml/4 tbsp orange juice
3 egg yolks, beaten
45ml/3 tbsp eau de vie de
  Mirabelle

1 Make the pastry. Sift the flour into a mixing bowl. Rub in the margarine and white fat until the mixture resembles fine breadcrumbs, then stir in enough cold water to give a soft dough. Wrap in clear film and chill for 30 minutes. Preheat the oven to 190°C/375°F/Gas 5.

2 Roll out the pastry on a lightly floured surface and line an 18cm/7in flan ring. Line the pastry case with foil and fill with baking beans, then bake blind for 12 minutes. Remove the foil and baking beans and bake for about 5 minutes more, until golden.

3 Make the filling. Mix the plums, sugar and orange juice in a saucepan. Bring to the boil, then lower the heat and simmer until the fruit is cooked and the mixture is thick.

4 Set the plum mixture aside. When it is cool, lightly stir in the egg yolks and eau de vie de Mirabelle. Spoon the mixture into the flan case.

VARIATION
This is equally delicious when made with strawberries and framboise or stoned cherries and Kirsch.

5 Whisk the egg whites in a clean grease-free bowl until stiff peaks form. Whisk in half the caster sugar. When the mixture is stiff again, fold in the remaining sugar.

6 Pipe or spread the meringue over the filling and bake for 15–20 minutes until golden.

ORANGE CURD TARTS *with* COINTREAU

These traditional English tarts combine a creamy filling with a hint of Cointreau.

SERVES 6

175g/6oz/1½ cups plain flour
40g/1½oz/3 tbsp block
   margarine, diced
40g/1½oz/3 tbsp white cooking
   fat, diced
30ml/2 tbsp caster sugar
1 size 3 egg yolk
2.5ml/½ tsp ground nutmeg
orange segments and thinly pared
   orange rind, to decorate

FOR THE FILLING

25g/1oz/2 tbsp butter, melted
50g/2oz/¼ cup caster sugar
1 egg
175g/6oz/¾ cup curd cheese
30ml/2 tbsp double cream
50g/2oz/¼ cup currants
15ml/1 tbsp grated lemon rind
15ml/1 tbsp grated orange rind
15ml/1 tbsp Cointreau

1 Make the pastry. Sift the flour into a large mixing bowl and rub in the margarine and fat until the mixture resembles fine breadcrumbs. Stir in the sugar and egg yolk and add enough cold water to make a firm dough. Wrap the pastry in clear film and chill for 30 minutes. Preheat the oven to 190°C/375°F/Gas 5.

> ### COOK'S TIP
> *Curd cheese is a soft unripened cheese with a milky, tangy flavour. To make a large tart use the pastry to line an 18cm/7in flan tin. Spoon in the filling and bake for 45–55 minutes.*

2 Roll out the dough on a lightly floured surface and line six 10cm/4in fluted flan tins.

3 Make the filling. Combine the melted butter, sugar, egg, curd cheese, cream, currants, grated rind and Cointreau in a bowl. Mix well. Spoon into the pastry cases, sprinkle over the nutmeg and bake for 30–35 minutes until golden. Serve decorated with orange segments and pared rind.

GRAND MARNIER PASSION PIE

Crisp puff pastry is teamed with a wonderfully creamy passion fruit and orange filling enhanced with Grand Marnier to make an unforgettable dessert.

SERVES 4–6

175g/6oz puff pastry, thawed
   if frozen
icing sugar, for dusting

FOR THE FILLING

60ml/4 tbsp apricot conserve
6 passion fruits
115g/4oz/½ cup cream cheese
300ml/½ pint/1¼ cup soured
   cream
2 eggs, beaten
75g/3oz/6 tbsp caster sugar
grated rind and juice of 1 orange
30ml/2 tbsp Grand Marnier

1 Preheat the oven to 190°C/375°F/Gas 5. Roll out the pastry on a lightly floured surface and use it to line an 18cm/7in flan tin. Prick the pastry base with a fork, then spread over the apricot conserve.

2 Cut the passion fruits in half. Using a teaspoon, scoop out the pulp and press it through a sieve into a bowl. Discard the seeds. Add the cream cheese, soured cream, eggs, caster sugar, orange rind and juice. Stir in the Grand Marnier.

3 Spoon the filling into the flan case. Bake for 25–30 minutes until golden.

4 Carefully heat some metal skewers. Dust the pie with icing sugar. Holding a skewer with oven gloves, press it on to the icing sugar, which will melt and caramelize. Continue to brand the topping, creating a lattice effect.

> ### COOK'S TIP
> *If you don't have time to brand the top of the pie, simply dust it with icing sugar, protect the pastry edge with pieces of foil and put the pie under a hot grill for a few seconds to caramelize the icing sugar.*

STICKY NUT PIE *with* DRAMBUIE

Drambuie is a liqueur which combines the flavours of whisky and heather honey – a delicious combination in this sticky pecan and macadamia nut filling.

SERVES 6–8

225g/8oz/2 cups plain flour
115g/4oz/¹⁄₂ cup butter, diced
30ml/2 tbsp strong black coffee
75g/3oz/³⁄₄ cup pecan nut halves
75g/3oz/³⁄₄ cup macadamia
  nuts, halved
ice cream, to serve
FOR THE FILLING
3 eggs
50g/2oz/5 tbsp molasses
50g/2oz/¹⁄₃ cup soft dark
  brown sugar
30ml/2 tbsp clear honey
30ml/2 tbsp Drambuie
25g/1oz/2 tbsp butter, melted
115g/4oz/1 cup pecan nuts,
  chopped
115g/4oz/1 cup macadamia
  nuts, chopped

1 Sift the flour into a bowl and rub in the butter until the mixture resembles fine breadcrumbs. Stir in the coffee and enough cold water to make a soft dough. Wrap in clear film and chill for 30 minutes. Preheat the oven to 200°C/400°F/Gas 6.

2 Roll out the pastry on a lightly floured surface to a long rectangle 40 x 16cm/16 x 6¹⁄₂ in. Lap the pastry over the rolling pin and use it to line a 35 x 11.5cm/14 x 4¹⁄₂ in oblong flan tin.

3 Make the filling by mixing all the ingredients in a bowl. Stir thoroughly, then spoon the filling into the pastry case. Arrange the pecan and macadamia halves in a pattern on top. Bake for 35–40 minutes until the pastry is golden. Serve with ice cream.

VARIATION
Use hazelnuts or walnuts
instead of the pecans.

APRICOT FRANGIPANE TART *with* KIRSCH

Take a light lime-flavoured pastry case, fill it with moist almond sponge generously laced with Kirsch and topped with fresh apricots and crushed macaroons, and the result is simply sensational. It is delicious warm or cold, served with yogurt or cream.

SERVES 6

225g/8oz/2 cups plain flour
115g/4oz/¹/₂ cup butter
10ml/2 tsp finely grated lime rind
12 fresh apricots, stoned, some
  halved, some thickly sliced
75g/3oz macaroons, crushed
natural yogurt or single cream,
  to serve

FOR THE FILLING
25g/1oz/2 tbsp butter, softened
30ml/2 tbsp soft light
  brown sugar
15ml/1 tbsp plain flour
50g/2oz/¹/₂ cup ground almonds
1 egg, beaten
45ml/3 tbsp Kirsch

COOK'S TIP

If you find the pastry difficult to handle, roll it out between sheets of non-stick baking paper or clear film.

---

1 Sift the flour into a mixing bowl, then rub in the butter until the mixture resembles breadcrumbs. Stir in the grated lime rind and add enough cold water to make a soft dough. Wrap in clear film and chill for 30 minutes.

2 Meanwhile, make the filling. Cream the butter with the soft brown sugar, then stir in the flour, ground almonds, egg and Kirsch. Preheat the oven to 200˚C/400˚F/Gas 6.

3 Roll out the pastry on a lightly floured surface to a 40 x 16cm/ 16 x 6¹/₂ in rectangle and use it to line a 35 x 11.5cm/14 x 4¹/₂ in rectangular flan tin. Spread the filling in the flan case and arrange the apricot halves and slices, cut side down, on top. Scatter over the crushed macaroons. Bake for 35–40 minutes until the pastry is golden. Serve warm or cold, with yogurt or cream.

DEEP APPLE *and* BERRY TART *with* GIN-LACED CRANBERRY SAUCE

Berries abound in this exciting medley of fruit flavours, given a special lift with a little gin.

SERVES 6–8

225g/8oz/2 cups plain flour
115g/4oz/¹/₂ cup butter, diced
10ml/2 tsp grated lime rind
egg or milk, to glaze
FOR THE FILLING
225g/8oz cooking apples, peeled,
  cored and grated
175g/6oz/1¹/₂ cups fresh or frozen
  cranberries
115g/4oz/1 cup fresh or frozen
  blueberries
50g/2oz/¹/₃ cup soft light
  brown sugar
grated rind and juice of 1 lime
15ml/1 tbsp gin
150ml/¹/₄ pint/²/₃ cup water
FOR THE SAUCE
175g/6oz/1¹/₂ cups fresh or frozen
  cranberries
30ml/2 tbsp clear honey
30ml/2 tbsp gin
300ml/¹/₂ pint/1¹/₄ cups fresh
  orange juice

1 Sift the flour into a mixing bowl. Rub in the butter, then stir in the grated lime rind. Add enough cold water to make a soft dough. Wrap the pastry in clear film and chill for 30 minutes.

2 Make the filling. Put the grated apples, cranberries, blueberries, sugar, lime rind and juice, gin and water in a large saucepan and bring to the boil. Lower the heat and simmer, stirring, until the fruit begins to pulp down and is very thick. Remove the pan from the heat and cool. Preheat the oven to 200°C/400°F/Gas 6.

3 Roll out three-quarters of the pastry on a lightly floured surface to a 25cm/10in round and use it to line a deep-sided 18cm/7in flan tin. Roll out the remaining pastry and cut thin strips for a lattice and small flower shapes for the decoration.

4 Spoon the filling into the pastry case. Make a lattice top with the pastry strips, brush them with a little egg or milk and attach the flower shapes. Brush the shapes with egg or milk and bake for 30–35 minutes. Remove the tart from the oven and leave to cool in the tin for 15 minutes.

5 Meanwhile, make the sauce by mixing the cranberries, honey, gin and orange juice in a small pan. Bring to the boil, then lower the heat and simmer for 10 minutes. Process in a blender or food processor until smooth. Serve hot or cold with slices of the tart.

COOK'S TIP

Give colour and flavour to pastry by adding grated citrus rind, ground nuts or spices.

MARSALA CUSTARD TART

The subtle yet unmistakable flavour of Marsala transforms a simple custard tart.

SERVES 6–8
175g/6oz/1½ cups plain flour
*40g/1½oz/3 tbsp block
  margarine, diced*
*40g/1½oz/3 tbsp white cooking
  fat, diced*
FOR THE FILLING
3 eggs
*30ml/2 tbsp soft light
  brown sugar*
250ml/8fl oz/1 cup creamy milk
60ml/4 tbsp Marsala
freshly grated nutmeg

1 Sift the flour into a mixing bowl. Rub in the margarine and fat until the mixture resembles fine breadcrumbs, then stir in enough cold water to make a soft dough. Wrap the pastry in clear film and chill for 30 minutes. Preheat the oven to 190°C/375°F/Gas 5.

2 Roll out the pastry on a lightly floured surface to a 25cm/10in round and use it to line a 20cm/8in flan tin. Line with foil and baking beans and bake blind for 12 minutes.

3 Meanwhile, make the filling. Whisk the eggs and sugar lightly in a bowl. Heat the milk to just below boiling point, stir in the Marsala and whisk into the eggs and sugar. Cool slightly, then strain into a jug.

4 Remove the foil and baking beans from the flan case, pour in the Marsala custard mixture and grate nutmeg over the surface. Bake for 25–35 minutes until the custard has set.

COOK'S TIP

*For a luxurious variation, use
single cream instead of milk.*

PRUNE *and* ARMAGNAC TART

Almond-and-apricot-stuffed prunes paired with armagnac and crisp orange pastry make for a superb sweet.

SERVES 4–6
225g/8oz/2 cups plain flour
115g/4oz/1/2 cup block margarine,
 diced
10ml/2 tsp grated orange rind
FOR THE FILLING
75g/3oz almond paste
3 ready-to-eat dried apricots,
 finely chopped
12 ready-to-eat prunes, stoned
2 eggs, beaten
150ml/1/4 pint/2/3 cup single cream
175g/6oz/1 cup soft dark
 brown sugar
45ml/3 tbsp armagnac

1 Sift the flour into a mixing bowl. Rub in the margarine until the mixture resembles fine breadcrumbs, then stir in the grated orange rind. Add enough cold water to make a soft dough. Wrap in clear film and chill for 1 hour.

2 Roll out the pastry on a lightly floured surface. Lap it over the rolling pin and use it to line a 20cm/8in flan tin. Line with foil and fill with baking beans, then bake blind for 10 minutes. Set the pastry case aside. Preheat the oven to 200°C/400°F/Gas 6.

3 Make the filling. Knead the almond paste with the chopped apricots on a clean work surface.

4 Press a little of the apricot and almond paste mixture into each stoned prune. When all the prunes have been filled, arrange them in the pastry case.

5 In a small bowl, combine the eggs and cream with half the sugar. Mix well and stir in the armagnac. Pour the mixture over the prunes, sprinkle the remaining sugar over the top and bake for 25–30 minutes.

COOK'S TIP
Fill a jar with ready-to-eat dried fruits, cover with armagnac or eau de vie and leave for a few days, to make a sauce that tastes superb with ice cream or yogurt.

WHISKY-LACED MINCE PIES

A little whisky enhances the fruit-laden filling for these traditional festive pies.

MAKES 12–15
1 size 2 egg yolk
5ml/1 tsp grated orange rind
15ml/1 tbsp caster sugar
225g/8oz/2 cups plain flour
150g/5oz/²/₃ cup butter, diced
beaten egg or milk, to glaze
icing sugar, for dusting
FOR THE FILLING
225g/8oz/1 cup mincemeat
50g/2oz/¼ cup glacé pineapple,
  chopped
50g/2oz/¼ cup glacé cherries,
  chopped
30ml/2 tbsp whisky
FOR THE WHISKY BUTTER
75g/3oz/6 tbsp unsalted
  butter, softened
175g/6oz/1½ cups icing
  sugar, sifted
30ml/2 tbsp whisky
5ml/1 tsp grated orange rind

2 Sift the flour into a bowl and rub in the butter until the mixture resembles fine breadcrumbs. Stir in the egg mixture and mix to a soft dough. Wrap in clear film and chill for 30 minutes.

3 Make the filling. Mix the mincemeat, glacé pineapple and glacé cherries in a small bowl. Spoon the whisky over.

4 Roll out three-quarters of the pastry. Stamp out fluted rounds and line 12–15 patty tins. Roll out the remaining pastry and stamp out star shapes.

5 Preheat the oven to 200°C/400°F/ Gas 6. Spoon a little filling into each pastry case and top with the star shapes. Brush with a little beaten egg or milk and bake for 20–25 minutes until golden. Leave to cool.

6 Meanwhile, make the whisky butter by beating the butter, icing sugar, whisky and grated orange rind in a small bowl until light and fluffy. Dust the mince pies with icing sugar and serve with the whisky butter or lift off each pastry star, pipe a whirl of flavoured butter on top of the filling beneath, then replace the star.

1 Start by making the pastry. In a small bowl, mix the egg yolk with the orange rind, caster sugar and 10ml/2 tsp water and set aside.

VARIATIONS
Replace the whisky in the filling and flavoured butter with Cointreau, brandy or an eau de vie. Use puff or filo pastry instead of shortcrust for a change.

CAKES AND GATEAUX

Sumptuous gâteaux create an impression of luxury, but are not necessarily difficult to prepare. A special cake is an essential feature of any celebration, whether the festivity is a birthday tea or a grand affair. For a striking effect, here is a pineapple and Kirsch gâteau that reveals dramatic spirals of cake and creamy filling. Cakes are for any occasion, of course, and gingerbread brownies with Canton ginger liqueur or Jamaican buns with Malibu are simpler but still tantalizing.

GINGERBREAD BROWNIES *with* GINGER LIQUEUR

Warm and spicy, ginger liqueur is an inspired addition to this gingerbread cake, with its gooey fudge topping.

SERVES 10–12

*175g/6oz/1 cup soft dark
  muscovado sugar*
175g/6oz/¹/₂ cup black treacle
50g/2oz/¹/₄ cup clear honey
175g/6oz/³/₄ cup butter
5ml/1 tsp bicarbonate of soda
275g/10oz/2¹/₂ cups plain flour
1.5ml/¹/₄ tsp salt
15ml/1 tbsp ground ginger
10ml/2 tsp ground cinnamon
2 eggs, beaten
115g/4oz/1 cup chopped walnuts
*50g/2oz/¹/₃ cup crystallized
  ginger, chopped*
*30ml/2 tbsp Canton ginger
  liqueur*
60ml/4 tbsp milk
*extra chopped walnuts and
  crystallized ginger, to decorate*
FOR THE FUDGE TOPPING
50g/2oz/4 tbsp butter
*45ml/3 tbsp Canton ginger
  liqueur*
*225g/8oz/1³/₄ cups icing
  sugar, sifted*

2 Sift the flour, salt, ginger and ground cinnamon into a bowl. Using a wooden spoon, stir in the melted ingredients until well mixed.

4 To make the fudge topping, put the butter, ginger liqueur and icing sugar into a heatproof bowl and set over a pan of barely simmering water. Stir until smooth and glossy, then remove from the heat and leave to cool. When the topping is cool, beat with a wooden spoon until it is thick enough to spread, then swirl over the cake. Cut into squares, slices or triangles, and decorate with extra walnuts and pieces of crystallized ginger.

1 Preheat the oven to 160°C/325°F/ Gas 3. Grease and line a 20cm/8in square cake tin. Put the sugar, treacle, honey and butter into a heavy-based saucepan. Stir over the heat until all the ingredients have dissolved, then cool. Stir in the bicarbonate of soda.

3 Stir in the eggs, walnuts, crystallized ginger and liqueur, with enough of the milk to make a stiff cake mixture. Spoon into the prepared tin, level the surface and bake for 1¹/₄–1¹/₂ hours until firm to the touch. Cool on a wire rack.

COOK'S TIP

Make this cake a few days before eating and store it in a tin prior to icing. The flavour will improve and the cake become stickier.

NUTTY MUFFINS *with* LA VIEILLE NOIX

Walnut liqueur gives a lift to these deep American muffins.

MAKES 12–14

225g/8oz/2 cups plain flour
20ml/4 tsp baking powder
2.5ml/¹/₂ tsp mixed spice
2.5ml/¹/₂ tsp salt
115g/4oz/²/₃ cup soft light
  brown sugar
75g/3oz/³/₄ cup chopped walnuts
50g/2oz/4 tbsp butter, melted
2 eggs
175ml/6fl oz/³/₄ cup milk
30ml/2 tbsp La Vieille Noix
FOR THE TOPPING
30ml/2 tbsp soft dark
  brown sugar
25g/1oz/¹/₄ cup chopped walnuts

1 Preheat the oven to 200°C/400°F/ Gas 6. Grease 12–14 muffin tins or deep bun tins (or use paper muffin cases supported in muffin tins). Sift the flour, baking powder, mixed spice and salt into a mixing bowl, then stir in the sugar and chopped walnuts.

2 In a jug, combine the melted butter, eggs, milk and liqueur. Mix lightly.

3 Pour the butter mixture into the dry mixture and stir for just long enough to combine the ingredients. The batter should be lumpy.

4 Fill the muffin or bun tins two-thirds full, then top with a sprinkling of sugar and walnuts. Bake for 15 minutes until the muffins have risen and are golden brown. Leave in the tins for a few minutes, then turn out and cool on a wire rack.

JAMAICAN BUNS *with* MALIBU

This popular rum-and-coconut liqueur makes an unusual and utterly delicious addition to rich sweet yeast-dough buns filled with pineapple, ginger and currants.

MAKES 14–16
450g/1lb/4 cups strong
  white flour
10ml/2 tsp ground ginger
pinch of salt
50g/2oz/4 tbsp butter
1 sachet easy-blend dried yeast
45ml/3 tbsp soft dark
  brown sugar
3 eggs, beaten
150ml/¹/4 pint/²/3 cup milk
FOR THE FILLING
50g/2oz/4 tbsp butter, melted
15ml/1 tbsp Malibu
75g/3oz/¹/2 cup soft dark
  brown sugar
115g/4oz/¹/2 cup glacé pineapple,
  chopped
50g/2oz/¹/4 cup currants
30ml/2 tbsp chopped crystallized
  ginger
FOR THE TOPPING
30ml/2 tbsp clear honey
75g/3oz/³/4 cup icing sugar, sifted
30ml/2 tbsp Malibu
10ml/2 tsp ginger syrup (from the
  jar of crystallized ginger)

2 Turn the dough on to a lightly floured surface and knead for 10 minutes until smooth. Put it back into the bowl, cover with oiled clear film and leave in a warm place for about 1 hour, until doubled in bulk.

3 Grease a baking sheet. Make the filling by mixing half the melted butter with the Malibu, sugar, glacé pineapple, currants and crystallized ginger in a small bowl.

4 Roll out the risen dough on a lightly floured surface to a 30cm/12in square. Brush with the remaining melted butter and cover with the fruit mixture.

6 Bake for 15–20 minutes until well risen and golden brown. As soon as the buns come out of the oven, brush them with honey.

7 Mix the icing sugar, Malibu and syrup in a bowl. Stir in enough cold water to make a smooth flowing icing. Pour over the buns and leave to set.

COOK'S TIP
The buns should just touch so that as they rise they join together. They can easily be separated for serving.

1 Sift the flour, ginger and salt into a large mixing bowl. Rub in the butter until the mixture resembles fine breadcrumbs, then stir in the yeast and sugar. Make a well in the centre and stir in the eggs, with enough of the milk to make a soft dough.

5 Roll the dough over the filling like a Swiss roll and cut into 14–16 slices. Arrange the slices cut side up on the baking sheet, so that they are almost touching. Cover with oiled clear film and leave to rise in a warm place for about 30 minutes. Preheat the oven to 220°C/425°F/Gas 7.

BANANA SPONGE SQUARES *with* CREME *de* BANANE

If you like bananas, you'll love these little cakes, where the flavour is given a wonderful depth by the addition of banana liqueur.

SERVES 8–10

SERVES 8–10

350g/12oz ripe bananas
175g/6oz/1 cup soft dark
* brown sugar*
2 eggs, beaten
30ml/2 tbsp crème de banane
30ml/2 tbsp milk
225g/8oz/2 cups self-raising flour
7.5ml/1½ tsp baking powder
pinch of grated nutmeg
175g/6oz/¾ cup butter
115g/4oz/1 cup chopped nuts,
* to decorate*
FOR THE FILLING
2 ripe bananas
115g/4oz/1 cup icing sugar, sifted
115g/4oz/½ cup butter
30ml/2 tbsp lemon juice
FOR THE ICING
225g/8oz/2 cups icing
* sugar, sifted*
30ml/2 tbsp orange juice
15ml/1 tbsp crème de banane

1 Preheat the oven to 160°C/325°F/ Gas 3. Grease and base-line a 20cm/8in square cake tin. Peel the bananas, slice them into a bowl and mash with the sugar. Stir in the eggs, liqueur and milk.

2 Sift the flour, baking powder and nutmeg into a mixing bowl. Rub in the butter until the mixture resembles breadcrumbs, then thoroughly beat in the banana mixture. Spoon into the cake tin and bake for 50–55 minutes until cooked. Remove the cake from the tin and leave to cool.

3 Make the filling. Peel and chop the bananas, place them in a pan and add the icing sugar, butter and lemon juice. Beat together over a low heat for 5 minutes, then remove from the heat and cool slightly. Slice the cake in half and sandwich back together with the banana filling.

4 Make the icing. Mix the icing sugar, orange juice and liqueur in a bowl and stir with a wooden spoon until smooth. Pour the icing over the top of the cake and decorate at once with chopped nuts. When the icing has set, cut the cake into squares.

GINGER *and* PEACH CAKE *with* PEACH SCHNAPPS

In the centre of this moist ginger Madeira cake is a luscious layer of peaches and peach-flavoured spirit.

SERVES 8

225g/8oz/2 cups plain flour
7.5ml/1½ tsp baking powder
10ml/2 tsp ground ginger
175g/6oz/¾ cup butter
175g/6oz/¾ cup caster sugar
3 eggs, beaten
3 fresh peaches, stoned and sliced
45ml/3 tbsp peach schnapps
FOR THE TOPPING
25g/1oz/2 tbsp butter
25g/1oz/¼ cup plain flour
30ml/2 tbsp caster sugar
50g/2oz/½ cup flaked almonds,
 crushed

1 Preheat the oven to 180°C/350°F/ Gas 4. Grease and line a 20cm/8in springform cake tin. Sift the flour, baking powder and ground ginger into a bowl. In a separate bowl, cream the butter with the sugar until light and fluffy. Beat in the eggs a little at a time.

2 Fold in the flour and spices and mix thoroughly. Spoon half the mixture into the cake tin. Arrange the peach slices in concentric circles on top. Pour over the peach schnapps and cover with the remaining cake mixture.

3 Make the topping in a small bowl. Rub the butter into the flour, then stir in the sugar and almonds. Sprinkle the topping over the top of the cake and bake for 1¼–1½ hours or until cooked.

VARIATION
Use nectarines or plums instead of peaches, or try stoned cherries with Kirsch.

HAZELNUT *and* APRICOT MERINGUE ROLL *with* APRICOT BRANDY

A soft, nutty meringue rolled around a creamy apricot filling spiked with apricot brandy.

SERVES 6

5 egg whites
150g/5oz/²⁄₃ cup caster sugar
5ml/1 tsp cornflour
50g/2oz/¹⁄₂ cup toasted
* hazelnuts, chopped*
icing sugar, for dusting
apricot slices and mint sprigs,
* to decorate*

FOR THE FILLING

300ml/¹⁄₂ pint/1¹⁄₄ cups double
* cream*
30ml/2 tbsp apricot brandy
60ml/4 tbsp apricot conserve, any
* large chunks chopped*
6 apricots, stoned and
* thinly sliced*

1 Preheat the oven to 110°C/225°F/ Gas ¹⁄₄. Grease a 30 x 20cm/12 x 8in Swiss roll tin and line it with non-stick baking paper. Whisk the egg whites in a clean grease-free bowl until stiff but not dry. Whisk in half the sugar and then continue to whisk until the mixture is stiff. Fold in the remaining sugar.

2 Fold in the cornflour and hazelnuts and spoon the mixture into the tin. Bake for about 45 minutes or until set. Leave the meringue in the tin to cool, uncovered, for 1 hour.

3 Meanwhile, make the filling. Whip the cream lightly in a bowl, then stir in the apricot brandy and conserve. Fold in the apricot slices.

4 Dust a sheet of non-stick baking paper with icing sugar and carefully turn the meringue on to it. Peel away the lining paper and spread the filling over the top of the meringue.

5 With the aid of the paper, and working from a short end, roll the meringue over the filling. Place the roll on a serving plate, dust with more icing sugar and decorate with apricot slices and mint sprigs.

COOK'S TIP

Add extra texture and flavour by turning the baked meringue on to a sheet of non-stick baking paper dusted with ground hazelnuts.

TIA MARIA GATEAU

Whipped cream and Tia Maria make a mouth-watering filling for this light chocolate and walnut cake.

SERVES 6–8

*150g/5oz/1¼ cups self-raising
 flour
25g/1oz/¼ cup cocoa powder
7.5ml/1½ tsp baking powder
3 eggs, beaten
175g/6oz/¾ cup butter, softened
175g/6oz/¾ cup caster sugar
50g/2oz/½ cup chopped walnuts
walnut brittle, to decorate (see
 Cook's Tip)*

FOR THE FILLING AND COATING
*600ml/1 pint/2½ cups double
 cream
45ml/3 tbsp Tia Maria
50g/2oz/⅔ cup desiccated
 coconut, toasted*

1 Preheat the oven to 160°C/325°F/ Gas 3. Grease and base-line two 18cm/7in sandwich cake tins. Sift the flour, cocoa powder and baking powder into a large bowl. Add the eggs, butter, sugar and walnuts and mix thoroughly, either with a wooden spoon or with a hand-held electric mixer, until the mixture is light and fluffy.

2 Divide the mixture between the cake tins, level the surface of each and bake for 35–40 minutes until risen and browned. Turn out the cakes and leave to cool on a wire rack.

3 Make the filling by whisking the cream with the Tia Maria in a bowl until the mixture forms soft peaks.

4 Slice each cake horizontally in half to give four layers. Sandwich together with some of the flavoured cream.

5 Coat the sides of the cake with cream. Spread out the toasted coconut on a sheet of non-stick baking paper. Then, holding the top and bottom of the cake securely, turn it on its side and roll in the coconut until evenly coated. Put the cake on a serving plate, spread more cream over the top and pipe the remainder around the rim. Decorate with walnut brittle.

COOK'S TIP

To make walnut brittle, slowly heat 75g/3oz/6 tbsp caster sugar in a pan. When the sugar has dissolved, stir in 50g/2oz/½ cup broken walnuts. Turn the mixture on to non-stick baking paper and leave to set. Break the brittle into pieces with a rolling pin.

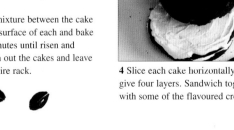

PINEAPPLE *and* KIRSCH CAKE

*A dramatic effect is created when this cake, with its Kirsch-flavoured creamy filling
is sliced to reveal the spiral pattern inside.*

SERVES 10–12

175g/6oz/³⁄₄ cup butter
*115g/4oz/¹⁄₂ cup caster sugar, plus
 extra for sprinkling*
2 eggs, lightly beaten
*115g/4oz/1 cup self-raising
 flour, sifted*
10ml/2 tsp grated lemon rind
225g/8oz ginger biscuits, crushed
*pineapple wedges and leaves,
 to decorate*

FOR THE FILLING AND COATING
*750ml/1¹⁄₄ pints/3 cups double
 cream, whipped*
30ml/2 tbsp Kirsch
*225g/8oz fresh pineapple, finely
 chopped*
*115g/4oz/1¹⁄₃ cups desiccated
 coconut, toasted*

1 Preheat the oven to 200°C/400°F/
Gas 6. Grease and line a 28 x 18cm/
11 x 7in Swiss roll tin. Also grease and
base-line a 20cm/8in springform cake
tin. In a bowl, combine 50g/2oz/4 tbsp
of the butter with the sugar, eggs, flour
and lemon rind. Beat until light and
fluffy. Spread the mixture in the Swiss
roll tin and bake for 10–12 minutes
until firm and golden.

2 Meanwhile, melt the remaining butter
in a small pan, stir in the crushed ginger
biscuits and mix thoroughly. Press the
crumb mixture evenly over the base of
the cake tin.

3 When the cake is cooked, turn it out
on to a sheet of non-stick baking paper
sprinkled with caster sugar. Remove the
lining paper.

COOK'S TIP
*Give a marbled effect to the cake by
colouring half the sponge mixture with
a few drops of food colouring. Put
alternate spoonfuls of plain and tinted
mixture into the tin and swirl with a
skewer before baking.*

4 Make the filling and coating.
Combine half the whipped cream with
the Kirsch and chopped pineapple.
Spread the mixture over the cake and
then cut the cake into four long strips.

5 Roll the first strip of cake and filling
and stand it on one end in the prepared
tin, on the biscuit base. Wrap the
remaining strips around to form a
20cm/8in cake. Chill for 15 minutes.

6 Remove the cake from the tin and
place it on a serving plate. Spoon some
of the remaining whipped cream into a
piping bag and spread the rest over the
cake. Cover with the toasted coconut.
Pipe swirls of cream on top of the cake
and decorate with the pineapple wedges
and leaves.

CARAMEL MERINGUE GATEAU *with* SLOE GIN

Two crisp flat discs of orange meringue, filled with a refreshing blend of cream, mango, grapes and sloe gin,
make a marvellous special-occasion dessert.

SERVES 8

4 egg whites
225g/8oz/1⅓ cups soft light
  brown sugar
3 drops of white wine vinegar
3 drops of natural vanilla essence
10ml/2 tsp grated orange rind
whipped cream, to decorate
FOR THE FILLING AND
CARAMEL TOPPING
300ml/½ pint/1¼ cups double
  cream
45ml/3 tbsp sloe gin
1 mango, chopped
225g/8oz mixed green and black
  seedless grapes, halved
75g/3oz/6 tbsp granulated sugar

1 Preheat the oven to 160°C/325°F/
Gas 3. Base line two 20cm/8in
sandwich cake tins. Whisk the egg
whites in a large grease-free bowl until
stiff. Add half the brown sugar and
whisk until the meringue stiffens again.
Fold in the remaining sugar, vinegar,
vanilla essence and grated orange rind.
Divide the mixture between the tins,
spread evenly and bake for 40 minutes.
Leave to cool.

COOK'S TIP
For home-made sloe gin, layer sloes
and sugar in clean jars and pour in
gin to cover. Seal and label, then leave
for a few months before filtering.

2 Make the filling. Whip the cream in a
bowl, then fold in the sloe gin, chopped
mango and halved grapes.

3 Place one meringue layer on a serving
plate. Spread with the cream and fruit
mixture, then place the second
meringue layer on top and press down
firmly but carefully.

4 Line a baking sheet with non-stick
baking paper. Put the sugar for the
caramel topping into a heavy-based
pan. Heat gently until it dissolves.
Increase the heat and cook, without
stirring, until it becomes a golden
caramel colour and a spoonful hardens
when dropped into cold water. Drizzle
some of the caramel on to the paper to
make decorative shapes and allow to
cool and harden. Drizzle the remaining
caramel over the gâteau. Decorate with
whipped cream and the caramel shapes.

ORANGE CAKE *with* CURACAO

A rich sweet yeasty cake full of orange flavour boosted with Curaçao.

SERVES 8

115g/4oz/½ cup butter
200g/7oz/1 cup granulated sugar
3 eggs
200g/7oz/1¾ cups strong
 white flour
pinch of salt
10ml/2 tsp easy-blend dried yeast
grated rind of 2 oranges
3 slices glacé orange, chopped
few drops of vanilla essence
15ml/1 tbsp orange juice
30ml/2 tbsp Curaçao
5 thin orange slices, peel and
 pith removed
5ml/1 tsp clear honey

1 Grease and base-line a 900g/2lb loaf tin. In a bowl, cream together the butter and sugar until soft and fluffy. Beat in the eggs a little at a time.

2 In another bowl, sift together the flour and salt and stir in the easy-blend yeast.

3 Stir the creamed mixture into the flour, add the orange rind, chopped glacé orange, vanilla essence, orange juice and Curaçao and mix thoroughly. Spoon the mixture into the prepared tin, then cover and leave in a warm place for 1 hour. Preheat the oven to 190°C/375°F/Gas 5.

4 Overlap the orange slices on top of the cake mixture and bake in the middle of the oven for 45–55 minutes or until cooked. When cooked, brush the orange slices immediately with the honey. Leave to cool in the tin for 10 minutes before turning out.

COOK'S TIP
This mixture may be baked in an 18cm/7in cake tin instead of a loaf tin.

STRAWBERRY *and* KIRSCH CHOUX RING

Kirsch and cream make a wonderful combination with succulent strawberries encased in featherlight pastry.

SERVES 4–6

150ml/¼ pint/⅔ cup water
50g/2oz/4 tbsp butter
65g/2½ oz/9 tbsp plain
  flour, sifted
2 eggs, beaten
75g/3oz/6 tbsp granulated sugar,
  for the caramel
175g/6oz/generous 1 cup small
  whole strawberries
icing sugar, for dusting
whipped cream, to decorate

FOR THE FILLING

150ml/¼ pint/⅔ cup double cream
30ml/2 tbsp Kirsch
10ml/2 tsp icing sugar, sifted
175g/6oz/generous 1 cup
  strawberries, sliced

2 Beat in the eggs, a small amount at a time, to form a dough. Pipe or spoon the choux pastry in rough balls, making a circle on the baking sheet (the balls should just touch).

3 Bake for 15 minutes, then lower the oven temperature to 190°C/375°F/Gas 5 and cook for 20–25 minutes more. Make one or two slits in the pastry to let the hot air escape and leave to cool.

5 Make the filling. Whip the cream in a bowl until it starts to thicken. Stir in the Kirsch and icing sugar and continue whisking until stiff. Fold in the sliced strawberries.

6 Slice the choux ring in half horizontally, spoon in the strawberry cream and replace the top. Dust with icing sugar. Serve in slices, with extra whipped cream and the caramelized strawberries.

1 Preheat the oven to 220°C/425°F/ Gas 7. Draw a 15cm/6in circle on a sheet of non-stick baking paper, turn it over and press it on to a greased baking sheet. Put the water and butter in a large saucepan. Heat until the butter has melted, then bring to the boil. Quickly tip in all the flour, remove the pan from the heat and beat vigorously with a wooden spoon until the mixture leaves the sides of the pan.

4 Put the sugar into a heavy-based pan, heat gently until it dissolves, then increase the heat and cook the syrup until it becomes a golden caramel colour and a spoonful hardens when dropped into cold water. Spear each strawberry in turn on a fork and quickly half-dip them in the caramel. Leave to cool on non-stick baking paper.

VARIATION

To make chocolate choux pastry, replace 15ml/1 tbsp of the flour with cocoa powder.

CARIBBEAN RUM CAKE

This marvellously moist fruit cake is filled with tropical fruits, rum and coconut.

SERVES 10–12

50g/2oz/¹/₃ cup sultanas
175g/6oz/1 cup ready-to-eat dried pineapple, chopped
175g/6oz/1 cup ready-to-eat dried papaya, chopped
175g/6oz/1 cup ready-to-eat dried mango, chopped
60ml/4 tbsp rum
225g/8oz/1 cup butter, softened
225g/8oz/1¹/₃ cups soft light brown sugar
4 eggs, beaten
225g/8oz/2 cups plain flour, sifted with 10ml/2 tsp mixed spice

FOR THE TOPPING

75g/3oz/1 cup desiccated coconut
50g/2oz/¹/₃ cup ready-to-eat dried papaya, chopped
50g/2oz/¹/₃ cup ready-to-eat dried pineapple, chopped

1 Combine the sultanas with the dried pineapple, papaya and mango in a glass bowl. Spoon the rum over, cover and leave for a day or just a few hours.

COOK'S TIP

If the cake mixture separates or curdles when the egg is added, just stir in a little of the flour mixture.

2 Preheat the oven to 180°C/350°F/ Gas 4. Grease and line a 20cm/8in round cake tin. Cream the butter with the brown sugar until light and fluffy. Beat in the eggs a little at a time.

3 Fold in the flour and mixed spice mixture, then stir in the soaked fruits. Mix thoroughly, spoon into the tin and level the surface.

4 In a small bowl, mix the coconut, papaya and pineapple together. Sprinkle the mixture over the top of the cake. Bake for 1¹/₂–1³/₄ hours or until a skewer inserted in the cake comes out clean. Cover with foil if the top of the cake begins to brown too much. Leave the cake in the tin for 15 minutes before transferring it to a wire rack to cool completely.

WHISKY-LACED RICH FRUIT CAKE

This classic whisky-flavoured Scottish cake is perfect for afternoon tea.

SERVES 12

175g/6oz/1 cup sultanas
175g/6oz/1 cup raisins
175g/6oz/³/₄ cup currants
150g/5oz/scant 1 cup mixed
  chopped peel
45ml/3 tbsp whisky
200g/7oz/1³/₄ cups plain flour
2.5ml/¹/₂ tsp baking powder
pinch of salt
10ml/2 tsp mixed spice
175g/6oz/³/₄ cup butter
175g/6oz/³/₄ cup soft brown sugar
4 eggs, beaten
grated rind of ¹/₂ lemon
50g/2oz/¹/₂ cup blanched almonds

1 Put the sultanas, raisins, currants and mixed peel in a bowl. Pour over the whisky, then cover and leave overnight or for several hours, stirring occasionally if possible.

2 Preheat the oven to 160°C/325°F/ Gas 3. Grease and line an 18cm/7in round cake tin. Sift the flour, baking powder, salt and mixed spice into a large mixing bowl.

COOK'S TIP

Cooking times can vary with slowly cooked fruit cakes. To test the cake, push a warmed skewer into the middle. If it comes out clean, the cake is cooked. If not, return to the oven for 10 minutes more, then test again.

3 In a mixing bowl, cream the butter with the sugar until light and fluffy, then beat in the eggs a little at a time.

4 Fold in the flour and spices, soaked fruit and lemon rind, then stir until thoroughly mixed.

5 Spoon the mixture into the prepared tin and level the surface. Bake for 30 minutes. Remove the tin from the oven and arrange the almonds on top, then return the tin to the oven and bake for 2¹/₄–2¹/₂ hours more or until cooked. Leave the cake to cool in the tin for 15 minutes before turning out on to a wire rack to cool completely.

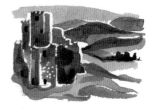

YEASTED FRUIT TWIST *with* PORT

This luxurious loaf, packed with dried fruits soaked in port and spiced tea, would make a marvellous gift.

SERVES 6–8

*175ml/6fl oz/³/4 cup orange-and-
  cinnamon flavoured tea
50g/2oz/¹/3 cup ready-to-eat dried
  figs, chopped
50g/2oz/¹/4 cup ready-to-eat dried
  apricots, chopped
50g/2oz/¹/3 cup sultanas
50g/2oz/¹/4 cup granulated sugar
30ml/2 tbsp port
225g/8oz/2 cups strong
  white flour
1.5ml/¹/4 tsp salt
50g/2oz/4 tbsp butter, diced
10ml/2 tsp easy-blend dried yeast
1 egg
milk
45ml/3 tbsp clear honey, to glaze*

1 Combine the tea, figs, apricots, sultanas and sugar in a bowl. Stir in the port, cover and leave for a few hours or overnight if possible.

2 Lightly grease a baking sheet. Sift the flour and salt into a mixing bowl and rub in the butter until the mixture resembles fine breadcrumbs. Stir in the easy-blend yeast.

3 Make a well in the centre and add the egg and the soaked fruit, with its liquid. Mix until the dough leaves the sides of the bowl, adding a little milk if necessary to make a soft dough.

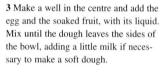

4 Knead the dough on a lightly floured surface for 5 minutes, then return it to the clean bowl, cover with oiled clear film and leave in a warm place for about 1 hour until doubled in bulk.

5 Roll out the risen dough on a floured surface to a sausage shape 30cm/12in long. With a sharp knife cut the dough lengthways in half. With each cut side facing up, twist the halves together. Lift the twist on to the baking sheet, cover with oiled clear film and leave to rise for 40 minutes. Preheat the oven to 200°C/400°F/Gas 6.

6 Bake for 25–30 minutes until the loaf is golden. Remove from the oven and brush immediately with the honey. Leave to cool, then serve in slices, with butter if liked.

SAVARIN *with* CHERRY BRANDY

Soaked in cherry brandy syrup and filled with fresh cherries, this savarin is quite sensational.

SERVES 6–8

150g/5oz/1¼ cups strong
  white flour
1.5ml/¼ tsp salt
15ml/1 tbsp easy-blend
  dried yeast
10ml/2 tsp sugar
3 eggs, beaten
75g/3oz/6 tbsp butter, melted
75ml/5 tbsp lukewarm milk
60ml/4 tbsp apricot jam
30ml/2 tbsp water
350g/12oz/3 cups fresh cherries,
  with stems if possible

FOR THE SYRUP

115g/4oz/½ cup caster sugar
250ml/8fl oz/1 cup water
45ml/3 tbsp cherry brandy
15ml/1 tbsp lemon juice

1 Grease a 20cm/8in savarin mould or ring tin. Sift the flour and salt into a large mixing bowl, then stir in the easy-blend yeast and sugar. Make a well in the centre, pour in the eggs, melted butter and milk and beat to a smooth, thick batter.

2 Pour the batter into the prepared mould or tin, cover with oiled clear film and leave in a warm place until the mixture has almost reached the top of the mould or tin. Preheat the oven to 200°C/400°F/Gas 6. Bake the cake for 35–40 minutes or until golden brown and firm to the touch.

3 Meanwhile make the syrup. Mix the sugar and water in a saucepan. Stir over the heat until the sugar has dissolved, then boil for 6–8 minutes without stirring. Remove from the heat and stir in the cherry brandy and lemon juice.

4 Turn out the warm savarin on to a serving dish and spoon over the hot syrup so that it will soak in. Put the apricot jam and water into a small pan. Bring to the boil, stirring constantly, then press through a sieve into a bowl. Brush the glaze over the savarin, then fill the centre with cherries and serve.

COOK'S TIP

The syrup is delicious on its own. Try stirring sliced fresh fruits into it when it is cold, and serving it with fromage frais or natural yogurt.

RUM *and* RAISIN CHEESECAKE

Spectacular to look at, and superb to eat, this light cheesecake is studded with rum-flavoured raisins and surrounded by diagonal stripes of plain and chocolate sponge.

SERVES 8–10

2 eggs
50g/2oz/¼ cup caster sugar
50g/2oz/½ cup plain flour, sifted
5ml/1 tsp cocoa powder, mixed to
*   a paste with 15ml/1 tbsp*
*   hot water*
115g/4oz/½ cup unsalted
*   butter, melted*
225g/8oz ginger biscuits, crushed
whipped cream and sifted cocoa
*   powder, to decorate*

FOR THE FILLING

45ml/3 tbsp water
1 sachet powdered gelatine
300ml/½ pint/1¼ cups double
*   cream*
30ml/2 tbsp milk
75g/3oz/½ cup raisins
60ml/4 tbsp rum
50g/2oz/½ cup icing sugar, sifted
450g/1lb/2 cups curd cheese

1 Preheat the oven to 200°C/400°F/ Gas 6. Grease and line a 28 x 18cm/ 11 x 7in Swiss roll tin. Also base-line a 20cm/8in loose-based cake tin. Cover a wire rack with a sheet of non-stick baking paper. Mix the eggs and sugar in a heatproof bowl. Place over a saucepan of barely simmering water and whisk until the mixture forms a thick trail. Fold in the sifted flour.

2 Pour half the mixture into a large piping bag fitted with a 4cm/1½ in plain nozzle, or use a paper piping bag and cut the end off. Pipe diagonal stripes of the cake mixture across the Swiss roll tin, leaving an equal space between each row.

3 Stir the cooled cocoa paste into the remaining cake mixture until evenly mixed. Fill a piping bag with the mixture and pipe as before to give rows of alternating colours. Bake for 10–12 minutes, then turn out the sponge on to the paper-topped wire rack. Peel off the lining paper.

COOK'S TIP
For an instant decoration pipe whirls of whipped cream on to baking sheets covered with non-stick baking paper and freeze until solid. Store in freezer boxes and use to decorate desserts and gâteaux.

4 Mix the melted butter and crushed biscuits in a bowl. Spread over the bottom of the loose-based cake tin and press down firmly. Cut the sponge in half lengthways and arrange the two strips around the sides of the cake tin. Set the tin aside.

5 Make the filling. Put the water into a small heatproof bowl and sprinkle over the gelatine. When spongy, place the bowl over a pan of barely simmering water and stir until the gelatine has dissolved. Remove from the heat and leave to cool slightly.

6 Whisk the cream with the milk in a bowl. Fold in the raisins, rum, icing sugar and curd cheese, then stir in the cooled gelatine. Spoon the filling into the prepared tin and chill until set. To serve, remove the cheesecake from the tin and trim the cake level with the filling. Pipe whirls of cream around the edge and dust with cocoa powder.

INDEX

Photographs

All photographs by David
Jordan, Janine Hosegood and
Paul Bricknell except pictures
supplied by Cephas Picture
Library: p6 and 7 Aviemore
Photography; p8 and 9 Mick
Rock; p12 (top left) Nigel
Blythe, (bottom left) Mick Rock
and (right) Stuart Boreham;
p13 Stuart Boreham; p60 (top)
John Heinrich, (bottom left)
Tripelon/Jarry and (bottom
right) Herve Champollion;
p61, 108 and 109 Mick Rock.

Thanks to drinkon.com for
supplying some bottles used
in the photography.

NOTES

NOTES